AN
INNOCENT
DELIGHT

AN INNOCENT DELIGHT

The Art of Dining in New Zealand

TONY SIMPSON

HODDER AND STOUGHTON
AUCKLAND LONDON SYDNEY TORONTO

Acknowledgements

An acknowledgement to some of those who have contributed to this book is in order. Certainly I could never have accomplished it if Fiona McAlpine had not prepared the sections on wine and on cheese. I thank Anne Kirker for researching and preparing the illustrations, and gratefully acknowledge the assistance of the Rare Books Room, Auckland Public Library, in providing reproductions of the Thomas Bewick woodcuts which appear as illustrations. And much appreciation is due to Rosemary Lowe for typing the manuscript.

Typeset by Saba Graphics Ltd, Christchurch.
Printed and bound by Singapore National Printers for Hodder & Stoughton Ltd, 46 View Road, Glenfield, Auckland, New Zealand.

This book is dedicated not only to Anne and to Jeremy who have eaten almost all that it contains, but also to Martine and Denis, May and John and all the others who came (and keep coming) to dinner.

On china blue my lobster red
Precedes my cutlet brown,
With which my salad green is sped
By yellow Chablis down.
Lord, if good living be no sin,
But innocent delight,
O polarize these hues within
To one eupeptic white.

— Sir Stephen Gaselee

Contents

Introduction

*So preoccupied are the majority of cooks with the good opinion which
people have of their abilities they imagine that so long as they disguise and
garnish their dishes in confusion they will pass for clever men but that is
where they are wrong (and) that is why you must try as much as you can to
diversify food by flavour and by the form in which you present it.*

— Nicholas de Bonnefons
Chef to Louis XIV in
Les Delices de la Campagne, 1654

SOME YEARS AGO, after a break of well over a decade, I found myself living
alone. This led to my rediscovery of many lost arts such as shopping, ironing
shirts and that most troublesome of all tasks, how to fold a double bed sheet
when there is only one of you. It also led to the need to cook for myself. Now
of course I could cook. What man thinks he cannot? But I made a discovery
long known to others. There was something of a difference between fiddling
about in the kitchen at rare intervals and providing sustenance for myself,
and eventually my teenage son, day in day out for years on end. I was thereby
constrained to tackle the matter in earnest. I bought a recipe book and began.
How often do we thus airily set out on a long and difficult journey?

In a very short time I developed a sympathy for Lady Barker who recounts
in *Station Amusements in New Zealand* how she likewise found herself
obliged to 'do' for herself:

> I want to lodge a formal complaint against cookery books. They are not
> the least use in the world until you know how to cook! and then you can
> do without them. Somebody ought to write a cookery book which would

1

tell an unhappy beginner whether the water in which she proposed to put her potatoes is to be hot or cold; how long such water is to boil; how she is to know if the potatoes are done enough; how to dry them after they have boiled, and similar things which make all the difference in the world . . . Of course in time, and after many failures, I did learn to boil a potato which would not disgrace me, and to bake bread, besides in time attaining to puddings and cakes, of which I don't mind confessing I was modestly proud.

There milady has the advantage over me. I have rarely trusted myself sufficiently to embark upon bread, although pastries hold for me no terrors. But I cannot forget my first essay into soufflés. I managed the separation of the yolks and the whites. A mere three ended up hopelessly scrambled in the cat's bowl. (The cat was an enthusiastic supporter in many of my early efforts; she seemed to get most of the benefit.) But I came then to the dread instruction: fold in the eggs, it said. Yes it did. Right there on the page. Ah. How wonderful. But what did it mean? The very nature of an egg either within or without its shell defies the concept of folding as this would normally be understood by any lay person. The notion of folding an egg as one would fold a sheet is absurd. It could not mean to stir in this fluffy egg white or surely the book would have said so. If I wished to swallow the soufflé I was obliged to swallow my pride. I telephoned a friend and asked. She was very sarcastic about the whole thing (as what feminist would not be with such an opening) but she finally vouchsafed the information. I cannot say that the soufflé turned out right, and neither have some since. The search for the perfect soufflé still goes on. Notwithstanding I think I have got the hang of folding in not only the eggs but even, in other circumstances, the gelatine. Of that latter more hereafter (for 'folding', see my section on soufflés). Suffice to say that, many cookbooks on, I am still learning.

And as I made my explorations I began to arrive at certain conclusions beyond mere food. Why is it that while we have in this country such a plenitude of ingredients for a wonderful cuisine we have so far failed to develop one? Why is it that when we dine out we do so upon the cuisine of other traditions, often so badly prepared that it really should be sent back and the chef admonished? Why, as with so much else, do we insist upon retaining a derivative and colonial culture in even this manifestation, the very food we eat?

Part of the answer to that of course is that we do not yet have a strong enough native cuisine to sustain us wholly. Partly too, eating Italian or Chinese food, if it is prepared properly, is a pleasant thing to do. Regrettably there is another side, however. We have inherited a lively tradition of cooking which we have chosen to bury beneath the sort of cultural snobbery which for many years prevented, for instance, our orchestras from performing the works of our own composers. Although those composers

2

had inherited a tradition and built on it they were felt somehow to be not quite proper, and indeed ever so slightly . . . incapable. So with our tradition in cookery. The reasons why this has happened are almost as interesting as the food itself, and take us immediately into the realm of our social history.

Much has been made in recent years, and rightly so, of our pioneers and the life they led: how they managed to turn out meals from camp ovens and adapt local ingredients to their requirements. But this technical detail will not tell you a great deal about the tradition of their cooking. If you try roast pukeko you find it has a certain novelty value but nothing else to commend it; it is damned stringy. To find what our forebears were about, one must go back to the introduction of new food technology in the 1860s and to the sorts of people who were coming to this country in large numbers in the two succeeding decades. The new technology was a very primitive form of the coal range, a shallow cast-iron cupboard built into the fireplace for baking, with the top left open for boiling and stewing. 'A sort of iron box with a wood fire under and over it' as the settler Adela Stewart recalled it in her 1908 reminiscence *My Simple Life in New Zealand*.

This stove was a part of a social process which architect and social analyst Siegfried Giedion called 'the mechanisation of the hearth'. Since the dawn of time, the centre of the household had been the fireplace. The nineteenth and twentieth centuries replaced it with at first an iron box, the gas and the electric oven and now the microwave cooker. Over the last one hundred and fifty years, a series of concentrations of heat sources has developed, combined with equally growing subtleties of control. All this amounts to a veritable technological revolution (which of course we take wholly for granted). Paradoxically this revolution has been accompanied by a progressive deterioration in our cuisine and an almost wilful refusal to take advantage of the potential it has released. If you want to see what colonial ovens developed into and what replaced them then you should visit Broadgreen House, the restored gentleman's cob residence in Nelson with its marvellously preserved kitchens of the period. As a technology these ovens were an enormous leap forward. But it was the notions brought with them by our immigrants about the same time in combination with this development which could have laid the foundations for a unique local cuisine.

This immigration has had consequences which reverberate still. Between 1872 and 1877 the colonial government of New Zealand allocated the equivalent of half a million dollars for the purpose of assisted immigration, an enormous sum in those days. In 1875 alone 31,785 immigrants were granted assisted passages; between 1877 and 1885 a further 36,653 were similarly subsidised. By the operation of a peculiar set of historical circumstances, almost all of these new settlers were labourers and their families from rural England. It is very difficult to imagine the extraordinary poverty of rural workers in the last century and to recollect that in fact they remained poor until within living memory. In *Lark Rise to Candleford*, her account of growing up in a farm cottage just before the First World War, Flora Thompson describes 'the three chief ingredients of the one hot meal a day — bacon from the flitch, vegetables from the garden and flour for the roly poly', this latter served first, 'the idea being that it took the edge off the appetite' so that less meat would be eaten. Until the Second World War and after, the experience was still much the same for those who lived in the poorer and more isolated parts of Britain.

Alan Millar grew up in a fishing village on the Scottish border and emigrated to New Zealand in the mid-fifties. He remembers the food of his childhood very well:

> We largely ate cheap things and it was a very stereotype diet with little variation, very simple, rather ordinary and boring looking back on it, compared to how even peasants in other countries might eat. We had for breakfast mostly porridge with milk. The younger generation of children, it was tolerated they might have some sugar with it but this was seen as rather weak and the elder people had salt. It was not unusual that the porridge, which was the real stuff you soaked overnight, be kept and eaten cold with salt in slices. The main meal often consisted of what was known as kail which was a very thick and nutritious soup — the stock was a sheep's head or some other bones, lots of turnips, lentils, barley. A great pot would be made, say on the Monday, and put on the hob and kept there and was heated up and got better and better as the days went by. And we had lots and lots of potatoes which was a major staple, in fact *the* vegetable. We didn't eat quantities of green vegetables; cabbage and brussel sprouts and cauliflower; turnips, but not the little ones you have in New Zealand, I'm talking about turnips as big as your head, what you feed to the cattle here, were a major item of diet.
>
> For meat we seldom bought a joint and I seem to have endless recollections of eating mince and sausages. We didn't eat a large number of eggs, they were quite expensive. We were fisherfolk, lived near the sea and therefore we ate quite a lot of fish which we got for nothing. We had things which other people would regard as luxury items like lobsters and crabs because in the off season they weren't worth selling and you still kept catching them so we ate them. There was a time of the year we never got to eat any, other times you could eat more than a millionaire. We didn't have much in the way of cakes. We would have occasionally scones and pancakes done on the griddle.
>
> Puddings were normally on a Sunday, mostly steam puddings and dumplings, otherwise it was tapioca, semolina, arrowroot and rice. Let me emphasise that it was a treat and you never normally saw them more than once a week if you were lucky. At Christmas and New Year, particularly New Year, there would be black bun. Funerals were rather

ritualistic, you would have cold ham and things like that after the funeral, it was Presbyterian Scotland I came from and they really weren't big on show. And weddings, if a reception was conducted at home, which for the poor it generally was, they would put on a bit of a spread with some biscuits and cakes.

When I came to New Zealand first of all I was amazed at the quantity of meat that was consumed. The fact that you sat down to roast meat virtually every day and sometimes two times and occasionally three times a day I found a bit sumptuous, it was really beyond what I expected of life. The fare was much more plentiful here and in bigger quantities, with much more generous helpings. Sausages were something that in New Zealand you had of choice rather than of necessity, it was something to sort of richen a thing up a bit. The first savaloys I ever saw were in New Zealand, they were unknown to me in Scotland and I wondered what they were. Also there was much more in the way of sweets and puddings and fruit and tinned fruit and that sort of thing, so here you rapidly adjusted to the fact that you had pudding every day, two helpings if you wanted it.

The childhood diet which Alan experienced was the common lot of the great mass of the working population in the previous century. The period of particular significance to us between about 1870 and 1900 was a terrible time for those who had no margin upon which to come and go. Severe agricultural depression meant there was much truth in the ironic grace:

Oh heavenly father bless us
and keep us all alive,
There are ten of us to dinner
and food for only five.

The desperation among rural labourers resulted in a rural revolt, a series of strikes led by Joseph Arch. What success they enjoyed was shortlived; the farmers combined to lock the labourers out and they were reduced to even more grinding poverty. The only way out for many was emigration. But where were they to find the wherewithal?

Into this breach stepped the New Zealand government which, through Arch's own organisation and with his active co-operation, provided money for the outfits needed for the journey and for assisted passages. This so alarmed the English gentry that they sometimes meanly refused to sign the required certificates of character for intended emigrants, or put it about that the agents of the colonial government were lying about conditions in the colony. One such agent, William Burton, reported repeated refusals, at the instigation of hostile farmers, clergy and squires, to rent him rooms to address meetings. Writing from Laceby in Lincolnshire in March 1875 he reported that it was 'a hand to hand fight whether we shall persuade them to go or the squirearchy intimidate them into stopping where they are.'

In the end, as the figures quoted show, Burton and his fellows had a remarkable success. One of their principal means of persuasion was the abundance of food in New Zealand. In the *Labourers' Union Chronicle* for example, of 28 November 1873, New Zealand is described in almost biblical terms as 'a good land, a land of oil, olives and honey, a land wherein thou mayest eat bread without scarceness: thou shalt not lack anything in it.' By 1875 the argument was being clinched by the reports sent home by those who had gone before. A quarter of fine beef, reported one Lincolnshire man, could be had at threepence the pound. You could buy your own cow, said another. Stephen Hutchings, a settler at Woodville, was reported as having twenty acres and a cottage freehold and 'chickens and ducks in abundance, and, if he have not now, he will soon have pigs, cows and a good farmyard'. These were experiences typical of settlers from all over rural England, an experience summed up in the words of the song attributed to early settler John Barr:

When to New Zealand first I came
Poor and dirty, poor and dirty,
When to New Zealand first I came
It was a happy day sirs.
For I was fed on porridge thin,
My toes they stickit through my shoon
I ruggit at the ponken pin,
But couldn't make it pay sirs.

But now it's altered days I trow,
I will I wot, I will I wot,
The beef is tumbling in the pot
and I'm both fat and full sirs.
At my door cheeks there's bread and cheese
I work or not just as I please.
I'm fairly settled at my ease
And that's the way of now sirs.

To the immigrants such abundance was astonishing. It should be observed however that once they got over their astonishment it was among their first cares to eat decently and well. That in its turn had certain consequences. The traditional cooking of rural England in the nineteenth century was a survival from an earlier period. Whereas in the towns the middle classes in particular had been affected in every particular in their lives by the industrial development, and in their diet no less than in others, this revolution had largely passed by those who had not joined the exodus to the factory towns. In culinary terms the rural English, both peasantry and gentry, were still living in the eighteenth century, as a comparison of the cookery books published in that and the next century makes clear.

Eighteenth-century cooking was based upon an abundance of fresh local materials such as eggs, cream and vegetables. Meats were not eaten every day but there was a great variety, particularly of game and poultry. Smaller animals which we now largely scorn were also more widely eaten. If any preservation was undertaken it was by drying (of fruits) or by salting or smoking (of meat and fish). This is the tradition which our nineteenth-century immigrants brought here, precisely at a time when the technology of cooking was taking a big step forward. For in nineteenth-century England, the stress came to be upon raw materials, which could be transported in bulk from supplier to wholesaler and thence to the urban kitchen.

Commenting on this, Anne Wilson, whose *Food and Drink in Britain* is basic to the study of English cooking, has drawn attention to transportation systems such as improved roads and railways. These allowed food to be moved quickly and in quantity and thus for the development of cities on a vast scale (before this, urbations simply could not feed themselves beyond a certain population size). The process was accelerated by the development of food preservation techniques, first by vacuum and then by freezing. These changes altered European diet beyond recognition. As time went on, not only did new products and raw materials become ever more widely available, but the processing of others for storage and transportation and, more recently, the development of high yield but sometimes poorly flavoured animal and plant varieties, created many food tastes which would be wholly unfamiliar to anyone from the eighteenth or earlier centuries, if they were suddenly to appear among us.

7

These changes are now so familiar to us that we take them for granted and forget their implications. Not all of them have been benign. The trench warfare of the First World War, George Orwell somewhere reflects, would have been impossible without the invention of tinned food. It all made a sense of sorts in nineteenth-century Europe, but on reflection one can see that it makes very little sense in twentieth-century New Zealand. Here, we might have been better to stay with those traditions which were brought here by the immigrants, straight from the eighteenth century.

There are two further features of eighteenth-century cooking which are relevant to our picture of early immigrant traditions in New Zealand.

The first consideration is that eighteenth-century English cooking is itself the culminating point of a development which stretches back at least to medieval times, when books of recipes first began to appear. Some of the medieval dishes are identifiable in later compilations from their spices or their cooking techniques; a dish boiled in a cloth and with ginger or cloves in it, for instance, is almost certainly medieval in origin. And although English cooking developed some interesting regional variations and peculiar dishes, prior to the late eighteenth century it was a part of a general European tradition of cooking. For instance, that apparently archetypal French dish *boeuf bourguignonne*, that is to say beef stewed in red wine with bacon, small onions and mushrooms, is first found in a published version in English. It also has its equivalents in most cuisines of Europe. Consequently, the tradition of English cooking, although dependent on available ingredients (there were no aubergines grown in northern Europe for example and therefore no English equivalent of ratatouille), is broad of base. What happened when this tradition came to New Zealand was that the kinder climate of this country allowed the development of a more eclectic tradition, within a general European framework.

An interesting parallel to our own circumstances and what might be made of them is to be found in the cooking of New England and the Chesapeake

Bay area of the eastern seaboard of the United States. Based squarely and for obvious reasons on seventeenth- and eighteenth-century dishes, this regional cuisine adapted itself very quickly to new materials — shellfish, corn, potatoes, tomatoes — and came up with something very rich and distinct. A number of New England recipes are included in subsequent chapters of this book, to encourage our emulation.

The second (and restraining) consideration in the development of our own cuisine is the point of reference from which the nineteenth-century settlers began when confronted by an abundance. They ate every day in the new country what their immediate betters had eaten on special but not quite festive occasions in the old. More specifically they began with something called the 'farmer's ordinary'.

This particular element in the English culinary tradition has been described by Mary Norwak in *The Farmhouse Kitchen*:

> In the past the 'ordinary' was the meal traditionally served to farmers in the market town on market day. Each eating-house offered a meal at a fixed rate for allcomers; sometimes the place itself was called an 'ordinary'. These meals were great favourites with the farmers. They usually started with a hearty soup followed by a pie or savoury pudding, roast meat or poultry. The meal would finish with a sweet pie or pudding and plenty of cheese. With the main course there would be an abundance of vegetables; creamed vegetables were particularly popular in the winter. In addition to potatoes a variety of savoury, starchy puddings were prepared to eat with the meat and soak up the gravy.

It is from this, among many other things, that our penchant for stuffed boned lamb shoulder, i.e. colonial goose, derives.

Combined with this was another farmhouse tradition, that of tea (served about six in the evening) and in particular high tea, which consisted not only of cold meats and pies, salads, sandwiches and cold sweets but a profusion of cakes, scones and biscuits. What this combination of traditions became in New Zealand is described by Judy Millar, who often went as a young child to stay on her grandparents' farm in Taranaki. The contrast between her childhood and that of her husband Alan, already described, is fascinating.

> Whoever got up first, which I think was grandfather, set the fire and of course the porridge was soaked the night before, so that was put on to cook and then the bacon and eggs. At 7.30 you were called and you were faced with a plate, a huge plate, of porridge. Breakfast was all over by about 8 o'clock and then nana would go and do the dishes and get all that tidied up and she would rush and do the housework and then she was back in the kitchen preparing scones for morning tea. And straight after, or even before morning tea, the roast was put into the oven and the vegetables like potatoes and carrots were prepared and all sort of left there to cook. The greens were put on later. Jellies made the night before

9

and custard which you could carve and which was lovely. So, after your morning tea, she would be back in the kitchen finishing off preparation and getting all that ready and onto the table by about a quarter to twelve. The table was something else. A long table, silver for everybody and serving spoons up and down the table. The vegetables were put into serving dishes and then the last thing brought in at five to twelve was the meat, in a big plate, set by grandfather, and then the plates were placed next to him and with great ceremony he sharpened the knife and at 12 o'clock precisely the fork went in and he started carving, and honestly it just did happen by the clock, it was incredible.

So we would fight our way through this enormous meal. Now it was invariably summertime that I stayed with them and you ate your way through all sorts of vegetables, greasy fatty meat, which I loved, and greasy gravy, which again I loved. The plate was handed around, you helped yourself to vegetables. Occasionally grandfather would bring out a bottle of cider, he was a great cider person. As soon as you had finished and put your knife down the plate was whipped away. So once all that was done and the table was cleared of the vegetable dishes and meat and everything, all that first course, while you were still wiping your face on the napkin, the pudding was brought on, which would again take about three or four dishes, and usually the dessert was dished up for you.

Then they used to have a siesta; they would go and lie down until something like quarter to two and nana would then get up and start preparing for the afternoon tea which was at 3 o'clock. In the morning, depending on the day of the week, she would make fruit cakes and so forth which were of course put in tins. Come 3 o'clock my uncle and grandfather would appear, didn't have to be called, and you would have an enormous afternoon tea.

Afternoon tea actually went through about half an hour or three quarters of an hour. And then grandfather would be back in the house just before 5, scrubbed up and sitting down for tea. Everybody would be highly organised and sitting down and listening to the BBC News at 6 o'clock. And that was how the day went. My grandmother organised the whole thing. I never realised until I was older and thought back on it the time she spent in the kitchen. Rhubarb jam, plum jam, apple and mint chutney, preserved fruit, there were a whole list of traditions. It was in this walk-in pantry that she kept all the pickles and preserves and of course they had no refrigerator.

It was a very rich and varied diet.

Curiously by the beginning of the nineteen-fifties this tradition had vanished, except among the elderly. My own mother, who knew most of what was involved in it, was not interested in exercising her skills. After twenty years of cooking for a wholly unappreciative husband and four sons, of whom I was the youngest, she had given up the ghost almost entirely. She could only be induced to cook elaborately on great occasions like funerals, or Christmas, or church bring-and-buys.

Those of an older generation, however, retained some sense of what good food could be. My grandmother, for instance, who had grown up in the reign of Queen Victoria, always refused to eat white bakery bread. She said it was rubbish and in retrospect I agree she was quite right. Whenever she came visiting she brought her own small wholemeal loaf with her, an act of almost anarchistic eccentricity for the time. As a child I always liked to eat at her house because the food was very good. My godparents, who belonged to the same generation, not only served quite unbelievable afternoon teas (twenty different varieties of cakes and biscuits was par for the course), but always, until they were both very elderly, grew all their own vegetables. As late as 1966 they were able to describe to me their very first experience of eating tinned peas 'and they were awful' the husband concluded firmly. Like my granny, he had excellent powers of discrimination.

There are a number of reasons why the New Zealand tradition of abundance died by the 1950s. In the first place, of course, we were going through the same sort of social change which had happened in Britain a century earlier. We were urbanising and industrialising and the whole pattern of our transport and communications was changing. There was no more local abundance of raw materials. Suburbanisation spelt the end of the kitchen garden with its mature fruit trees and a few chooks. Neighbours complained about the rooster and the dog got into the run and ate the eggs. Home preserving, always a chore, was abandoned in favour of available tinned fruit. There began to develop processing and distribution industries which had a vested interest in urging us to buy their product. Some few people kept up the old ways but most stopped bothering. Their energy went into 'protecting their asset', i.e. laying concrete, putting up fences or painting the house. And there were other reasons for the deterioration in what we eat.

Two demons stalked the land, casting their evil blight over kitchens everywhere — nutrition and 'home science'. How this ghastly cult of wholesome food came to undermine the walls of culinary delight is a horridly fascinating story. The outline is given here as a cautionary tale. In 1906 one John Studholme, wealthy farmer of Canterbury, offered funds to the university college, so that a chair in Domestic Science could be set up. Outraged by the growth of secondary and tertiary education for women, but unable to stop it, Studholme felt that if women could not be prevented from going to school then they ought at least to be taught there something which fitted them for their proper role as wives and mothers. One of the matters he proposed for inclusion in the curriculum of the course he would endow, along with the bandaging of wounds and the beauty of the house, was 'the composition and cost of foods'. Canterbury College, to their lasting credit, declined his offer.

At Otago Studholme had better luck. He was abetted by Sir Truby King (who thought that the education of women in the same subjects as men was 'a preposterous farce') and a Dr F.C. Batchelor (who thought that 'after the age of puberty the education of women should be directed chiefly to domestic management, domestic economics, physiology and hygiene' and a 'home life which tends to the rearing of a healthy and happy population'). A course in 'home science' was thus set up in 1912. It was subsequently smuggled into the school syllabus and an arbitrary decision made, now changed thank heaven, that only girls would have its benefits. As if that were not bad enough, the story does not end there!

Following a series of reports by the health authorities early this century, commencing with an inquiry into some of the questions raised by the influenza epidemic of 1918 and continuing in investigations into the health of rural children in the twenties, horrifying conclusions emerged. It was found that the children of the poor, and in particular of poor farmers, were not getting enough to eat. There was significant malnutrition. The abundance found by the colonists was, it seemed, beginning to lose something in the distribution. The real solution would have been to increase incomes at the bottom of the social scale, but that would have meant unacceptable reforms. Instead it was decided to undertake that amazing liberal feat — effecting improvements without actually changing anything. Scores of enthusiastic interfering busybodies, i.e. social workers, descended upon the poor, particularly during the depression of the thirties and after, to explain to them that if they spent their money wisely then they could be adequately fed, without having an increase in the family income. After three decades and more of this there emerged triumphant the 'food as fuel' school of culinary thought. Any suggestion that eating might be an enjoyable experience either at home, or (horrors!) in a restaurant, was stamped on immediately.

It seems inconceivable now, but in the nineteen-fifties Eric Linklater could write of a visit to Central Otago and the problems of finding a public eating house as though he was an anthropologist describing the queer habits of an obscure tribe at the ends of the earth. Perhaps he was. 'The natural quality of the food is so good that it deserves both skill and reverence in the kitchen. What lordly dishes a French housewife would make of it! But the New Zealanders, like the Scots, think that baking is the better part of cookery and spend their ingenuity, exhaust their interest on cakes and pastries and ebullient vast cream sponges. Soup is neglected, meat mishandled.' And he went on to refer to a waitress who, when asked what she recommended, 'snorted at me "I wouldn't recommend a thing and I never touch their fish".' To such were we reduced by a malign coalition of Sir Truby King and assorted women's magazines. The rampant non-conformist conscience is a terrible thing.

But, I can hear you saying, all that surely has now changed? Well, not quite. It is perfectly true that restaurants now abound, but alas when we choose to eat out, like good colonials we take our point of reference from an urban metropolitan culture somewhere else. There is nothing wrong of course with French or Greek or some other national cuisine provided it is truly and well done. But in our attempts at *haute cuisine* we seem largely unaware that the tradition upon which we think we are drawing is itself decadent. In her fascinating book *The Cookery of England*, Elizabeth Ayrton mentions this decadence thus:

> From the time of Chaucer until the end of the eighteenth century the steward or housekeeper in palace or castle, the mistress of the manor, and the rich farmer's wife would have countenanced nothing slipshod in their great kitchens: every dish received exactly its traditional herbs and seasonings and had its proper gravies and accompaniments. It is when the mistress of a house which cannot support steward or housekeeper leaves the kitchen that the food loses its savour, and this is what happened to English food in the nineteenth century. It happened for two main reasons: rapid urbanisation which undermined the tradition of good farm housekeeping so that women with growing pretensions to gentility went out of their kitchens, and sat in their parlours; and a vast increase in prosperity for the great landowners and the ruling classes in general, which sent the gentry to Europe in search of education. As a result it became fashionable to import foreign chefs as well as foreign art treasures and Frenchmen such as Carème in the late eighteenth century, Ude in the Regency period, Alexis Soyer in Victorian times, and Escoffier in the Edwardian era became celebrities in England. . . . The results were that English, urban middle class cooking became debased by inept imitation of the fashionable and upper class world which could afford to import its chefs.

And those chefs, it might be added, despite their many admirable qualities, were schooled in a courtly tradition which derived from renaissance Italy and which had long since parted company from its roots in the age-old European tradition. A hundred years on, we are guilty of similar inept imitation.

Eric Linklater went on to say in his account that in giving addresses to groups of one sort or another he 'was tempted more than once to say something about cooking but as a guest in the country I thought criticism would be ungracious and might even be resented.' Those of us who live here should not feel constrained by a similar inhibition. Our failure to deal well with our culinary advantages is not a burning issue of the day. But it is significant enough; all of us eat at least once every twenty-four hours. It needs our attention.

Good cooking, like charity, begins at home. This book is directed to that

end. It is not, like some books of recipes, a jackdaw collection, but is designed for those who like to entertain or who would like to do so more regularly. There is more to it than cooking and eating. The meals it contains are not for every day (although some of the dishes, particularly those of vegetables) might very readily be adapted to that. Rather, they are for those who wish to sit down with friends to an entertainment complete in itself, not to eat but to *dine*, something we have largely yet to learn how to do. The Balinese say: We have no art we just do everything as well as we can. That applies to dining as to anything else, provided one important thing is always borne in mind. Food is one of the nicest things I know. It is not actually meant to be a punishment but a pleasure. A gentleman named Sir Theodore de Mayerne once remarked: 'It was an odde saying of a mad fellow, who having first well dined clapt his hand upon the board, and protested, that this eating and drinking was a very pretty invention, whoever first found it out.' As he was not only court physician to both James I and Charles I but the author of a cookery book which commences with the words quoted he ought to know what he was talking about. Paying heed to his advice will do you no harm although you might consider we have now wandered far in time and space from myself, forlorn, wondering how to fold an egg into a soufflé. I think not however. One of the pleasures of cooking is the discovery of its continuities, a feeling of relationship across the centuries to other cooks long dead in the flesh but alive in their recipes. It is a neverending process and one of the motivations for the writing of this book has been to add another brick to the culinary pyramid.

It is not the sole motive. To reduce the damage for the future that our recent history has done to our national diet is another. And as well to enable the not-quite-tyro cook to sit six people down to a meal of four courses without going stark mad and to emerge content at the end of a further three hours or so. Finally, perhaps, to feed that sprite in all of us which insists upon the sharing of what is known. Anyone who can read, as I discovered, can begin to learn to cook but there is more to dining than that.

Dining is a socialist activity; it requires not only humour to cope with its failures but a certain amount of central planning. This ensures not perfect cooking but at least minimal opportunity for disaster. So we have not yet got to the food. We need first to spend a little time considering what comes before in the matter of preparation.

Getting it Right

I write these precepts for immortal Greece,
That round a table delicately spread,
Or three, or four, may sit in choice repast,
Or five at most. Who otherwise shall dine,
Are like a troupe marauding for their prey.

— Archestratus
fragment from the lost poem
'Gastronomy'

IT IS THE OLDEST cliché in the world to say that you can't do the job if you don't have the proper tools. No one in their right mind would try to hammer in a nail with a brace and bit. But the number of people who attempt the culinary equivalent is really rather astonishing. 'Oh, I don't bother with a lot of cookery books', they say airily. 'I just throw in a bit of this and a bit of that and it comes out all right. But I couldn't tell you how I do it.' They are making it up. The only thing you would get from that method is a disgusting mess —unless you happen to be extremely good, and that takes years of experience and great skill. The fact is that if you want to cook successfully you shouldn't try to make custard in a frying pan. And if you want to go on and not only eat but *dine* then of course there is even more to it. Fundamentally four things are necessary: the right tools; the best ingredients; plenty of time and patience to devote to the task; and a sense of style fitting to the event.

16

Batterie de Cuisine

The right equipment is not the same thing as elaborate equipment. Some people have kitchens which are more complex and sophisticated than a hospital operating theatre. They frighten the life out of me and some of the owners of them couldn't scramble eggs. Actually that isn't fair, because scrambling eggs is one of the most difficult of all dishes to get right, but you will understand what I mean. The task is to cook, not to show off your possessions.

Unfortunately down at the ad agency they have cottoned on. The semi-literate snobs who make up too great a proportion of the market fall for it every time. Remember that the great chefs from Varenne to Soyer to Carème did all of that magnificent cooking without once seeing a microwave oven or a crockpot or any other similar gadget. That's not to say that certain recently invented items such as the ones I've just mentioned or whirligigs with a sharp blade in a plastic bowl or electric beaters aren't useful adjuncts to any kitchen. But they aren't *necessary* to good cooking. All you really need is two sources of heat, that's to say an oven and a cooking top (preferably gas, which is easier to control) and some pots, and you're in business. The equipment need not be the latest. I have an ancient oven; I know it and it knows me and we get on fine together. That said, however, the following kitchen advice may help you on your way.

If you want to buy decent equipment don't go to gifte shoppes. In most large towns there is a specialist supplier where professional cooks go to buy what they need. Find out where it is and go there. Most of these suppliers don't mind in the least dealing with individual domestic customers. And you'll discover two or three things. Firstly the quality will be high. Chefs and the owners of restaurants certainly aren't going to buy shoddy junk which won't do the job. Secondly everything you want and need (and a few highly specialist items, e.g. a machine for drawing wine corks, necessary in a busy restaurant, not in your home, that you do not) will be there in one place. If you ask at most retail kitchen outlets for a fish kettle they'll only gawp at you or tell you fish don't use kettles; wholesalers supplying the trade will know at once what you are talking about. And it may also surprise you to discover that professional equipment is often cheaper, because professionals have no intention of paying through the nose for their tools of trade. Wholesalers can keep prices down because they invoice in bulk and do their own warehousing. Nor do they have the same overheads, since they are not paying exorbitant rent in some trendy city arcade. The same goes for crockery and napery — for these too, go to the restaurant supplier. In fact for some items you can go a step beyond this. For kitchen glassware and related equipment try a chemical supplier. Laboratory beakers and flasks not only look good but you'll be surprised at how cheap they are (for the same reasons as above and also because much of it is imported from China where they want the foreign exchange). They are also very easy to keep clean and are in heat-resistant materials; they are designed for laboratory use after all. Besides, it adds a bit of 'high-tech' class to your table to decant your wine into a three-cornered flask marked off in millilitres!

Or you can go from the sublime to the ridiculous and buy some of your equipment from shops specialising in tramping gear. Those who engage in hardy outdoor pursuits can't be bothered with trumpery rubbish. They want something practical and sturdy and so do you. Many of the items they use for stewing possums or whatever they do in the hills were once the universal item for the job. The classic is the so-called camp oven which was the most widely used of all kitchen items well on into the nineteenth century. A small cast-iron camp oven makes a very good large casserole although it needs proper care and oiling, otherwise your stew will taste of rust, which is not very nice. And of course camping/tramping shops don't charge fancy prices.

If you really want to go into the subject in depth then I commend to you *Pot and Pans* by Gertrude Harris, which will tell you all about why silver chafing dishes are best or why you don't need a lot of copper bowls except for whisking egg whites. It can all get very high-falutin' and some of it is beyond me although it is interesting enough in its way. That aside, here are one or two tips from my own experience which you might find useful if you're setting up as a cook.

Saucepans and Frying Pans

These should be made of a material which conducts heat evenly and be heavy enough not to buckle with constant use, or to dent. Aluminium with copper bottoms is the best for saucepans, balancing expense with practicality, and cast iron for frying pans. Your frying pan should have a snug lid. Handles which don't burn you when you pick them up are also very desirable. Specialist items depend on your own needs. The fish kettle which I've already mentioned, for instance, makes the poaching of fish much easier, because it is the right shape and has a device for lifting out the cooked fish and transferring it to a serving dish without it coming apart before your very eyes. It is also expensive, however, unless you poach a lot of fish. Two other items I find particularly useful are a steamer and a double boiler. This latter, which the French call a *bain marie*, is essentially one saucepan fitting snugly inside another, with the lower one of the two containing water. The point is to ensure that the effects of direct heat are minimised and this can be very helpful if you are making a custard or a sauce with eggs and cream. It won't stop your dish from curdling, any more than any other item of equipment will turn you into a good cook, but it will minimise the opportunities for disaster. A steamer is for vegetables. I actually use a collander above a saucepan of simmering water but you can buy special saucepans for the purpose. If you use a wok then you may be familiar with the circular bamboo steamers with lids which can be stacked up. I don't much care for that system because I think it taints the food and isn't really very efficient; a good deal of the steam escapes and runs down the kitchen wall.

It is also convenient to hang up your pots and pans, which saves bending down or opening cupboards all the time. There's no need to buy some fancy gadget for this purpose. I use a piece of aluminium towel rail fixed to the wall and some butcher's hooks. I have never gone in for pressure cookers although my mother has used one all her life and still finds it convenient. To tell the truth I'm afraid of the things. They're not a new invention, incidentally. John Evelyn records in his diary for 3 July 1679 that he went along to the Tower of London to visit his friend Samuel Pepys (who was locked up on a charge of handing over naval secrets to the French, but subsequently exonerated). He was bringing Pepys a leg of venison, and intended to dine with him there. Afterwards he went on to the newly founded Royal Society, where he saw a demonstration of cooking under pressure with a 'digester'. This was the invention of Denis Papin, a Huguenot refugee from Blois. If you should ever visit Blois you will find that the local citizens have erected a statue to the gentleman (and to his device, which is also depicted), a most civilised and very French act. Evelyn dined on some pigeons cooked this way: 'Nothing exceeded the pigeons which tasted just as if baked in a pie, all these being stewed in their own juice without any addition of water save what swam about in the digester.'

Casseroles

About a decade and a half ago a strange plague broke out in this country. It may be loosely described as a visitation of potters. They are with us still, as are their wares. Many of these are misshapen and ugly (the wares, not the potters) and others leak, and are badly glazed. But some are all right and among these are earthenware casseroles. Some people swear by them and say that they add to the flavour of the food. Happen they do but I don't use them myself. This is not only because I keep dropping the lids and breaking them but because cast iron is better. You get a more even heat, and they have an additional advantage — they can also be used on top of the stove as a high-sided frying pan. The ones lined with vitreous enamel are best because they are easiest to keep clean. A casserole is a very important item for the sort of cooking I am talking about in this book, because it can be used to prepare dishes which do not have to be timed too precisely. If you can deal with one course of a dinner in that way then that is often very helpful, particularly if you are slow-cooking. I actually have three casseroles of different sizes and I use them more than any other kitchen vessel.

19

Knives

A set of knives is a most important requirement. Carbon steel combined with molybdenum takes the best edge and knives should be kept very sharp because paradoxically you are less likely to cut yourself that way — a sharp knife will not slip. But do warn any friends who happen to be using your kitchen. Not everyone keeps their knives like razors and an unfamiliar knife makes the user clumsy. As with pots and pans there are different ones for different purposes. I have two different sizes of carver, a vegetable knife and a boning knife. You can get as elaborate as you like. Some people use the knives that freezing workers use; another friend of mine has bought surgical knives, which are very good for carving, but that seems a bit macabre to me. Good knives cost money but they last for ever. You will need a good steel as well. There are various gadgets for sharpening, some of them electric, but to my mind they distort the blade. My father always used to declare at Sunday lunch apropos of the carving knife: 'You could ride to China on this damn thing and do yourself no harm' and to the outrage of my mother he would go and sharpen it on the concrete back doorstep. I wouldn't recommend that, no matter how spectacular it might be. My father knew what he was doing because he'd been a cook in forestry camps in his time, but he was an exception.

Miscellaneous

As you go along you will of course be tempted by exotica which you don't need — grapefruit knives, salamanders, couscous steamers; you name it, and there'll be some salesman in white vinyl shoes ready to palm it off on you. That notwithstanding, a couple of moulds, a pestle and mortar (from the chemical supplier), a mincer and a really good set of scales will set you up a treat. The old-fashioned balance scales with a shallow curved removable container are the best, and two sets of weights, one metric and the other avoirdupois. American weights and measures are a bit of a pest because they use a standard 'cup' so you may need a measure for that. It's also a good idea to get yourself a standard set of 'spoons' for the same purpose. As you go along through this book you'll find other items you may require. Personally, I've always adopted the principle of never buying something until I need it and then asking myself whether I already have something which can be adapted And when faced with a choice of items, it has always been my rule of thumb to choose the design which was in use in my mother's time. Cooking is a severely practical business; a utensil which won't do the job goes to the scrap-heap pretty quickly. Conversely, if it's still around after a generation or two and the professionals use it, then it almost certainly works.

Materials

Chippendale couldn't have made his furniture if all he'd had was laminated chipboard. Cooking is the same. You can't make a good meal out of tired vegetables and tough meat. It's also not advisable to substitute one item for another in a recipe. The flavour is never the same (to invent something equally interesting takes a good deal of experience), and it will more likely come out like nothing on earth, or worse.

The first criterion for food is freshness. In particular that creates problems with vegetables and some of the more exotic meats and fish. Deep freezing can help availability but it tends to have an effect on flavour. Many vegetables and fruits have come long distances before you see them, and have wilted. The best thing is to grow your own but that takes a lot of time. Nor does everybody have the space. If you have fruit trees they should be looked after. The best thing is to go out into the countryside and buy from the supplier even though that may mean buying in bulk. Vegetable co-ops are quite good from that point of view.

I'm not one of those fanatics who won't have anything to do with sprays and chemicals and I don't bother with 'naturally grown' materials even though I have a supplier very close. But that isn't to say that items don't need to be carefully washed. And there's another problem, a classic example being the tomato: since about 1880, when they first became popular, tomatoes have been more selectively bred than almost any other vegetable, but for the wrong reasons — that is, for the purposes not of eating but of agribusiness. They've become larger, of standard size, of thicker skin and of increasingly jelly-like internal consistency. They're not usually allowed to ripen on the plant, because they bruise in mechanical picking if they do. The net result of this has been the development of tomatoes which taste like cotton wool.

Many other vegetables and fruits suffer the same fate. Just what can be done about this I don't really know. Perhaps it's time that consumer organisations in this country took it up. The trouble is we've all grown so used to insipid tomatoes, frozen peas, etc. that we don't notice their deficiencies any more, except when we chance to get the real thing from time to time. Mostly we have to make do with the poor stuff which is all that's available on the market. The effect can be minimised by finding good greengrocers who care about the quality of their produce, and sticking with them. If they know you are interested then you will get good service, and even market information. Failing that, cultivate your rural acquaintance.

The same goes for butchers. A supplier of meat who knows what he is doing is a pearl beyond price. Develop a personal relationship with him or her. My butcher, Ernie, was a little nonplussed by my original requests for some out-of-the-ordinary items but now he responds with considerable enthusiasm. He also cares about the *presentation* of his meat and that can't be said of every butcher in this country by any means. If your butcher turns

surly when faced with a request for a pig's head or an ox heart then go elsewhere. It's pleasing to note that there's a better variety of meat on the market over recent years. This is partly because of economic circumstances; people have less money, so the cheaper cuts and items of offal are now more regularly asked for. At the other end of the market, cuts which previously went for export exclusively, for example, lamb fillet, are now also available, so it's an ill wind that blows nobody good. Rabbits and venison can be got too, although the farmed variety are not as good as the wild. For more exotic items such as hare or trout you may have to rely on huntin' shootin' fishin' friends although a search will usually unearth a source of supply in the larger cities. The same goes for the general run of fish and most of the rarer dry goods.

Finally, a brief comment on herbs and spices. The ideal is a herb garden just outside the kitchen door, but that might be expecting rather too much. If you can get fresh herbs then the difference will astonish you and it won't do you too much harm to grow a pot of parsley and some mint. But beyond that most of us can't really manage and we have to buy the dried variety. Herbs do lose potency after a while so keep them sealed up and replace them at regular intervals. The same goes for spices. The best thing with these latter is to buy them in their natural state and grind them as you need them. The value of freshly ground pepper goes without saying but the same is true of say nutmeg or cinnamon. And stay right away from monosodium glutamate.

Planning

If you are giving a dinner party on Saturday it's obviously no use sitting down to think about it at 2 pm on the day. Preparing a dinner is a co-ordinated operation and proceeds in several stages, some of them commencing well beforehand. For instance, I find it convenient to prepare meat stocks in bulk and to freeze them in convenient quantities to be thawed out as I need them. Equally, some desserts can be made well in advance, like ice creams and sorbets.

But mostly to me giving a dinner begins two or three days before when I sit down with some cookery books and plan the menu. Obviously the first thing you will need is a decent collection of such books. The rule of thumb is that the glossy large format ones are to be avoided. There are certain classics, too, which you will discover as you go along — the works of Jane Grigson or Elizabeth David for instance. As with pots and pans you can get very involved, particularly as there are now a range of reprints of medieval works or eighteenth-century classics as well as a host of magazines, some good, some bad. The over-riding purpose is to cook rather than to read, although there's much to be said for the pleasures of the latter. Assuming however that you now have a small collection in front of you, here are some basics.

The first is *timing*. It would be very foolhardy to select four dishes, all needing elaborate last-minute preparation such as sauces. Even if you could manage them, your guests wouldn't see you because you'd be in the kitchen all the time. It is much more sensible to choose a combination of hot and cold, slow and fast dishes. For instance, a soup can often be prepared in advance and served cold, or heated up when the guests arrive. A second course might be something quick to cook, the main course a slow-cooked item and the dessert cold too. You can ring the changes on all of these. In summer it's sometimes good to have everything cold but well-flavoured. Second courses can be cold and desserts put in to cook after the main course has been taken from the oven. The point is not to try doing seventeen things at once.

The second rule is that of *appropriateness*. Try and keep your cuisine consistent, both within the one course and between courses. Pasta doesn't go with roast beef and cabbage. A Chinese soup doesn't normally go with a Hungarian main dish and vice versa. Sometimes things like that can be made to work but it takes a fair bit of experience and skill. You also have to choose your menus to suit your guests. Not everybody has a granny sophisticated enough to cope with a pheasant braised in gin (although some of my friends have), preceded by escargot with buttered noodles. And there also needs to be a balance struck between flavours, the light and the heavy. A leguminous soup followed by a pâté en croûte, a beef Wellington and a Sussex pound pudding is not a good menu. You would have to hire some porters with trolleys to remove your guests from the table afterwards. And again, unless you are making a feature of it, have a sophisticated group of diners and know what you are doing, you shouldn't have a single flavour like orange in every dish of a four-course meal.

Once you've chosen your menu you will then have to check what you will need and *make a shopping list*. It's no use finding at the last minute that you haven't any nutmeg or savory. They are in the dish for a reason and it detracts from the flavour if they are left out. Better still, make several lists and shop over several days rather than coming home at the last minute festooned with parcels like a Christmas tree. It helps to buy certain stores in bulk and to have them always on hand, like some tinned goods and certainly many dry goods. I don't know why the institution of the pantry ever went out of fashion.

Above all, allow yourself *plenty of time*, particularly when it comes to the cooking itself. Good food can't be hurried. If the recipe says beat the egg whites until stiff then either do that or don't make pavlova at all. Read the recipe several times right through before you even begin, and work out a sequence of preparations. If the cream is coming to the boil and you haven't yet separated the eggs then I wouldn't be surprised if your sauce curdles. I like to have almost everything prepared at least four or five hours prior to the guests arriving and then to have the last minute things carefully programmed. This allows me to waft about drinking sherry without an apparent care in the world.

In the end it becomes routine. The main dish has been cooking all day. As the last guest arrives you can turn on the soup. The pâté is in the refrigerator. As the soup is served the vegetables, ready prepared in their steamer, are turned on. As the main course comes out of the oven, the tart in its blind-baked case goes in. Sometimes it goes wrong of course and the only thing to do then is to confess all to the guests and pour them another glass of wine while you correct it. No one will care; the intention is conviviality, not to make an obstacle course for the cook. What I can't stand is to go out for dinner at eight, be given the first course at ten and still be waiting for dessert at midnight. By that stage everyone is not only irritable but so sloshed they don't know what they are eating.

Style

The table should be ample, and above all solid, with no squeaks and shiverings. Plates, too, should be large, and the silver heavy rather than light, with smooth simple lines to it. Plain linen, ample as the table, plain colours in the flowers and the fruits, glasses no more ornamented than the bubbles they imitate — all should be adequate as the food and drink served there.

Thus writes M.F.K. Fisher in *Serve It Forth*. What she is describing is the style associated with dining.

Just because you've got the right equipment, the best ingredients and have planned everything to the last detail, don't think that makes for a perfect dinner. How would it be if you then served the meal off paper plates in people's laps? Some people like to live like that, but to me eating a dinner with friends needs just a tiny element of formality to make it work properly. A sense of an occasion somewhat out of the ordinary if you like. This is where style comes into the picture. That doesn't necessarily mean Georgian silver and dinner jackets. I want to keep emphasising that point — a dinner party should be an enjoyable experience, not an ordeal or a punishment.

Everybody has a different style and everything they do should express it, but there are some basic rules to be observed.

The great French savant and master of taste and style, Jean Anthelme Brillat-Savarin, remarks in his *La Physiologie du Goût* of 1825:

> The pleasures of the table must be carefully distinguished from their necessary antecedent, the pleasure of eating. The pleasure of eating is the actual and direct sensation of a need being satisfied. The pleasures of the table are considered sensations born of the various circumstances of fact, things and persons accompanying the meal. The pleasure of eating is common to ourselves and the animals, and depends on nothing but hunger and the means to satisfy it. The pleasures of the table are peculiar to mankind and depend upon preliminary care over the preparation of the meal, the choice of the place and the selection of guests.

And he ends with the comment: 'At the end of a good dinner, body and soul both enjoy a remarkable sense of well-being.'

Brillat-Savarin is, incidentally, one of the most interesting of all writers on the subject of food, as much for himself as for what he wrote. He was born into a family of lawyers in Belley in south-eastern France in 1755. This family were all renowned gourmets; his sister died at the age of one hundred sitting up in bed having just finished a good dinner and calling loudly for her dessert. A splendid way to go! Jean studied law at Lyon and Dijon, became public prosecutor in Belley and was a delegate to the famous Versailles parliament in 1789. But he was a royalist by inclination and narrowly escaped the guillotine. In 1793 he found it prudent to decamp to the United States for a few years. In 1796 he returned to France, was pardoned, and began his culinary career when he became caterer to the French general staff. He served with distinction in high civic office under both Napoleon and the restored Bourbons. He was famous throughout Paris for his dinners. It was he who said: 'The discovery of a new dish does more for the happiness of humankind than the discovery of a star.' His book, translated as *The Philosopher in the Kitchen,* repays the experience of dipping into it.

What Brillat-Savarin was trying to impress upon his readers was that there is an approach to dining which makes it one of the most pleasurable of human experiences. That is not to say that there is a right and a wrong; on the contrary. The nature of the meal should express the essence of the host or hostess and this should be instantly recognisable to the guests. This is a truth that the Chinese and Japanese realised many centuries ago. We are only now catching up with it.

How many people should come to dinner? Archestratus thought no more than five. Four is too few and eight too many. M.F.K. Fisher in *An Alphabet For Gourmets* says:

> I feel that gastronomic perfection can be reached in these combinations: one person dining alone, usually upon a couch or a hillside; two people of

no matter what sex or age dining in a good restaurant; six people of no matter what sex or age dining in a good home. . . . The six should be capable of decent social behaviour: that is, no two of them should be so much in love as to bore the others, nor at the opposite extreme should they be carrying on any sexual or professional feud which could put poison on the plates all must eat from. A good combination would be one married couple, for warm composure; one less firmly established to add a note of investigation to the talk; and two strangers of either sex, upon whom the better acquainted diners could sharpen their questioning wits.

This is excellent advice, but let me add some further to it. They should meet one another over a well dressed table.

It is vital consequently to have adequate accoutrements. A table and chairs, naturally, but what is to go on the table itself? The starching and ironing of damask linen tablecloths is one of the silliest activities known to humankind. Nevertheless the effect of such an item covering a table and in its turn as base for gleaming glasses and cutlery is unparalleled. That is to say for a European meal of the modern period. It would not be appropriate, I feel, for a Chinese dinner or a meal of the medieval or classical periods. Some people have a separate dining room. I like my guests to come into the room and to see the dining table and to have it before them as a constant reminder of the pleasure to come as they take their apéritif. A single rosebud as centrepiece? Some like to dine by candlelight but I confess that I do not. I like the lighting effect, but the candles get in the way of the serving and divide the table.

And then there is the matter of the dinner service. It has become fashionable recently to compete over this, and we now have the dinner service as status object. One can pay vast and unnecessary sums for a German or French service. But the purpose is to eat, not to read the imprint on the bottom of the plates. That is like buying clothes with the label on the *outside* so that no one can be in any doubt about the couturier (when in fact the famous designer has never set eyes on the garment and has done no more than sell a licence to use the name). Next time you are in a restaurant look at the crockery. You will find that it is hard-wearing, heavy-duty, easy to wash and therefore well-fired, and heat-resistant. You might do worse than to emulate this example. As already remarked, a restaurant supplier is the best place to buy such things. You will amost certainly find them much easier on the pocket as well.

Many of the items of dinner service we now take for granted are relatively recent in origin, and that includes plates. Until the late middle ages thick slices of bread were universally used to serve food. They were called trenchers, and were only gradually replaced with plates and bowls, made of silver or pewter for the wealthy, and wood for the poor. In the eighteenth century, when China was opened to trade with Europe, crockery became fashionable, and the original dinner services were either imported from China or copied from items which the Chinese (who regarded the Europeans, not without reason, as barbarians) had mass-produced for the purpose. To the Chinese it was low-grade junk; to the crowned heads of Europe chinoiserie became all the rage. In the end the market became flooded, however, and Europe was swamped in an avalanche of porcelain carried as ballast in merchantmen returning from the east. This trade continues.

The history of cutlery is even more surprising. The use of spoons did not become widespread until the late middle ages and guests brought their own knives to a meal. The fork took even longer to catch on. It first appeared in Italy and Spain in the fifteenth century but was widely regarded elsewhere as decadent and over-civilised. An English traveller who brought one back from Italy in 1608 became the object of derision among his friends. No forks appear in English inventories before 1660 and their use only became general after 1750. As for individual glassware, in many places it was unheard of before the seventeenth century. Instead a large glass used to be handed along the table and a servant kept it full as it progressed. The passing of the port is a survival of this custom. The philosopher Montaigne was astonished to find, travelling in Germany in 1580, that 'everyone has his goblet or silver cup at his place; the man serving takes care to refill this goblet immediately it is empty without moving it from its place, pouring wine therein from a distance away out of a tin or wooden vessel with a long spout.'

Just what people did have in their houses in earlier times has become much clearer through a project undertaken by Caroline Davidson in respect of the historic Ham House on the outskirts of London. Ms Davidson has been restoring the kitchen and larder as they would have been in the 1670s and 1680s when the house was home to Elizabeth, Countess of Dysart, and her second husband the Duke of Lauderdale, who was Secretary of State for Scotland under Charles II. If you are interested in following this up you can find the details published in issues 12 and 15 of an excellent cooking periodical entitled *Petits Propos Culinaires*. And of course if you are in England a visit to the kitchen at Ham is intensely interesting. (Another kitchen which is even more so, in my view, is the one at the Brighton Pavilion.)

Even the serving of meals in courses is a fairly recent phenomenon, as is the giving of dinner parties itself. Until the early eighteenth century there was no division of a meal into courses as we would understand them. All of the main dishes, both sweet and savoury, were served at once. One took a little of what was before one and then helped one's neighbour to it and so everything was passed around the table. There is an interesting diagram for setting out a table for a cold wedding feast in one of the household books for Ingatestone Hall in Essex in the sixteenth century. In the middle of the table is a vast 'piramid of sweetmeats' surrounded all around with fruit jellies, pigeon pies, custards, 'hambs', tarts, cold chicken, salmon and so on.

This sort of setting out of dishes was carried, as with much else, almost into the realm of high art in France in the seventeenth and eighteenth centuries. One of the more fascinating handbooks published on the subject was published by Antoine de Courtin in 1695. It contains such vital information on etiquette as when to wear your hat at table (always except when grace was said — except the King who ate bareheaded) and how to get the ash off a truffle (blowing it was out, it should be scraped off with a knife). And it goes on to caution gentlemen not to put their elbows on the table, nor their fingers in their food, not to gnaw bones, and to *always* tip their hat to a lady when offering her an item. However, by the middle of the eighteenth century these vast and formal meals (one of Louis XIV's chefs committed suicide when a dish went wrong) had been largely replaced by the *souper intime*. That well-known cad, Giacomo Casanova, has left a description of such a supper at Venice. The dishes were prepared in advance and kept warm over hot water baths. No servants were present and the ladies mixed the salad *with their own hands*. Knowledge of such improper behaviour must have sent a *frisson* through polite society.

One of the great aficionados of intimate dinners was the philosopher Voltaire who described himself as an exponent of *nouvelle cuisine* and came down very hard on the hearty cooking of an earlier age and in particular its chefs, whom he described as poisoners. When he was ensconced at Ferney scholars came to visit as much for his dinners as for his wit and learning. This may be pardoned in them. In one letter of invitation to a friend he offers 'a truffled turkey as tender as a squab and as fat as the bishop of Geneva'. In fact his suppers became so famous that he complained that they were killing him and that he had become the innkeeper to Europe. He did not stop giving them, nevertheless.

At his table one day he perforce entertained the young James Boswell, taking the grand tour. Boswell had invited himself to dinner but seemed mainly intent on making off with the chambermaid which, on his own admission, he did. He may not have appreciated the food much: dinners in England at this time and later were too often characterised by much drinking and ended to the drunken snoring of those who had slid gracelessly beneath the table.

I wouldn't want to suggest that the English on the other hand were behind the French in the niceness of their table settings. Many eighteenth-century cookbooks have advice on how to set out the dishes on the table. The most elaborate is Charles Carter's *The Complete Practical Cook* of 1730 with its sixty copper engraved plates of table settings. Less complicated but more charming is Sarah Harrison's *The Housekeeper's Pocket Book* (1739) or Alice Smith's *Art of Cookery* (1758). Alice remarks: 'We have learned many little arts of the French and it is a pity that we do not a little more carefully follow them in this. The best dinner will have but an ill aspect if the dishes are not properly disposed on the table, and in this we are very deficient. We have a John Trot method, in which we go on with perfect sameness; they have a great variety.' And she goes on to explain how dishes might be differently served for as many as thirteen different courses — 'for these the table is to be of a square, and they are to be placed in three rows, five down the middle of the table and four on each side.' This may not have done much however to improve the manners of the diners who hawked and spat, drank at least two bottles of claret each, ogled the maid-servants and brought their large hunting dogs inside.

By the middle of the next century, however, the work of religious reformers had cleaned up the English dinner to such an extent that Lord Melbourne was heard to complain indignantly that things had come to a pretty pass when religion was allowed to invade private life. The conviviality of Sydney Smith and Parson Woodforde had been replaced by the starchy formality we have come to associate with the high Victorian era. At about the same time the 'Russian service', as it was called, replaced the 'French service' of yore. That is to say, whereas previously all the dishes were served higgledy-piggledy they were now served in the manner we would today recognise as courses. We would find some Victorian menu habits a little strange however. It was considered unmanly for the gentlemen to have the sweet and the dinner invariably ended with a savoury, which ladies usually missed, it being considered too robust for them. What the Victorians ate as savouries we might now eat as an entrée, but they are not quite equivalent. Sardines on toast, or pear and Stilton, would be thought a bit odd as second course I think. But Victorians thought nothing of polishing off a meal of eight courses, upon which the ladies retired and the men sat about drinking port and telling one another the latest blue stories.

It took the Prince of Wales, later Edward VII, a man of no discernible merit in any other regard, to reintroduce convivial dining to society. It is understandable that he should have done so. Such an exuberant Francophile and leader of fashion could hardly fail to bring his England such a feature of the *belle époque*. No one could dine like the French of that period. It is just a pity that Edward introduced bad French *haute cuisine* at the same time. It was not a trap into which two of the greatest exponents of dining at home of the period would ever have fallen.

The first of these was Henri de Toulouse-Lautrec, member of *le tout Paris* and the *demi-monde*, friend of the cook and art dealer Maurice Joyant and no mean cook himself. He also used to paint a bit. No one could turn on a dinner party like Lautrec. He invented the cocktail, kept careful records of the recipes he discovered and took extreme pains over his table settings. He even designed his own menus, a new one for each meal, and lithographed them. They are now fought over by collectors everywhere. There is one in the National Gallery in Wellington. On one occasion he offered as dessert a showing of a new painting by the symbolist Paul Leclerc. Crucially, however, he always based his cooking on his own rural tradition.

He is surpassed only by his near contemporary Alexandre Dumas, once at the centre of a celebrated culinary scandal. His cook, Sophie, claimed darkly that the Dumas culinary reputation was undeserved. Apprised of this canard during a visit to the Café de Paris by a malicious Dr Veron, the outraged Dumas invited the entire company to dinner the following day to watch him cook. Among those present was Albert Vandam who wrote it all down and remained throughout his life charmed by the sight of Dumas, an enormous man, with chest bared and clad in an apron, turning out *soupe de choux, carpe farcée, ragoût de faisan à la hongroise* and *salade japonaise*. Of Dumas more hereafter. But these two were only the doyens of an enormous tribe —Emile Zola, for instance, whose taste for exotic food was not appreciated by everyone. The novelist Daudet once compared a hazel hen he ate with Zola with 'the scented flesh of an old tart marinated in a bidet' which makes one wonder how Daudet was able to make the comparison; I hope the writer and his friend Jeanne Rozerot never invited him to dinner again. Zola's novels are studded with dining episodes of which the most famous is undoubtedly the dinner party in *Nana*. Not perhaps a good omen for this book. There were too many guests, too many courses, too much to drink. Let it be a warning to the pretentious.

For myself I prefer the simplicities of Sydney Smith who knew how to combine the splendid English food of the eighteenth century with wit and sparkle, and of James Woodforde who one night at dinner laughed so

immoderately at the pleasure of it all that he choked (not fatally) on the hot gooseberry pie. And on another personal note: it is my custom to keep a dinner book. This records the menu and at the end of the meal the guests sign it. It serves several functions. Firstly, you know not to serve the same meal or dish twice to the same guests and, secondly, it is a splendid conversation piece as it is passed around the table and the dishes in it compared. Of course it also has its funny side and its attendant dangers. Some of the signatures are next day indecipherable for obvious reasons, nor can the more boisterous always forbear to make written remarks. I have had to entirely give up serving port with the coffee since one diner fulsomely admired the port. This has since led to loud demands for port and faced with the ruinous expense this entails I am constrained to serve sauternes instead.

The hilarity which accompanies the end of many meals is part of their charm. On one occasion this stimulated my cat, which usually runs a mile, to join in the proceedings. She emerged into the dining room clutching a large and not quite dead rat as her contribution to the general brouhaha. She seemed surprised at the curses this attempt at bonhomie called down upon her.

Planning an Unusual Meal

Let's assume that you're setting out to give a small dinner party and you crave to do something entirely different. How about a meal as it might have been eaten in Rome during the early Empire, say at the time of Tiberius or Claudius Augustus? A four-course dinner for six.

You must begin by putting out of your mind all that you learned or have heard about larks' tongues in aspic. Of course it's perfectly true that Julius Caesar in a single election campaign spent five million sesterces on meals for his political supporters, but having now observed a number of election campaigns in the United States I know that Caesar was an amateur. And besides, politics is something else. Certainly the Emperor Heliogabalus sent hunters into Lydia offering two hundred gold pieces to anyone who came back with a phoenix, and fed his prized conger eels on the living flesh of his slaves. Certainly Mark Antony gave his chef a town of thirty-five thousand people as a reward for his paste of flamingo brains. Petronius Arbiter has one of his characters say: 'Only command him and my cook will make you a fish out of the pig's chitterlings, a wood pigeon out of the lard, and turtle-dove out of the gammex, and a hen out of the shoulder.' Lucullus had trout brought alive from a mountain stream to expire in front of those who were to eat them. His style when eating grapes stimulated Juvenal to write:

> Stretched on unsocial couch he rolls his eyes
> O'er many an orb of matchless form and size,
> Selects the fairest to receive his plate,
> And at one meal devours a whole estate.

These were the decadent and depraved, inventors of the dread vomitaria. We know of them only because their contemporaries found their behaviour so outrageous they wrote it down so that future generations might marvel at the bizarre nature of it all. And we do. 'Are you astonished at our innumerable diseases?' asked Seneca. 'Then count the number of our cooks.'

Most Romans, even of the wealthiest class, dined simply, sitting on stools at table. Most did not recline on couches; this was a habit from Lydia (in Western Turkey), much beloved of the Athenian aristocracy of the time of Socrates, but excoriated by most right-thinking democrats, along with the wearing of silk and perfume by men.

So here we are sitting at a plain wooden table covered with a simple linen cloth. We may begin with wine but it should have water in it. The Romans thought the drinking of unadulterated wine a nasty barbarian habit only suitable for Germans and suchlike. The fact that the Emperor Tiberius drank his wine unwatered was considered so peculiar that it was mentioned in Seutonius' history of the early Caesars.

The recipes which follow are drawn by and large from the only extant cookery book of Roman times — *De re coquinaria** — attributed to the gourmet Apicius, a first-century contemporary of Tiberius Caesar, the Caesar of the New Testament. It is in fact a fourth-century compilation. Most of what we know about Apicius comes from Pliny the Elder, who was a bit sniffy about him, regarding him as a jumped-up *equites* whereas Pliny was a patrician. There is much of interest in Apicius. Quite apart from anything else he had great style. He inherited a fortune which even by the standards of the early Empire was excessive, and in ten years managed to spend one hundred million sesterces, mainly on food and high living. One morning the ancient Roman equivalent of his accountant told him that all he had left was about ten million. If he pulled in his horns and retreated to his country estate he could survive. No thanks, said Apicius, and committed suicide. The meal that follows is the sort which would have sustained him if he'd taken the other option.

BARLEY SOUP

This is the classic soup of antiquity. The Spartans, they say, ate nothing else, but then everyone at the time found them rather odd. Their hobbies were running, fatigue, hunger, thirst and putting down any incipient uprisings among the peasantry they ruled.

100 g chick peas
100 g green lentils
100 g dried peas
100 g pearl barley
2 leeks

---

*Apicius, *The Roman Cookery Book: A Critical Translation of the Art of Cooking*, B. Flower and E. Rosebaum, 1958.

olive oil
coriander, dill, fennel, oregano, asafoetida, lovage, garum
200 g broccoli

Soak the chick peas, lentils, barley and peas overnight, cover well with water and simmer until tender. Add the chopped leeks, a tablespoon of olive oil, coriander, dill and fennel. Cook the flowerets of broccoli separately. Mix together the other herbs. As far as we are aware the Roman herb *silphium* is asafoetida which can be bought at your pharmacy as an essence. It's very strong so just a few drops will suffice. Garum is a little more problematical. It was actually a rather nasty substance — the innards of fish mixed with anchovies and salt and left to ferment in the sun — and this I cannot recommend. Nor I think would the Medical Officer of Health. But it was the universal seasoning of those times and your dish will be inauthentic without. The nearest modern equivalent is a south-east Asian spice *blachan*. If you can't obtain that then anchovy essence will do, to the amount of a couple of teaspoons. Add this mixture to the soup along with the broccoli. Throughout the meal as well as with this soup the Romans would have served bread (no butter).

Italian bread for the upper classes was made from soft white wheat and sometimes had chalk added to ensure that it was as white as possible. The lower orders ate a darker bread. 'To know the colour of your bread' was the Roman expression for knowing one's place in the class system. If you like making bread then this recipe may interest you. If not then any wholemeal loaf will be more or less authentic for recreating a Roman meal.

BARLEY BREAD

You should be able to obtain the required quantities of barley flour from a health food shop:

450 g strong plain flour
120 g barley meal
15 g yeast
1 teaspoon salt
340 ml tepid water
3 tablespoons milk or buttermilk

Mix the two meals and the salt very thoroughly together in a heat resistant dish and put it in a very low oven for just a few minutes, to warm. Put the yeast in a cup and pour a little bit of tepid water over it to cover. In a couple of minutes it will soften enough to mix to a cream. Let it work for about ten minutes or so. If you are using dried yeast add a little sugar. Pour the yeast into the flour, add some more water and stir it in. Now pour in the rest of the water and the milk and mix until the dough is lithe and elastic. Mixing with your hands is the only real way to do it. Form it into a ball, sprinkle a little flour on it and leave it covered with a plate to rise. In a couple of hours it should have doubled in volume. Slap it down and knead it again by sprinkling it with flour and folding it over itself several times. Do this firmly and thoroughly. Have a loaf tin ready lightly greased and knead the dough into it. Leave it to rise again for about 45 minutes. Then bake it at 220°C in a pre-heated oven for 15 minutes, reduce the heat to 200° and give it another 15 minutes. Shake the loaf out of the tin, put it back in the oven on its side and give it another 20 minutes at 180°C. Bread is done if it 'booms' when you tap the side of the loaf. Leave it to cool on a rack. This is not quite how the Romans made bread two thousand years ago but it is essentially the same. Barley bread, although more typical of the northern areas of the Empire such as Britain, was made everywhere. Carbonised loaves found at Pompeii were round and about eight inches in diameter and it is from analysis of these that we know the ingredients. There is some debate about whether the Romans made cake. One cake-like bread called *libum* seems to have been a combination of cheese, flour and egg. They did not however succeed in inventing the pastry pie. That had to wait about a thousand years.

MUSHROOM ENTRÉE — GUSTATIO

The Romans were inordinately fond of mushrooms. Too fond. The Emperor Claudius poisoned himself eating some of the wrong kind. Some say it was done on purpose by his wife, the mother of Nero, who thus became Emperor owing to the unfortunate decease of his stepfather. Pliny remarks that Roman gentlemen would condescend to cook this dish themselves in front of their guests. Perhaps they just wanted to be quite sure what was going into it. The Romans seem not to have cooked mushrooms in plain oil. They either simmered them in water and then transferred them to another pan for final cooking in a sauce, or they may have cooked them in the sauce itself. Favourites for these sauces were mixtures of:
(a) pepper and garum moistened with a little oil;
(b) pepper, oil and vinegar. To this would be added a substance called *carenum* which was made by boiling down sweet white wine to about a third of its volume. It seems a wicked waste of sauternes.
(c) pepper, lovage, honey and *carenum* with perhaps a little coriander.
Any of these three cooking methods would turn out a perfectly acceptable second course. The Romans were also extremely fond of truffles which they cooked with leeks.

MAIN COURSE — LENTICULA ET SFONDYLIS

Or lentils and mussels to you. The Romans liked shellfish. There is an old tale to the effect that Caesar's invasion of Britain in 41 BC was on account of the succulent oysters which used to be sent from there to Gaul.

250 g brown lentils
250 g grape juice boiled down to half quantity
1 teaspoon honey
½ teaspoon each ground coriander, cumin and mint
1 tablespoon anchovy essence or blachan
1500 g mussels
4 tablespoons each vinegar and olive oil mixed

Lentils should not be soaked. Cover them with cold water, bring to the boil and then simmer them for about half an hour or until they are tender. Don't put in any salt. If you do this with dried vegetables it makes them go hard. When the lentils are done, drain them and add the honey, vinaigrette, spices and anchovy. Then add the mussels and return to the heat until they are warmed right through. Add the grape juice just before serving. The Romans called this seasoning *de frutum*.

With this there should be a vegetable dish. The Romans ate a lot of salads which might have contained a combination of garlic, onions, radish, lettuce and cucumber. The Emperor Tiberius along with several less endearing habits was an enthusiastic grower of cucumbers, which he had wheeled out into the sun each day in movable beds. But no tomatoes of course. Salads were dressed with a mixture of *garum* and wine.

If you would prefer a cooked vegetable dish as an accompaniment you might try a *patina* of broccoli. The Romans were very partial to this vegetable which they called *cymae* or *coliculi*, usually but wrongly translated as cabbage. It is quite clearly, from Pliny's description, a primitive form of broccoli. Cook a sufficient quantity of broccoli and combine it in a pan with the following: pepper, lovage, a little salt, minced onion, garum, vinegar, oil and a little wine. Heat it through and then stir into this four beaten eggs. Cook until just set. A paella dish is probably best for this cooking.

DESSERT — MENSAE SECUNDAE

This would have been simply fresh or dried fruit and a cheese. We don't know what cheeses tasted like in Roman times but they seem to have eaten quite a lot of cottage and cream cheese. Fresh grapes and apples of course. Dried figs, raisins and possibly apricots. In Greece and further east there was a grand tradition of little cakes with honey and sesame — not unlike the same things eaten in the same places today.

Well-to-do Romans might have eaten a meal like this in the villas at Chedworth in Gloucestershire or Lullingstone in Kent. The meals were fairly leisurely family affairs which began some time in the late afternoon and went on for several hours. Sometimes there was roasted meat. In Britain wine was a luxury and beer was quite commonly drunk; although the Emperor Julian, on a visit in the fourth century, didn't care for it. He thought it smelt like a goat.

Roman meals of this sort illustrate the sorts of principles which have been applied in writing this book and selecting the recipes for it. Their combination into a meal and the manner of its serving is for the individual in the end. But one might do worse than remember the advice of the Greek poet, traveller and gourmet Archestratus:

> Many are the ways and many the recipes
> For dressing a hare; but this is best of all:
> To place before hungry guests
> A slice of roasted meat, fresh from the spit,
> Hot, seasoned only with plain salt, a little,
> Not overdone. Do not be disturbed
> To see it rare, but eat it up.
> All other ways are unnecessary.
> Especially with a lot of damned sticky sauce poured over.

I think I would have liked Archestratus. He could have come to dinner any time.

Soup

Beautiful soup so rich and green,
Waiting in a hot tureen,
Who for such dainties would not stoop,
Soup of the evening, beautiful soup.
Beautiful soup! Who cares for fish,
Game, or any other dish?
Who would not give all else for two
pennyworth only of Beautiful Soup?

— the Mock Turtle sings 'Turtle Soup'
from *Alice's Adventures in Wonderland*

THE MOCK TURTLE, whatever else one may think of its opinions, was perfectly right when it came to soup. Properly done, soup surpasses all. It must also be the earliest of dishes. For millenia the greater part of humankind dined on nothing else but herbs in water thickened with gluten and some fowl or meat when they could get it. This is the pottage for which Esau sold his birthright. Given the right ingredients I might be tempted to do the same. Its constituents have however changed over the centuries. In medieval times the wealthy thickened their pottage not with flour but with the pounded cooked meat of a chicken, in which case the dish was a cullis. One recipe which has survived the centuries and continues to make use of breadcrumbs is gazpacho. The very word soup is from 'sop', the bread contained in the liquid.

Some time in the seventeenth century, the practice began of taking the meat from the liquid and eating the two separately. The invention of the fork must have helped. Vegetables were added to the liquid, a bread roll was served with it and it was treated as an appetiser. Interestingly this first began, it seems, in England, as the traveller François Misson remarked upon it in 1690. It was the French however who developed the habit of eating soup to a peak of perfection. Meanwhile in England by the nineteenth century soup had got itself a bad name as a suitable means of patronising the poor. During the Irish potato famine one philanthropic soul suggested that the starving peasantry might conveniently dine on boiled water and curry powder. Things of that sort take a good deal of forgiving. Although soup kitchens were set up during the Irish famine the substance served in them bore little relation to soup. An economical version invented by the bailiff in Castleconnell, County Limerick, consisted of small quantities of beef, barley, peas and turnips and *190 quarts of water*. Alexis Soyer, the noted chef, had a similar version which he said 'has been tasted by numerous noblemen, members of parliament and several ladies who have considered it very good and nourishing' although none seem to have volunteered to actually live on it. Another horror visited on the indigent was 'sky blue and sinkers' made by mixing a little flour and skimmed milk with great quantities of hot water and sinking a small square of barley bread in it. 'When meat's short we puts plenty of potherbs', remarked a Cornishwoman early this century, 'and when potherbs is short we puts plenty of salt. Salt and water's never short in these parts.'

Eating such dishes became a badge of lower-class status in England and so soup tended not to be important as a separate course. Consequently English soups rather differ from those of French *haute cuisine* and again from the provincial soups of Europe, which have remained closer to their origins. In this section therefore I will be drawing some distinctions along those lines, and another (which overlaps) into hot and cold soups. The latter are obviously most suitable for summer although they can be eaten in winter too in the appropriate circumstances. Most of these soups are intended to be a first course. Sometimes however it can be entertaining to 'muddle' the courses and to serve, say, a vegetable-based dish for the last course, a soup for the main, meat for the first and so on. There is a dessert, described later, in which the main ingredient is meat. You should I think practise a little before doing this.

And before we proceed here is an item for your 'useless knowledge' file. I suppose everyone has heard of Florence Nightingale and the sterling work she did among the sick in the Crimea. Less well known is the fact that what saved many lives was not Ms Nightingale but soup. Among those who arrived at Scutari in her party was Alexis Soyer, already mentioned, fresh from the Reform Club. He discovered to his outrage and disgust that the daily ration of meat provided according to commissary regulations was boiled and served by the lump to the sick (who could not eat it) and the liquid in which it was cooked was poured away. Soyer changed all this overnight.

The liquid, suitably strengthened, was served to the sick instead and of course greatly contributed to their recovery; many survived who would previously have starved to death. For the first few weeks after his arrival, Soyer was to be descried rushing from mess to hospital mess sweeping aside scandalised commissary officers and himself tasting the meat broth. The subsequent report of the inquiry into the disasters of the Crimea drew a pointed contrast between the arrangements made for feeding the French and English armies. The former were served by gleaming field kitchens which accompanied the troops almost onto the field of battle and which could feed them instantly on nourishing and hot food. The latter issued their soldiers salt beef and hard biscuit, and expected them to forage for whatever else they could find, and to cook the result over small and inadequate camp fires. When epidemic struck the English died like flies in winter.

Which takes us rather far from soup. To return to the point: in many of the following recipes you will need a base of stock. These stocks are simply prepared. They can be made up in quantity and stored in a freezer for subsequent use. Either use a carcass or scraps of the appropriate meat, poultry or game, or buy the desired items accordingly. The inclusion of some bones is essential if your stock is to be sufficiently rich. Some butchers will give you beef bones outright or sell them to you for a nominal sum. Chicken giblets can also be obtained cheaply (but avoid livers in making stock). The meat should be covered with water in a large pot and brought to the boil. Skim the grey foam which rises to the top and as much fat as you are able. When that is done, for each litre of water add two large chopped carrots, two onions, two stalks of chopped celery and salt and pepper to taste. Put in a bouquet garni, that is, a sprig each of parsley and thyme, and a bay leaf. Rinse but don't skin the onions. The skins give an excellent colour to the stock.

Simmer this for three hours, allowing a certain reduction. Strain it into a bowl and allow it to cool. When it is almost cold, skim the remaining fat. Discard the bones and vegetables and separate the liquid into 600 ml freezer containers. Remember that the stock will expand as it freezes (a peculiar property of water) so leave room for this. When you want to use the stock, thaw it out in the refrigerator the day before. You will find incidentally that any last remaining fat will have risen to the top and solidified. It can be easily picked off the frozen stock and discarded.

Beware the dreaded bouillon. The invention of reduced stock is recorded as early as 1694. It was known variously as 'veal glue' or portable soup. This is still sold at some shops specialising in provisioning hunters or trampers, and at a pinch will do. But the stock cubes sold in general grocers are loaded with monosodium glutamate and other synthetics and this makes them very nasty, as well as their bearing little resemblance to the original idea of soup reduced to a solid substance. There are one or two exceptions, mostly imported from France. These are hard to lay hands on and as long as you have a freezer and can plan in advance there's really no need to use stock cubes except *in extremis*.

If you want to clarify your stock before use, boil it vigorously with a white of egg and the crushed shell, whisking it as you do so. Then let it infuse for about fifteen minutes and strain it. The resulting liquid should be relatively clear. This is particularly important if you are making a consommé.

English and Scottish Soups

My friend Helen McNeish once remarked to me that she was sorry that she discovered English soups only later in her life, and it was only then that I realised how separate a tradition there was. Helen's quite right, and the distinction also applies to the Scots. The reasons for the difference between British and Continental soups have already been remarked, *viz.* that although the English stopped serving pottage and began taking the meat out of the liquid earlier than the French, they left off this before they got to the consommé. Curiously enough until a decade or so ago you could not get English soup in an English restaurant any more than you could get a Yorkshire pudding. There is an essay by George Orwell (there's *always* an essay by George Orwell), 'In Defence of English Cooking' published in the *Evening Standard* in December 1945. This concludes: 'It is not a law of nature that every restaurant in England should be either foreign or bad, and the first step towards an improvement will be a less long-suffering attitude in the British public itself.' And he remarks *inter alia* that you can't get good English cooking outside a private house. That is no longer the case in Britain but it still isn't possible to get a decent English or Scottish soup in a restaurant in New Zealand. This is a pity because there are some very fine soups of that provenance.

SCOTCH BROTH

This was a dish which impressed even the redoubtable Samuel Johnson, who was not overly fond of things Scottish. He suggested that the only good thing to come out of Scotland was the road to London. He also defined 'oats' in his famous dictionary as a food in England fed to horses and in Scotland to people. That notwithstanding, Boswell recounts in his *Journal of a Tour to the Hebrides* in 1786 that at Aberdeen Johnson ate several plates of Scotch broth with barley and peas in it 'and seemed very fond of the dish'. When Boswell asked his mentor if he had ever eaten it before Johnson replied: 'No sir, but I don't care how soon I eat it again.' Perhaps walking in the open air improved his appetite. This recipe is from *Lady Clark of Tillypronie's Cook Book* published in 1909. All the vegetables should be chopped.

1 kg of neck or breast mutton
5 onions
5 turnips

3 carrots
barley (about a handful)
1 leek
2 sticks of celery

Stew together for three hours the meat, 3 onions, 3 turnips, 2 of the carrots, 1500 ml of water and seasoning to taste. Let it cool and remove all the fat. Strip the remaining meat from the bones, discard the latter and set aside the meat. Cook the remaining ingredients in the liquid for about half an hour, then adjust the seasoning, add the meat and simmer for five more minutes to heat through before serving. Dr Johnson would have been surprised by the absence of peas. These can be added at the same time as the barley if you like. Soaked dried peas would be better than frozen I think. This combination of mutton and vegetables is basic to a number of such soups. Some of these say that the leek should be added at the same time as the meat so that it is still crisp when it is served. One recipe I know also suggests that a teaspoon of sugar will bring out the flavour.

The origin of soup is imply illustrated by the above recipe, which is very close to some traditional stews such as Lancashire Hotpot. Until the eighteenth century a lamb's head was cooked in much the same fashion and then boned, the meat cubed and served in a brain sauce made from some of the stock. In Wales this combination of meat and vegetables is called *cawl* and in French *pot-au-feu* or *garbure*. It was usually regarded as food for the poor, although not necessarily. That extraordinary seventeenth-century English courtier Sir Kenelm Digby (of whom more hereafter) remarks that Queen Henrietta Maria (wife of Charles I) drank 'a good porringerful of broth every morning for her health'. At the other end of the social scale was game soup, theoretically only available to the rich because of game laws, but I suspect that that didn't mean a great deal to most people, particularly as an alternative name for this dish is poacher's soup.

GAME SOUP

The ingredients are not easy to come by, and will be expensive, but the result is worthwhile.

200 g venison minced or chopped
meat from a pheasant and from a rabbit, chopped (200 g each)
50 g butter (twice)
2 onions
3 sticks celery
bouquet garni
12 peppercorns
large glass red wine
1 litre beef stock

100 g mushrooms
2 egg yolks
150 ml cream
1 tablespoon redcurrant jelly

Brown the meat in a casserole on the stove in the first lot of butter, remove and brown the onions and celery in the same butter. Return the meat to the casserole with the bouquet garni, the peppercorns and the wine, cover and cook in the oven at 150°C for one hour. Fry the mushrooms in the remaining butter and when the hour is up, add these to the pot together with the stock and the jelly. Season to taste and simmer for a further hour on top of the stove. About ten minutes before serving, beat the cream and egg yolks together and combine with a ladle of the soup (if you put the egg and cream directly into the soup it will curdle). Sprinkle with fresh parsley and serve with triangles of toast.

There are almost as many variations on this recipe as there are cooks. If instead it is made with the flesh and carcass of a hare combined with shin of beef it becomes *hare soup*. That this is regarded as a peculiarly English dish is seen by the name by which it is known in France *potage de levraut à l'anglaise*. The Scots add cloves and cayenne as well and call it 'bawd bree', 'bree' meaning soup, although with Gaelic perversity this is not the only word used for soup, as the next recipe shows.

FEATHER FOWLIE

This is also from the redoubtable Lady Clark of Tillypronie, who died nine years before the publication of the cookery book which bears her name. It was compiled from a stack of manuscript notebooks which she kept for her own use. These are a veritable Aladdin's cave of traditional recipes and include many otherwise unknown items, e.g. Parmesan cheese biscuits.

This particular soup takes us about as far in the direction of consommé as traditional British cooking will allow. An expert on Scots cuisine, Marian McNeill, thinks that 'fowlie' is a corruption of *volaille* because the soup is so similar to *velouté de volaille* and suggests that it may be 'a legacy of the Auld Alliance'. That's rather too fanciful I suspect but a pleasing thought nevertheless.

1 fresh chicken
1 slice ham
1 stick celery, chopped
1 sliced onion
mace, thyme and parsley
seasoning to taste
3 egg yolks
2 tablespoons cream

Joint the chicken and let it soak in salted water for one hour. Rinse it well then cover it with fresh water in a pan and add the other ingredients, except the eggs and cream. Bring it to the boil and then simmer gently for an hour and a half. Strain it and let it cool. Strip the meat from the carcass and chop finely. To remove the fat from the stock, blot it three or four times with several thicknesses of paper kitchen towels. Return the meat to the pan, and bring gently to the simmer. Beat the eggs and cream and stir in a ladle of the soup stock, then return this mixture to the pot and cook stirring for another five minutes before serving.

CRAB SOUPS

Another soup similar to the fowlie which really is called 'bree' is *Partan Bree*. The Scots have always earned a good measure of their living from the sea and that they should have a traditional crab soup (partan = crab) is therefore hardly surprising. Like some of the other soups mentioned this one is also enriched with cream. If you pick all the meat from the carcasses of two cooked crabs this can then be combined in a blender with about 150 g of rice cooked in milk. Heat this in a litre of chicken stock, seasoned with salt and *white* pepper and a tablespoon of anchovy sauce. Two tablespoons of cream are added just before serving.

In Southern Europe they make their crab soup quite differently, adding white fish to the crab and flavouring the stock with onion, garlic, mace, lemon and cayenne. They also add white wine and fresh fennel or marjoram. I think the Scots soup has both more flavour and greater individuality. The Chinese make yet another crab soup named for the Wangpo river at Woosung, near the mouth of the Yangtse, where the best crabs are said to be found. That region has always been a byword in China for its cooking, particularly the pleasure city of Wangchou with its west lake where many famous dishes were invented. If you see a Chinese dish denominated 'west lake' you will know it is from there. The cultivated poets of the late T'ang loved to sing of this part of their country, particularly its soft spring.

But of all soups from the sea the most luxurious is turtle. That said, I do not propose to give a recipe for it but rather to tell you about it. Turtle as an item of cuisine first made its appearance in the eighteenth century. It was such a luxury dish that it was reserved for the annual Lord Mayor's Banquet when it was served in five different ways: thick, clear, calipash, calipee and fins. It needed two days to prepare, and included not only the whole turtle but veal, chicken and ham and a variety of spices. Alas, the depredations of seamen upon turtles made this an ever-diminishing resource. Helen Bradford, who went to sea on a whaling ship with her father at the age of nine in the 1870s, notes in her memoir *When I Went A'Whaling*: 'We reached Europa Island in the Mozambique Channel and some of the boats went on shore for turtle. They brought off some and there was a change of diet for all hands, soup, and cake and custard from the eggs . . . whenever we passed islands where there were turtles we would send a boat's crew ashore to patrol the beach for a night and turn over on their backs any turtles coming up to lay their eggs.'

Turtles are now of necessity protected. Turtle soup still appears occasionally, usually in tinned form, but should be spurned by all conservationists. I have read that a dish called Turtle Lady Curzon, a turtle consommé with curry powder and cream, was served on transatlantic liners in the thirties. Why anyone would want to curry turtle soup I cannot think, it seems a barbarous thing to do.

MOCK TURTLE SOUP

This is not, as Lewis Carroll would have you believe, made from mock turtles but from a calf's head. Asking for one will get you a funny look from your butcher but do persist. The soup makes it worthwhile. This particular recipe incidentally was used for a banquet in 1850 at which the Russian ambassador to the Court of St James was the guest of honour.

half a calf's head
1 litre beef stock
8 spring onions
90 g butter
60 g flour
300 ml madeira
chives and parsley, chopped
salt, pepper and cayenne
2 teaspoons soy sauce

1 tablespoon mushroom ketchup
lemon juice

Boil the head for half an hour and then remove it, let it cool, strip the meat from the bones and cut it into small pieces. Put this to one side. Boil the bones in the stock for about an hour and then strain. Fry the spring onions lightly in the butter, remove and stir in the flour to make a roux. Cook it for a couple of minutes and then stir it into the stock broth. Bring this back to a simmer and add the meat and the other ingredients. Just a squeeze of lemon juice will do. Be easy on the cayenne, which is ground, dried chilli pepper. It used to be used in infused form in the eighteenth century as an alleged cure for chronic alcoholism. The thought of the treatment probably frightened people entirely off the thought of drinking too much. Some people don't like it at all and others can take quite a lot of it. Prepare for this eventuality by serving chilli sherry. This is a strained infusion of dried chillis in dry sherry. A few drops sprinkled on soup will bring out the flavour. It was very popular in the messes of the Indian Army in the last century. That probably explains all those choleric colonels.

One of the characteristics of English soups is the way they use items, such as a calf's head, which would otherwise be discarded. Another is the incorporation of elements of foreign cuisines from conquered lands into something which then becomes typical of English cooking. The next two soups, oxtail and mulligatawny, illustrate these respective characteristics.

OXTAIL SOUP

half an oxtail cut into joints
2 carrots
1 large onion with 3 cloves stuck in it
bouquet garni
60 g butter
90 g flour
1 large glass of sherry
1 teaspoon redcurrant jelly
2 teaspoons tomato purée
seasoning to taste

Fry the oxtail and the carrots in a little of the butter until they are well browned. This will make your soup richer in taste as well as appearance. Then add 1500 ml of water, the onion and the bouquet garni. Simmer it for two hours, skimming off any foam which rises. Strain it and let it get quite cold so that you can remove every bit of fat without burning your fingers. Strip the meat from the oxtail. This is rather a messy business. Discard the vegetables and the bones. Make a roux with the butter and flour, stir into the stock and bring it to the boil. Then add the remaining ingredients and the meat. Serve very hot.

MULLIGATAWNY

When I served briefly in the army (with which I parted company abruptly by mutual consent) I was told off to work in the kitchen of the officers' mess. There the cook made 'mulligatawny' soup by taking the soup left over from the previous day and putting in more water and plenty of curry powder. Not to be recommended. The name for the real thing comes from the Tamil *milagn-tannir* which means pepper-water and may have prompted the ghastly suggestion earlier noted that the famine-stricken Irish should drink curry powder in water. The soup came from India with the returning nabobs of the Honourable East India Company in the eighteenth century, and has stuck fast in the English cuisine since. This recipe is adapted from one in Eliza Acton's *Modern Cookery* of 1845. The original, which calls for among other things six cucumbers and three pounds of marrow, is obviously designed for a rather large dinner party. Interestingly it contains no meat except in the form of stock, whereas most other recipes for this soup involve a jointed chicken.

> *2 large onions, chopped*
> *60 g butter*
> *500 g marrow, peeled, seeded and chopped*
> *2 large cucumbers, peeled, seeded and chopped*
> *2 tart apples, peeled, seeded and chopped*
> *lemon juice*
> *2 tablespoons cream*
> *¼ teaspoon cayenne*
> *½ teaspoon paprika*
> *1 teaspoon turmeric*   *combined as a curry powder*
> *½ teaspoon mace*
> *½ teaspoon ground ginger*
> *1 litre beef or chicken stock*
> *6 cloves, 20 peppercorns, salt and pepper to taste*

Brown the onion, marrow, cucumber and apple in butter in a large pan until they are soft. Then add the curry and cook for a further ten minutes, stirring to ensure the mixture does not catch. Add the stock, seasonings, cloves and peppercorns. Simmer gently for an hour and then strain into a bowl. Rub the vegetables and the apple through a sieve into the liquid (or purée them in a blender first). Add the lemon juice and cream and serve with a side bowl of boiled rice and another of mango chutney, which those present should add at their own pleasure. Sometimes coconut milk is used instead of cream at the last.

PEA AND HAM SOUP

There are quite a number of English traditional soups based on vegetables rather than meat but containing the latter as a secondary flavour. One of the best known of these is pea with ham.

In the days before canning or freezing, vegetables were preserved by drying. One of the most useful vegetables for this is peas. They have been stored dried from at least the early medieval period and were a great winter standby for soups. Jane Austen records in one of her letters that when the doctor called at her father's parsonage unexpectedly she sat him down to a dinner of pea soup and spare-rib of pork. The two flavours go very well together and in the eighteenth century they formed the base of a very fine soup. Incidentally, Jane Austen's great friend and eventually sister-in-law Martha Lloyd was a fine cook and collected a large number of manuscript recipes. These were finally published in 1977 as *A Jane Austen Household Book*. This recipe is adapted from the same period, from Somerset about 1750.

500 g dried peas
250 g frozen peas
1500 ml water
fresh mint and thyme (or dried)
2 sticks celery
2 lettuces
150 g butter
3 onions, chopped
1 cucumber, peeled and seeded
45 g flour
chopped parsley, pepper and salt
6 slices ham
sour cream

Soak the dried peas overnight and drain. Put these in the water with the mint, thyme, celery and one of the lettuces, washed and shredded. Cook this for twenty minutes, strain and put the vegetable residue through a blender before returning it to the soup. Melt half the butter and fry the cucumber, the onion and the ham, cubed, until the vegetables are tender but not browned. Then add the shredded second lettuce and fry for another minute or two. Add these to the soup with the seasonings. Make a roux and stir this into the soup. Bring it back gradually to the boil and then add the frozen peas.

47

Simmer for ten minutes and serve with chopped parsley and a sour cream knob in each bowl. Don't add salt to dried peas until they've been cooked. If you do they are liable to cook hard instead of tender.

GARDEN SOUP

Another eighteenth-century soup which was a great favourite was garden soup, which also includes cooked lettuce. We find this rather odd but only because we are so used to it fresh in salad. I usually serve this soup if a vegetarian comes to dinner, although in that case I have to base it upon a vegetable stock.

It takes two days to prepare but is nevertheless fairly uncomplicated. On the day before the dinner, simmer all the following for about five hours.

1 kg knuckle of veal
a few lamb bones
300 g shin of beef
2 large onions (no need to peel)
12 peppercorns
dessertspoon salt
teaspoon mace
12 cloves

Strain and allow to cool. Remove all fat. About an hour before serving bring to the boil and add the following, washed and finely chopped:

1 large lettuce
12 heads of spinach (or some watercress)
2 endives
2 bunches spring onions

Simmer this until ready to serve. Shortly before serving, add a drained tin of cooked asparagus, some chopped parsley and some thyme. Sour cream and chives in each bowl adds the finishing touch.

Endive isn't always easy to get: when you see it you'll know it because it looks like lettuce with curly hair. If you cannot obtain it, try chicory instead (which you may find equally difficult to lay hands upon). Not everybody likes endive because it has a slightly bitter taste. It has been enjoyed by those who do since the time of the ancient Egyptians, who called it *kebsher* or *tybi* meaning 'January', because it came to maturity then, in winter. Notwithstanding, this is a real summer soup; the fresher the vegetables the better. But best of all in the summer is beginning a meal with a cold or iced soup.

Cold Soups (And Their Hot Variants)

GAZPACHO

Possibly the most famous of all cold soups is the Spanish gazpacho, not one soup but many. Gourmets have long debated the origin of its name. Most seem agreed that it's of Roman origin from *caspa* meaning remains or bits and pieces with *acho* a simple diminutive. Théophile Gautier encountered it on a visit to Spain in 1840 and initially turned up his nose at it. 'At home, a dog of any breeding would refuse to sully its nose with such an uncompromising mixture.' But he ended up liking it. It is simplicity itself to prepare and should be left to mature for at least twenty-four hours in the refrigerator before eating.

> *1 large chopped onion*
> *1 green pepper, seeded and chopped*
> *3 cloves of garlic, chopped*
> *1 cucumber, peeled and chopped*
> *8 chopped tomatoes*
> *three slices of stale bread, crumbled*
> *parsley*
> *fresh mint*
> *pine nuts*
> *2 tablespoons olive oil*
> *1 tablespoon wine vinegar*
> *salt and pepper*

Blend all these ingredients and stir the resulting purée into about 700 ml of water. When you are ready to serve, give it a good stir and add half a dozen ice cubes. Separate bowls of finely diced raw onion, cucumber, green pepper and green olives should be served with it for the guests to add. The taste will truly surprise you. It needs plenty of salt and pepper or it may be a little insipid. It also needs a dry white wine to wash it down.

VICHYSSOISE

For the best known of 'foreign' soups this must run gazpacho close. What may surprise you is that it is not strictly speaking a French soup at all. It was invented *by* a Frenchman, Louis Diat, for the patrons of the Ritz-Carlton Hotel in New York in the nineteen-twenties. Its basis of leeks and potatoes is however very European (again it is not specifically French, being common in English cooking too) and is widely served as a peasant dish in its hot version. Diat named it for Vichy, the town near which he had grown up.

2 large leeks
1 chopped onion
50 g butter
1 teaspoon salt
1 teaspoon pepper
2 large potatoes, peeled and diced
600 ml water
300 ml milk
300 ml cream
chopped chives

Chop the white parts of the leek. Stew them with the onions and the butter, covered, in a heavy pan for about five minutes without browning. Then add the milk, water, potatoes and salt. Simmer until the potatoes are well cooked and put through a blender. The resulting substance is leek and potato soup, or *potage parmentier*. To convert it to Vichyssoise, bring it back to a simmer and stir in the heated cream. Cook it for a few minutes stirring to prevent it catching, then cool and chill it. Adjust the seasoning and sprinkle with chives before serving. Cold dishes in general need more salt than hot. Experience will teach which potatoes to choose. Some cook very stiff and this makes the soup unpleasantly gluey. The soup is equally good served hot and there are many variations. For instance the substitution of kumara for potato makes a particularly flavoursome local dish which I am in the habit of serving to dinner guests from overseas. It is also possible to substitute cucumber for the leeks in which case a bunch of watercress might also be included. Some like to cook the vegetables in chicken stock rather than milk and water.

ICED CUCUMBER JELLY

To my mind one of the best dishes for summer is an iced cucumber jelly.

2 large cucumbers, grated
1 large onion, grated
1 tablespoon lemon juice
salt, pepper, finely chopped mint
aspic jelly
a few cooked prawns

If the cucumber is of the hothouse variety you can grate it skin and all. Otherwise you will have to peel it. Combine all the ingredients and stir into some prepared aspic jelly. Excellent recipes abound for aspic, but there are some perfectly acceptable prepared and powdered ones available and I usually use one of those. Pour into individual bowls for serving, preferably glass. The combination of cucumber and prawns (or shrimps) may sound odd but they complement one another perfectly. One of the simplest and most elegant hot soups I know consists of three ingredients: water, peeled cucumbers and dried Chinese shrimps simmered for thirty minutes. A little chilli sherry completes the flavour (the shrimps are usually quite salty).

In general we do not use cucumbers in sufficiently adventurous ways. They are one of the oldest known vegetables. Ur-Nammu, ruler of Mesopotamia in the second millenium BC, built a temple to the god Nanna in his cucumber garden to preserve it should his city be sacked but it didn't help — when the city was put to the sword the garden went west with everything else. Cucumbers have survived fire, sword and much else and flourished.

GELÉE DE COCHON

If you are truly intent upon making your own aspic you can try this recipe for a jellied cold consommé.

pork bones and trotters
large glass white wine for each guest
large chopped onion
1 bay leaf
2 cloves crushed garlic
¼ teaspoon mixed spice
1 tablespoon lemon juice

Wash the bones and trotters thoroughly in case they have been pickled, otherwise your jelly will be inedibly salty. Put all the ingredients in a pan except the lemon juice and bring to the boil. Skim and simmer for six hours. Strain the liquid and reduce to about 500 ml. Add the lemon juice and a *little* salt after tasting carefully. This should set when it is cool, and can then be broken up and piled in individual glasses and served as an entreé. If you want to be more elaborate you can pour a thin layer of the hot jelly into the bottom of ramekins and let it set. Then layer some sliced boiled egg, olives, chopped ham, etc. and finally melt the remaining jelly again, add a little sherry or madeira and pour over. When these are set they can be turned out. Which takes us rather far from soup. I like a cold beetroot soup which can also be done as a jellied consommé; or in the following rather less usual version.

SWEKOLNIK

This is very Russian, although most of northern Europe makes a similar dish. The recipe here is quite basic; in the Russian cuisine it is usually more elaborate.

200 g beetroot leaves
4 beetroots
half a fresh cucumber
3 pickled dill cucumbers
tarragon, chives, mint, fennel
tarragon vinegar
150 ml cream
salt and pepper to taste

Cook the leaves in a little water and then drain and chop them finely. Cook the beetroots and when they have cooled peel and dice them. Put them in a bowl with the leaves and pour on about 100 ml of tarragon vinegar. Dice and add both sorts of cucumber and the cream. Chill this for some hours. Just before serving add the chopped herbs and seasoning and then sufficient water for a good bowlful each. Float a few ice cubes in it. For summer this is magnificent; in winter there is its much better known cousin — bortsch.

BORTSCH

I first ate bortsch (which can be served hot or cold) in Moscow in 1973. Among the other foodstuffs I had on that visit it stood out as a spectacular success and I kept hinting that like Dr Johnson with his broth I didn't care how soon I had it again. To my chagrin it was only served once, but I have since made up for this disappointment by making it and eating it many times for myself. The ingredients are simple.

1 litre beef stock
4 raw beetroots, grated

Grating beetroots is a messy business: the red juice seems to have an uncanny ability to penetrate every corner of the kitchen, even when you are using an electric blender. Cook the ingredients for about an hour, then if you want it cold, add a little gelatine and leave it to set overnight. A spoonful of sour cream and a light dusting of ground cloves completes the cold soup later. If on the other hand you want it hot, then just add a chopped frankfurter for each guest and again serve with sour cream.

No bortsch would be complete without *vatroushki*. These are little pastries stuffed with cheese and are traditionally served as an accompaniment. Sift together 200 g of self-raising flour, a tablespoon of sugar and a pinch of salt. Rub about 180 g of butter into this and mix with enough cold water to make a stiff dough. This is the short pastry. For the filling, mix together 500 g cream cheese, an egg, a tablespoon of sugar, a pinch of salt and 2 tablespoons of plain flour. Roll out the pastry very thinly and cut into rounds (the bottom of a tumbler is a quite convenient template). I usually take a greased cookie tray, and put a round of pastry in the bottom of each cup. Then put a spoonful of the mixture in each one, cover with another round of pastry and pinch the join together. Continue until all the pastry or all the filling (or both) are used up, glaze the tops and bake for about 20 minutes in a pre-heated oven at 190° C. Served hot with hot bortsch these are a real winter's day treat. In pre-revolutionary Russia these same pastries were served in Lent but stuffed with vegetables rather than cheese.

Of course, because nothing is ever quite what it seems, bortsch is no more traditionally Russian than vodka. Both are Ukrainian by origin. In old Russia the traditional drink was *Kvas*, a beer made of wheat or rye, although after several vodkas flavoured in the traditional way with a variety of herbs who cares. The traditional Russian soup is either *shchi* or *okroshka*.

OKROSHKA

If you are ever in Moscow try to inveigle your hosts into taking you to a restaurant about fifteen miles outside the city and called Russkaya Izba which means 'the Russian peasant cottage' and which specialises in traditional Russian food. They have there a particularly good cold *okroshka*. Traditionally it is made out of *Kvas* which is quite unprocurable in this country but this version is at least an approximation of the original.

1 cup diced, peeled and seeded cucumber
3 or 4 diced frankfurter sausages
or *half a cup of cooked chicken meat, diced*
½ cup cooked shrimps
2 tablespoons chopped spring onions
fennel
dill pickled cucumbers
parsley
2 hard-boiled eggs
150 ml plain yoghurt
1 cup of milk
salt and pepper

Mix the milk and yoghurt until it is smooth and add all the other ingredients except the eggs. Leave to chill in the refrigerator. Just before serving, put in one or two ice cubes, the chopped eggs and some more parsley. Nothing could be simpler for a summer dinner.

Yoghurt is an excellent accompaniment to many cold soups and is usually added cold at the end of the cooking and cooling. It is widely used for that purpose on the southern shores of the Mediterranean. Scientifically speaking yoghurt is the result of the effects of two baccilli (*Lacobacillus bulgaricus* and *Streptococcus thermophillus*) on milk. Don't let that put you off. It didn't affect the Aryan peoples of Central Asia who have been eating it for at least ten thousand years. In fact the word 'ambrosia' is actually derived from 'homa' a fermented yoghurt drink flavoured with a strong herb and made long ago by the forerunners of the folk who through immigration and time became the Greeks of the classical period. It has always been used as a cooking ingredient in the area and spread from there into India and with the Turks as far west as Hungary; it is now eaten throughout the world. It is to be preferred to cream as an ingredient of cold soups because it does not contain so much fat, and has a sharper taste.

Another soup follows which also uses yoghurt and is an unusual but delicious combination of flavours — carrot and orange.

POTAGE CRÉCY À L'ORANGE

The appearance of the name Crécy in a dish tells the cook at once what is the main ingredient, *viz.* carrots.

To the English it is also likely to conjure up one of Edward III's battles; the French of course do not remember it for that, probably because one prefers to forget one's defeats. Rather, it is because the sandy soil of northern France is said to be excellent for growing carrots.

> *2 chopped onions*
> *60 g butter*
> *500 g carrots, peeled and chopped*
> *1 litre chicken stock*
> *400 ml (approx) pure orange juice*
> *150 ml natural yoghurt*
> *mint, salt, pepper*
> *sour cream*

Fry the onion in the butter until it softens, add the carrots and the stock and cook until the carrots are soft. Put the cooked carrots and onions in a blender with a little of the stock blend to a purée, then recombine with the stock and bring to a simmer. Add the orange juice, pepper and salt. Cook for a few minutes and then cool. To serve, stir in the yoghurt thinned with a little water and float sour cream and a mint leaf on each plate. This soup can also be served hot if you stir in cream rather than yoghurt at the same time as the orange juice. Be certain that the orange juice you use is pure and unsweetened, although pure juices are becoming increasingly elusive these days.

Carrots are one of the most versatile and useful of vegetables; they are also one of the oldest. The Romans ate them with enthusiasm, although as far as we can tell theirs were not reddish in colour but white. Our carrots were developed from a purplish variety which came into Europe through Spain with the Moors. In Spain carrots of this type are still commonly sold in the markets. In northern Europe carrots were rather exotic in the fourteenth century and court ladies decorated their hats with the green tops. Carrots combine very well with tomato to make a hot or cold soup.

PEANUT SOUP

Yoghurt also goes very well in this soup, which is one of the more unusual I know and which always delights dinner guests. It comes from the Caribbean island of St Kitts and is I think an adaption of a European recipe to suit a plentiful local ingredient.

300 g roasted peanuts (without skins)
1 litre chicken or vegetable stock
tabasco sauce to taste
300 ml cream or yoghurt
1 tablespoon Angostura bitters
dry sherry
chopped chives

Blend the peanuts and a little of the stock to a smooth paste and add this to the rest of the stock, the tabasco and some salt and pepper. Bring it to the boil and simmer for fifteen minutes, stirring. Stir in the bitters, and the cream if you are using it (but not the yoghurt). Allow this to cool and at that point stir in the yoghurt, the sherry and the chives.

Angostura bitters, you may be interested to know, are not manufactured in Venezuela although they were invented there in the town of Angostura in 1824 by Johan Siegert, a Silesian military surgeon and friend of Simon Bolivar. Just to confuse matters further, the town was renamed Cuidad Bolivar in 1846. In 1875 Siegert's sons moved the business to Trinidad where it has been manufacturing the bitters to the same recipe ever since. The present owner is the great-grandson of the founder. Among admirers of the product was Mark Twain who did not however want it to put in soup. Whisky was rather more what he had in mind. And finally, for unusual but delicious cold soups, here is a favourite.

SOUR CHERRY

This is Hungarian and is known there as *meggyleves*. The cherries won't be easy to get and they'll be fiendishly expensive but the tinned ones won't do because they are for desserts, and are done in far too sweet a syrup.

300 g stoned cherries
1 litre water
salt, pepper, cinnamon, cloves
120 g sugar
20 g flour
chopped lemon zest
6 tablespoons sour cream
the cherry stones and a little red wine

Bring the stoned cherries to a simmer in the water, add the pepper, salt, a pinch of cinnamon, one or two cloves and the lemon zest. When the fruit is cooked press the whole to a pulp with a potato masher. It should then be thickened by heating the flour alone in a frying pan until it begins to brown and mixing this to a paste with the sour cream thinned with a little water. Stir this into the soup and bring to the boil. Crack open some of the cherry stones and simmer the kernels gently in red wine. Strain this into the soup. Allow it to cool, chill it and serve with more sour cream.

Fruit soups of this sort are a Hungarian speciality. This is not because of a quirk of the Hungarian palate but because of the geography and history of Europe. Fruit as an ingredient in soup was very common in the medieval period, particularly during Lent, when meat was forbidden. In metropolitan Europe this practice fell out of fashion however and largely only survived, as is often the case, on the relatively isolated fringes in places such as Hungary. As with most cold soups of course they can be served hot as well. One such hot soup made with fruit did survive in the centre of things, notwithstanding, at least in England — apple and barley, or 'rota'.

Hot Soups

ROTA

This soup is interesting as much for its longevity as anything else. The recipe that follows comes from Eliza Acton's *Modern Cookery* of 1845 but the same soup also appears in an early fifteenth-century recipe in manuscript in the Bodleian Library. From there it has found its way more recently into *Fabulous Feasts: Medieval Cookery and Ceremony*. As there is not the slightest evidence that Eliza Acton ever went near the library in question but drew upon domestic manuscript books, one can only assume that the recipe had been handed down to her through the generations in complete form.

1500 ml beef stock
350 g Granny Smith apples

½ teaspoon ginger
pepper and salt to taste
90 g soaked pearl barley

Peel and core the apples and cook them in the stock until they are soft. Let them cool, purée them and return them to the stock. Add the ginger, seasonings and barley and return to a simmer until the barley is cooked, then serve. For some reason Eliza Acton calls this soup 'à la Bourguignonne' although it seems to have no obvious connection with France. Perhaps she first came across it when she was on a visit there in the 1820s.

Eliza Acton is one of those interesting personalities who seem to crop up in cooking; daughter of a brewer, and born in 1799, she was a poet and journalist and published a book on bread. Her recipes include some innovatory Jewish dishes of Central European origin so she was clearly adventurous for her time in her social acquaintance. She actually suggests rice rather than barley, but barley is in the original.

Barley soup has been in vogue for a long time. There is the recipe already mentioned from Apicius' *De re Coquinaria*. This called, you will recollect, for the combination of chick peas, lentils, green peas and barley with leeks, fresh coriander, dill, fennel and *coliculi* which was similar to what we now know as broccoli. There was also the ubiquitous *garum*, the closest to which would be found nowadays in a Chinese grocery in the form of *blachan*. This recipe has survived (in a slightly different form) as leek and barley soup.

LEEK AND BARLEY SOUP

This pops up for example in the manuscript recipe book which Emily, Lady Shaftesbury, kept between 1855 and 1872. Her husband, Anthony Cooper, was the famous reformer, the 7th Earl, who not only had a miserable childhood (his parents were given to starving and beating him and his sisters cruelly) but lived most of his life in straitened circumstances. The frugal Emily was the daughter of Lady Cowper, a member of the bohemian and eccentric Lamb family. There was some dispute about who Emily's father was but the general consensus was that it had been Lord Palmerston. It was Lady Cowper who contributed this soup to Emily's recipe book. For some reason she says it is German but it seems general to European cooking.

60 g pearl barley
2 litres chicken stock
60 g butter
4 trimmed and sliced leeks
bunch of celery trimmed
nutmeg, salt and pepper
150 ml cream
1 egg yolk

Soak the barley overnight, strain it and simmer it in the stock until it is soft — about an hour. While that is going on stew the leeks and celery in butter in a covered pot. Do this gently so that they do not brown but soften only. Add them to the stock and continue to simmer gently. Flavour with the nutmeg and seasoning. Beat the egg and cream together and blend it with a ladle full of the liquid from the soup. Then stir this into the soup itself. When the whole is blended, serve with small pieces of toast. Barley in its primitive forms goes back to Neolithic Europe where it was used not only in soups and pottages but as a cereal in bread (as in the Roman recipe given earlier) and of course for brewing, in the form of malt.

CABBAGE AND FRUIT SOUP

Some vegetables even make an excellent soup in combination with fruit. This recipe found its way into this book by a rather circuitous route. In 1983 while I was staying with a friend in a loft in Greenwich Village, New York, we made the acquaintance of a very pleasant neighbour, Ruth Richards. During the course of a social drink the conversation turned to food and it transpired that she too was preparing a book of recipes. Hers, rather unusually, was to comprise entirely cabbage dishes. We exchanged recipes for pepperpot, hers from Philadelphia (her home town), mine from the West Indies, and she promised to send me a favourite cabbage recipe to put in my book. This is the one.

4 tablespoons butter
70 g sugar
2 chopped onions
half a small cabbage, well shredded
3 tart apples, peeled, cored and sliced
3 peaches, peeled, stoned and sliced
2 tablespoons wine vinegar
½ teaspoon grated nutmeg
salt and pepper to taste
200 ml chicken stock
whole cranberry sauce
sour cream

Cook the onions in the melted butter with the sugar until golden and well combined. Add the cabbage, fruit and vinegar, with water to cover, and cook covered over a low heat for ten minutes. Add some stock, nutmeg and seasonings, cook slowly for an hour and then purée in a blender. Serve hot with a dollop of sour cream and a spoonful of cranberry sauce in each bowl. 'The amount of sugar used', remarks Ruth, 'will vary depending on the tartness of the apples. Adjust to your taste.'

PUMPKIN SOUP (POTAGE DE CITROUILLE)

Combinations of green vegetables in soup can be quite delicious and very refreshing. Rather less usual vegetables, however, make equally delicious soups. Some of these have entered the general cuisine since the introduction of the main ingredients to Europe. The classic example given of this is usually the pumpkin, which is believed by many to have been introduced from the Americas. In fact this is not so, pumpkins having been native to Europe for centuries. The English however, for reasons which are unclear, presently despise them as a food.

I discovered this shortly after I went to live in London and entered a shop in Chelsea to ask for a slice of the pumpkin displayed in the window. The greengrocer was surprised, and enquired why I wanted it. When I told him that it was for soup he explained, as to the mentally afflicted, that pumpkin was a horse and cattle food and those in his window were for display only. Nevertheless I prevailed upon him to sell me some. He became so interested that I returned later with the recipe, not only for this soup but for pumpkin pie. I don't know whether he ever overcame his aversion and tried them.

I hope so, because his ancestors have been eating pumpkins since the late medieval period. They used to remove the pith, stuff the space with apples and bake the whole. The colour of pumpkin certainly makes a fine decorative effect in a shop window or anywhere else. The French call pumpkin *potiron* but also in rural districts *citrouille* which is always to me very evocative of their colour. When it comes to eating pumpkin the Americans also have no foolish prejudices. This recipe is from their part of the world.

1 medium good looking pumpkin
2 tablespoons softened butter
1 onion, sliced
60 g rice
750 ml chicken stock
nutmeg, salt and pepper
4 chopped and fried bacon rashers
2 tablespoons mozzarella cheese, grated

It's the nutmeg that makes the flavour of this dish. Cut a small lid in the stalk end of the pumpkin and scoop out the seeds and pith. Rub the inside with butter, sprinkle with salt and pepper and set it in an ovenproof dish. Put in the onion and rice and the heated stock. Replace the lid and bake it for two hours at 190°C. Then add the nutmeg, bacon and cheese. It should be brought to the table as it is, and served direct, by inserting a ladle and scraping the flesh into the liquid.

This dish requires some care in preparation. If the pumpkin is too big it will split in cooking. The hole in the top should not be too large, but large enough to get the pith out and to get a ladle in to serve. Don't try and remove the pumpkin from its dish to bring it to the table, or it will at once disintegrate. Instead, choose a cooking dish on which to carry it in.

A word on nutmeg *(Myristica fragrans)*, whose outer husk also provides mace. Buy it in berry form and grate it as you need it. You will be surprised at the difference this makes to the flavour of the completed dish. Its medicinal use according to older herbals was as a carminative, so don't use too much of it. George Orwell, discussing the use of words, recounted how he always thought that 'carminative' referred to the deep red colour of the dose he was given as a child. It was only in later life, after he had several times used it as a synonym for red, that he discovered to his acute embarrassment what the word on the label actually meant.

My mother, who was an enthusiastic organic composter, usually created several heaps of noisome vegetable matter at the end of the garden at any one time. When she decided that one of these was ready to 'cook' she would cover it with earth and leave it for a season. She always however sprinkled pumpkin seeds on top and before very long the compost heap would be a mass first of green tendrils and then of swelling brilliant pumpkins. This ease of growth close to the earth may explain the French *potiron* which meant originally 'great mushroom' from the Arabic for the *morel*. Mushrooms themselves make a quite delicious soup.

MUSHROOM SOUP

It's very difficult in these days of mass-produced food to get decent mushrooms. The cultivated varieties are so bland as to be almost flavourless. If you can get some fresh field mushrooms then these should be used instead. But take care; although there are many more edible fungi around than you will ever see in the shops, others are deadly. Recall the fate of the Emperor Claudius and consult a guide. An excellent work is *The Mushroom Feast* by Jane Grigson (which incidentally contains seventeen recipes for soups in which mushrooms are a principal ingredient). This is one of the simplest although unusual enough in its way. It is adapted from *The Gentle Art of Cookery* by C.F. Leyel and Olgar Hartley, originally published in 1925.

300 g chopped mushrooms
1 sliced onion
1 litre chicken stock
60 g butter
30 g flour
150 ml cream
150 ml milk
100 ml Sauternes
salt and pepper

Simmer the mushrooms and the onion in the stock for about 20 minutes.

Purée the vegetables and return them to the stock. Make a roux, cook it gently for two minutes and stir it into the soup. Add the milk and cream and season to taste. The wine should be added at the last minute just before serving. You can drink the remainder later with your dessert. Mushrooms make an excellent consommé and an iced soup.

CALLALOO

Above are the more obvious vegetables to use in a soup. Others, equally delicious, are less often considered. One of these is callaloo.

This is a very famous creole soup well known in the West Indies where it is also spelt callilu or calalou. For years I had wanted to make it but thought I would never be able to get the main ingredient. At last however all was revealed. It turned out to be the leaves of — taro. These are fairly readily available in the northern part of New Zealand but if you live in Invercargill *nil desperandum* because you can also use Chinese spinach (yin-choi to the Chinese, bhaji to the Indians) or even plain ordinary spinach. In any event you will end up with a delicious soup. This is a version which comes from Guadaloupe.

1½ kg of callaloo (i.e. taro) leaves (or spinach)
200 g okra chopped
1 aubergine chopped
4 tablespoons vegetable oil
125 g diced pork
3 green bananas, peeled and chopped
2 onions, chopped
2 cloves garlic, chopped
2 tablespoons chopped chives
½ teaspoon thyme
½ teaspoon ground cloves
1 seeded chilli pepper
1 tablespoon white wine vinegar
200 ml coconut milk
salt and pepper

Cook the chopped greens, okra and aubergine in a little lightly salted water until just done. In a heavy casserole heat the oil and fry the pork a little, then add the bananas, onion and garlic. Cover and cook until tender. Take out the pork and add the other ingredients and cook gently for five more minutes. Put both this and the vegetables previously cooked through a blender and mix the two purées. Return the pork and adjust the seasoning. If it seems too thick, add a little chicken stock. This should then be heated again just before serving.

Taro grows in most tropical or sub-tropical countries throughout the world. Its availability is a welcome consequence of the Polynesian influx of the last thirty years.

Green bananas are also something we ought to use more in our cooking. Bananas appeared in Europe in modern times in the seventeenth century but they had been known before. Alexander the Great came across them at the farthest reaches of his conquests on the banks of the Indus, and Pliny referred to them although he didn't know what they were. They've never much caught on in European cooking although they go well with fish, in omelettes and in fritters. I am told that they are also eaten with frogs' legs although I have never tried that. Okra is a green pod which grows on the tropical tree of the same name. It is known as gumbo in the Caribbean, and grows in the Pacific also. You will have to buy it tinned: I have only ever seen it on sale fresh once.

A number of new fruits and vegetables have joined our cuisine in recent years, in particular from South America. One thinks of the carambola, or the sapodilla for instance. Or perhaps one doesn't. For some reason, however, one item has enjoyed an immense vogue, and that is the avocado. These flourish not only in Mexico but in parts of Africa where they are so plentiful that they fall from the trees and are eaten by stray animals. Spare a curse for the pariah dogs of Kenya the next time you pay an outrageous price for an avocado. Again, for inexplicable reasons, people *will* drown them in oil and vinegar. Frankly I don't much care for them in that way but they do make a delicious soup. This from Mexico.

SOPA DE AGUACATE

1 litre chicken stock
2 large avocados
300 ml cream
sour cream, spring onions, parsley
nutmeg
salt and pepper

Peel and stone the avocados, mash them and heat in the chicken stock. Make sure there are no lumps and then stir in the cream, a little nutmeg and seasoning to taste. Serve hot or cold with sour cream, chopped spring onions and parsley.

BASIC AVGOLEMONO SOUP

Using fruit or vegetables in soup is a tradition known in most parts of the world but the most famous of all such soups is to be found in the Mediterranean where the basic ingredient is the lemon. Avgolemono soup, to give it its Greek name, is general to the Mediterranean. One of the memories I shall cherish for a lifetime is sitting in a taverna on the harbour front in Chania, Crete, and eating iced lemon soup. But, like the famous fish soups (which are really stews) of the same area, there are many varieties. Below I give a basic recipe and a few variations.

2 litres chicken stock
90 g rice
3 eggs
juice of a large lemon
salt to taste

Cook the rice in the stock. While this is happening beat the eggs well, then beat in the lemon juice, then *very gradually* two ladles of the hot stock. Just before serving the soup beat this sauce back into the soup and simmer it gently. Let it cool slightly before serving. This is a very vexing soup no matter how simple it may sound, because it will curdle without warning and for no apparent reason. I have found that praying helps and also keeping it just at a simmer. A little of the grated lemon zest can also add to the lemon flavour. Jane Grigson in *Fish Cookery* recommends a variation using fish stock instead of chicken stock and this is also very interesting. In combination with fennel it is devastating — just add a teaspoon of Pernod, six thin lemon slices and some chopped fennel leaves. This can also be served cold.

Fennel grows wild in many parts of this country but is rarely used as a herb. This is probably because it is a weed and therefore widely regarded as poisonous. In fact it is a superb accompaniment to fish in particular. In Italy and France its lower stalk is eaten as a vegetable. It can also be made into a herb tea.

In Egypt where avgolemono is called *Beid di Lamoun* there is another lemon soup called *Hamud*. This combines chicken stock with leeks, garlic, lemon juice, courgettes and rice. The combination of lemon and garlic is very North African and brings us close to another cuisine, the yassa cooking of Senegal, which is not within the scope of this book. But for my money the two Greek variations on the basic avgolemono which follow are truly superb.

MAYIERITSA

Easter soup. The Greek Church is one of the few which still enjoins a strict Lenten fast. This is traditionally broken by eating this soup after the Christos Anesti service, which signals the end of Lent and the beginning of the Easter celebration.

lamb tripe, heart and two shanks
60 g butter
parsley, dill, spring onions
100 g rice
juice of two lemons
salt and pepper
egg and lemon soup as in the basic recipe

Simmer the meat in two litres of water flavoured with the lemon juice until you have a strong stock. Then strain off the liquid. If you like you can also chop the meat from the shanks and add this. Your cat will thank you for the remaining solid ingredients. Add the rice. Meanwhile fry the herbs and onions in the butter and when the onions are tender add these also. Bring it once more to a simmer and then add the egg and lemon prepared as already described. Things that curdle can sometimes be restored by rapid cooling and whisking. This is effective with a sauce but a soup is rather more problematical.

PSAROSOUPA ME AVGOLEMONO

This is essentially the soup recommended by Jane Grigson, using fish stock. As a prelude, about a kilo of fish cut into neat pieces is poached in the stock and when it is cooked it is removed and kept hot while you proceed. The fish is then added again at the end. In that case the recipe will sometimes leave out the rice, but I keep it in.

SHRIMP AND TOMATO BISQUE

Shellfish make excellent soup, particularly in combination with the right vegetable. Two which go particularly well together are shrimp and tomato, and they combine well in a bisque which was a favourite soup of Alexandre Dumas (1802-1870). Dumas *père* was an extraordinarily hospitable man who entertained such crowds of visitors in his home at Port-Marly outside Paris that the railway receipts fell by twenty thousand francs a year when he moved away. His dinners served in the middle of the day lasted from 11 am to 4.30 pm. He did all the cooking himself. He was indeed one of the most formidable amateur cooks of his century and his posthumously published *Grand Dictionnaire de Cuisine* is still a standard reference work. Sometimes the painter Courbet, who was a good friend of Dumas and also an enthusiastic cook, would join him. They would cook together, talking through and at one another continuously. At least so Monet says, for he often joined them too. The *Dictionnaire* is full of the most diverse culinary information imaginable. This soup Dumas invented for his two painter friends; he used to prepare it for them at an establishment near Le Havre where he went every year in the summer for a holiday.

200 g shrimps
700 g tomatoes, chopped
500 g onions, chopped
750 ml white wine
500 ml beef stock
salt, pepper, cayenne

Cook the shrimps in half the white wine. Strain and cool, retaining the liquid. Peel the shrimps and put the crushed debris back in the wine. Simmer to extract the flavour and to concentrate it, and strain again. Meanwhile cook the tomatoes and onions in the remainder of the wine and when they are soft purée them and then combine this with the beef stock, the shrimp and wine stock and a quarter teaspoon of cayenne. Season to taste and bring back to a simmer. At the last moment add the peeled shrimps and serve. Prawns are just as good.

Tomatoes also go extremely well with mussels. About 500 g of mussels cooked in 500 ml of fish stock and 500 g of cooked and puréed tomatoes suitably seasoned is a delicious combination. In Catalonia they make a slightly more complicated and flavoured version.

SOPA DE MUSCOS DE LITORAL CATALA

about half a dozen mussels for each person
olive oil
1 chopped onion
4 chopped tomatoes
4 slices dry toast, crumbed
small glass of brandy
2 garlic cloves
2 sprigs parsley
½ teaspoon cinnamon
salt and pepper

Fry the onions and tomatoes in the olive oil in a heavy casserole. When they are soft strain in the mussel liquor and add a little water. Bring it to the boil and add the crumbs and brandy and simmer. Pound the garlic, parsley, cinnamon, salt and pepper in a mortar (the resultant paste is in Spanish a *picada*) and add this to the soup. Finally add the mussels and heat them through thoroughly. Some sprinkle this with grated cheese but I don't.

OYSTER SOUP

Of all the shellfish soups the best is oyster. At least it is when the Bluff oystermen are not having a row with their employers about the price per sack. Whatever the outcome the price never seems to go *down*.

Given the shocking price of oysters, this is a soup I eat very rarely. The last time I did so with a clear conscience was the day I won the pub raffle and staggered home burdened down with oysters. Expense aside, the soup which results is not only delicious but illustrates most admirably the tenet that in cooking simplest is best.

2 dozen oysters
60 g butter
2 tablespoons flour
600 ml milk
1 teaspoon anchovy essence
150 ml cream
salt, pepper, nutmeg, cayenne, lemon juice, parsley

Reserve the liquor from the oysters. Make a roux with the butter and flour and cook it for a couple of minutes. Heat the milk and gradually blend it with the roux. Season with the anchovy, nutmeg and cayenne and stir in the cream. Simmer for thirty minutes. At the very end add the oysters and the liquor and just heat them through. The secret of successful oyster soup is to serve the oysters cooked *only by this warming*, otherwise they will become tough. Squeeze in a little lemon juice and sprinkle chopped parsley for serving at once. Some people prefer to use chicken stock rather than milk. Rye bread and a lightly salted butter goes very well with oyster soup.

HAMBURGER AALSUPPE — EEL SOUP

If you prefer to be adventurous and more complicated in your fish soup, try this North German speciality, which is virtually a meal in itself. Certainly it would do very well as a main course.

Conger eel, the proper sea eel, is not to everybody's taste. Apicius liked it but drowned its strong flavour in wine, honey, cumin, onion and garum. Those who have read *The Tin Drum* might not care for it either. But if you can get past such unpleasant associations you will be pleasantly surprised by this dish which is really a matelote, i.e. a stew. It is also the only fish dish I have tried which uses a dried fruit in this way. The French have a version in Anjou which uses prunes, I am told.

200 g dried pears
250 ml white wine
500 g chuck steak with any fat removed, cut into about six pieces
2 leeks, trimmed and chopped
3 carrots
4 celery stalks
bouquet garni
1 sliced onion

parsley, sage, salt and pepper
250 g green peas
the florets of half a small cauliflower
1 kg of eel skinned and boned and cut into lengths of about 5 cm
white wine vinegar
3 small whole onions, each with a clove
peel of a lemon in strips
2 tablespoons sugar
4 egg yolks

Soak the pears in the wine overnight. The next day put in a large pan the beef, leeks, carrots, celery, bouquet, sage and onion. Add 2 litres of water and season lightly. Simmer for two hours and then remove the beef and bouquet and add the cauliflower and then ten minutes later the peas. Simmer until these last two are cooked. Meanwhile in a separate pan and about an hour before serving barely cover the eel with water, add a dash of vinegar, and the onions and cloves. Simmer until the eel is cooked (20 minutes). In yet a third pan put the pears to cook in their wine with the lemon peel. Now combine all three by removing the eel from its liquid and adding it to the first pot and to this add the pears in their wine but not the lemon peel. Add the sugar gradually and more salt and pepper to taste. Beat the egg yolks and a ladle of the soup liquid. Combine and then stir carefully into the main pot. Do not let it boil or you will curdle it. Serve with plain bread. If you suspect some of your guests will baulk at conger eel don't tell them what they are eating until later.

Conger eel is one of the cheapest fish items at your fishmonger simply because it is unpopular and most people don't know how to cook it. In France they use red wine instead of white and a tablespoon of anchovy essence but this seems to me to be an unnecessary refinement.

DUMPLINGS

Finally, some soups, especially the lighter variety, are better for the addition of dumplings. These are quite easy to make and particularly for winter eating add an extra touch.

100 g flour
50 g suet
salt
2 teaspoons dried parsley

Mix the ingredients thoroughly and make a soft dough by adding a little water. Roll out into a long 'snake' and chop off inch pieces. These can then be dropped into the soup about twenty minutes before serving. They are a particularly English refinement and are not suitable for many non-English soups. Avgolemono soup and dumplings wouldn't be right somehow. On the other hand they go very well with the eel soup, at least in my estimation. Doubtless North Germans reading this will suppress a delicate shudder at the thought, but food is after all what one cares to eat.

Fish

What female heart can gold depise,
What cat's averse to fish?
— Thomas Gray, 'Ode on the Death of a Favourite Cat'

JUST AS HE is wrong in attributing meretriciousness to one sex, so Thomas Gray is not, I trust, ascribing love of fish solely to cats. It is the most delicious of foods. Not however that one would know it, living here.

I never fail to be astonished that in an island nation, surrounded for thousands of kilometres by seas which contain an abundance of fish of every variety, the staple of our diet continues to be meat. Not only do we not eat much fish but we prefer to allow others from great distances to come and fish our waters with methods which will, within a decade or two, deplete our stocks beyond recovery. And foreign fishermen do this largely for the purpose of making protein meal to feed to animals. In addition we pollute our shores with industrial or urban wastes which destroy the shellfish beds. In a world where the problem of inadequate daily protein is a major cause of starvation this is scandalous. Most New Zealanders do not only not care, they have never even considered the matter. We would rightly laugh out of countenance any person who, when confronted by a lamb chop and a steak, couldn't tell the difference between them; but most New Zealanders confronted by hake and cod could not tell you which was which, and no one thinks anything of it.

I suppose that this ignorance to an extent reflects the habits of our antecedents. Most of our settler population came from rural England or from Ireland, where the tradition was that of eating meat when you could get it. If they came from elsewhere it was from places where fish was for poor

69

people to eat and the chance to eat meat every day was not to be passed up. Only the Maori continue to have a strong tradition of fish eating and until the appearance of Italians and other Southern Europeans among our immigrant population the eating of fish on a regular basis was regarded as a curious eccentricity, with the exception of regional delicacies such as oysters, crayfish or whitebait. Looking back towards my childhood I have no recollection whatsoever of eating fish, although I am sure I did from time to time. And I am equally sure it was buried in a gluey disgusting substance denominated 'sauce'. This was believed to be particularly suitable food for invalids; why they were picked on I don't know, because it was suitable for nobody. Perhaps they were too feeble to protest.

There was one exception to this rule; the English habit of the fish supper, which consisted of fish deep-fried in batter, served with chipped potatoes similarly abused. Fish cooked in this manner is, if done properly, an acceptable, if unremarkable dish. With a very few exceptions it is not done properly here. On the contrary it is done frightfully and it pleases me little to know that in England, mother of this tradition, they generally do it worse. I am consoled only by the thought that I live within walking distance of a shop where they do do it properly. The proprietor is from Crete and knows how to treat fish with respect. His cooking reminds me of sitting in that harbour-front taverna at Chania where you could eat fried sardines fresh from the sea. Despite the best efforts of the industry itself, to whom all credit, as cooks we still cannot be induced to draw fully upon the riches of our seas.

Partly the problem is one of supply. Although no one in New Zealand is terribly far from the sea, commercial fishermen only operate and return with a sufficient variety in certain areas. They are not to be blamed for this: if people won't buy variety then why bother bringing it ashore? People still tend to turn their noses up at not only squid, paua and crab but at varieties of cod or even anything which is not ready filleted. Wellington, with its Italian and Greek populations, is particularly well-served; there are excellent fish shops where variety is not only abundant but the less usual varieties are relatively cheap. It's better to eschew the fashionably expensive fish shops which don't often justify the high prices charged. Now that Saturday shopping is here to stay one of my pleasures is to tuck a cookery book under my arm, saunter along to my fishmonger and see what he has for sale that's unusual, find a recipe for it and continue down the street to the delicatessen to purchase the remaining ingredients for that evening's meal. It's surprising what can be done with whole mullet, eel or even herring.

In one particular only we are at a disadvantage. With the exception of the eel, we have no abundant freshwater fish. This is a pity because not only are most people deeply prejudiced against eels but they are missing a real treat in water-souchy which is the English equivalent of the French bouillabaisse. There are of course introduced freshwater fish and in particular the trout.

The way we have dealt with its supply is a curiosity. The Acclimatisation Societies constitute a powerful lobby, the principal objective of which seems to be the protection of privilege, by bitterly opposing fish farming (on entirely spurious grounds) and thereby ensuring that mostly it is the wealthy who eat trout. Unless one has a friend who will catch it and supply you with it, trout is virtually unprocurable. The development in a democratic society of a local equivalent of the eighteenth century English game laws is quite shameful. Cooks of New Zealand should unite against it.

While they are doing that, and before we get to the recipes, a note on why this chapter is in this particular place. Tradition only demands it. Fish comes after the soup and before the entrée, which precedes the main course. Many of the recipes given here are entirely suitable for a main course themselves and should be so served. Contrariwise, fish need not be preceded by a soup, or if it is may just as easily become the entrée. In that case a smaller quantity should be prepared than is given here, since these quantities are mostly for main courses. About two-thirds of the amount should do, if the fish is to come earlier in the meal. If the recipe calls for a whole fish you will have to rely upon eye and judgement at the fishmonger.

Baked Fish

Baking with an appropriate stuffing is one of the most neglected but simplest ways of cooking a whole fish. It is also one of the more spectacular dishes to serve. To appear bearing a whole fish on a platter wins one an instant reputation for culinary skill. Some of the stuffings which follow may seem odd, but all are delicious. First, however, a word on the preparation of the fish.

Fish need to be scaled, if the fishmonger has not already done this. There are special implements for scaling but you don't need them. Lay the fish on a spread-out newspaper. (This is to catch the scales which will fly in all directions.) Cut off the spiky fins with scissors or a sharp knife and then push the scales firmly the wrong way with the back edge of a large knife or a cleaver and they will come off easily. You may have to go over the fish several times to get them all. Slit the fish down the belly, pull out the gut and rinse thoroughly in running water. If you are not going to use the fish immediately you can immerse it in water to which a little vinegar has been added. Remember however that the fresher the fish the better it will taste. Purists excoriate frozen fish in any form but usually I find it acceptable; we have little option in any event.

If bones in fish irritate you then a fish is very easily boned before cooking. After cleaning, cut through the backbone just below the head and just above the tail with sharp scissors. This needs some care. Then turn the fish gutted side down on a board and press it firmly along the backbone. Turn it back over and you will find that most of the bones are sticking up and can be fairly easily picked out. Warn your guests, however, that you have almost certainly missed one or two.

Cooking a whole fish is simplicity itself. Parcel it up with appropriate seasonings, and a little butter in foil, pressing the joins firmly together. Pop it in the oven. A slow oven is best because the fish can be cooked for several hours without having to worry about it, the flavour will stay in and the fish will not overcook or dry out. This gives flexibility to deal with other dishes, or even just to sit and talk to guests while dinner is cooking. This is always an impressive trick because non-cooks think that cooking is a complicated business with sauces and what-have-you being prepared at the last moment. The real skill is in the preparation, some hours previously.

STUFFED TROUT, TRUCHAS RELLENAS

Cooking trout using a European cookbook is a startling experience. The recipes almost always instruct the cook to 'take eight trout for four people'. This is because European trout are brook trout and quite small by comparison to ours, which are salmon (or pink) trout. Usually one will do; I got hold of such a monstrous fish on one occasion that not only did it do for a main course for six, but I had the remains cold for lunch the next day. These two recipes are both Spanish, respectively from Asturias and from Galicia. They will do equally well for a terakihi (which has a superbly delicate flavour).

Incidentally the doyens of angling are supposed to be Isaak Walton and his friend Charles Cotton, who did the cooking. Feminists might like to note that long before these two gentlemen had appeared on the scene, Dame Juliana Berners had written a similar work on the subject of catching and eating fish.

For *Truchas Rellenas*, make your stuffing with the following:

2 slices cooked chicken
2 slices smoked ham
1 small onion
8 stoned olives
100 g crushed almonds
1 chopped red pepper
butter, salt, white pepper
lemon juice

White pepper goes better with fish than black. Regrettably it must be bought ready-ground. White and black pepper are the same thing prepared differently, white pepper being the core of the berry, and sharper in flavour.

Sprinkle the inside of your fish with lemon juice and salt. Mince together the chicken, ham, onion, olives and pepper. Add the almonds, salt and pepper. Stuff the fish with this mixture. You will need then to seal the cavity otherwise the stuffing will ooze out during cooking. Trout has a very tough skin so unless you have a larding or sailmaker's needle you will have trouble penetrating even with skewers. It's better to truss it. This can be done very easily with thread which can be snipped away before serving.

Bake in foil. The best way to serve is simply to put the parcel on a warmed platter and unwrap it at the table, which always draws appropriate appreciative noises from guests.

TRUCHAS CON TERNERA

This combination illustrates, as did the previous recipe, that the serving of meat with fish is not confined as a tradition to English cooking:

1 small onion
2 pieces steak or veal
12 cooked and shelled prawns
2 tablespoons breadcrumbs
2 cloves garlic
chopped parsley
salt, white pepper, butter
lemon juice

73

Prepare as for the preceding recipe by mincing the onion, garlic and beef (and a slice of smoked ham if you wish) and mixing them together with the other ingredients to make the stuffing. Steak with a game fish was a new one on me, but most successful.

The varieties of stuffings are almost endless. Here are one or two which you may find of interest.

DUXELLES

2 cups breadcrumbs
300 ml milk
2 chopped onions
30 g butter
2 tablespoons white wine
bunch of spring onions
100 g chopped mushrooms
1 tablespoon parsley
2 eggs
salt, pepper, nutmeg

Soak the breadcrumbs in the milk and press them dry. Press the liquid out of the mushrooms also. Soften the onions in the butter and cook the spring onions in the wine and strain away the liquid. Mix these several ingredients with the parsley, eggs, salt, pepper and nutmeg to make the stuffing and sauté this until it has no moisture left in it. Then stuff the fish with it and bake it in the usual way.

SOFT ROE STUFFING

100 g soft roe
30 g breadcrumbs
milk
small chopped onion
30 g butter
tablespoon chopped fresh rosemary (if you can get it)
teaspoon lemon zest
teaspoon anchovy essence
salt, white pepper, lemon juice

Soft roe can sometimes be bought but usually in a quantity somewhat larger than required here, because the whole sac is sold. The balance can be frozen. It needs to be fresh rather than smoked. Tinned roe is rather expensive and doesn't taste quite so flavoursome.

Mix the roe and the breadcrumbs with just enough milk to make a soft paste. Combine thoroughly with the other ingredients and stuff fish after sprinkling internally with salt and lemon juice. This stuffing is particularly good with cod.

TZAVAROV LETZONADZE TZOOK

This is not a traditional English stuffing, but comes from the Caucasus. What makes it so interesting is the use of burghul instead of breadcrumbs and the nutty flavour that results. Burghul is hulled wheat steamed until partially cooked, dried and ground coarsely. It's sold under a variety of names in health food shops, the most usual of which is 'bulgar wheat'. In its original home it is known as *tzavar*.

30 g butter
1 finely chopped onion
200 g burghul
3 hard-boiled eggs, shelled and chopped
parsley, dill, salt and white pepper

Soften the onions in the butter, combine with the other ingredients and stuff the fish in the normal way. Just before serving warm through 300 ml of yoghurt stabilised with a tablespoon of plain flour and squeeze the juice of half a lemon into it. Serve this separately as a sauce.

FENNEL STUFFING

Another rather unusual stuffing from Umbria is that involving *fennel*. To most of us, fennel is a weed and a nuisance. In Italy and France they make a virtue of necessity and use the root (a larger, plumper one than our weed here) as a vegetable. I have rarely seen it on sale here but that should not stop you digging ours up for the purpose. It was introduced into England in the eighteenth century by the world's most disastrous diplomat ever, the 3rd Earl of Peterborough, friend of Locke and Newton and enthusiastic vegetable gardener, but it never caught on. Similar failure dogged Thomas Jefferson, an equally enthusiastic gardener and cook, when he tried to popularise it in America. Fennel goes superbly with fish.

3 slices of smoked ham
2 large cloves of garlic
1 head of fennel
olive oil
60 g breadcrumbs
1 egg
salt and pepper

Chop the first three ingredients very finely together with a large heavy knife to make what the Italians call a *battuto*. Stew this gently in a little oil in a covered pan until it is soft. Mix with the crumbs and seasoning and the egg to bind and stuff your fish with it. Bake as earlier described.

GOOSEBERRY STUFFING

Of all the stuffings which can be used for fish the most interesting are those which involve fruit. And of these the best are, in my view, those using gooseberries. That of coure is an odd suggestion to English ears. We are used to gooseberries with sugar in tarts or pies and with cream. The French on the other hand regard *that* as an odd thing to do and have always eaten their gooseberries, which they call *groseille à maquereau*, i.e. mackerel berries, with fish either as a sauce or a stuffing. In fact in English cuisine it's not so odd at all. In Eliza Acton's *Modern Cookery* (1845) you will find a recipe for gooseberry sauce for fish. Although it contains rather too much flour for today's taste I have used it not only for fish but for venison. The English have simply got out of the habit of using the sharpness of gooseberries as a flavour, partly because they have bred them for sweetness. They still retain a sufficient tartness to be suitable for fish and the habit needs returning to.

150 g gooseberries
100 g breadcrumbs
1 clove garlic, chopped
1 small onion, chopped
30 g butter
1 tablespoon fresh parsley
1 egg
marjoram
salt, pepper, lemon juice

Top and tail the gooseberries and chop them coarsely. Soften the onions in the butter and mix with the other ingredients. Stuff and bake the fish in foil in the usual way. Incidentally, when buying fish don't despise herrings. They are small but very juicy. You will need two per person to make a meal. Two can be cooked in their own foil parcels and will greatly surprise dinner guests who had only met them hitherto in a tin swimming in half rancid oil or in an apology for tomato sauce. They are actually one of the cheapest fish on the market. They are not seen often (although plentiful around our coasts) because people don't buy them. In the middle ages nerring was a staple because it was so available and could be easily salted or smoked. They have contributed the kipper to our cuisine (a noble addition in my view). Archeology now tells us that it was intrepid Portuguese fishermen seeking herring on the Newfoundland banks who visited North America in modern times at least a century before Columbus set foot there. They had settlements ashore for both salting and smoking. Some of these, when excavated, have turned out to be substantial in size. The north-eastern seaboard of the American continent has a submerged but significant Portuguese sub-culture as a result. So much for the Pilgrim Fathers! But of the stuffed seafood it has been my pleasure to eat, there is one item superlative above all else, which comes next.

STUFFED SQUIDS

Jules Verne has much to answer for. Most people have a vision of a squid as an enormous creature, a veritable monster of the deep, embracing a submarine. There are squid of such a species but they are not the ones I have in mind. Rather, I prefer the variety known to coastal folk of the world since the dawn of time: the calamari of the Mediterranean, or botanically speaking *Loligo vulgaris.* As something to eat we have only come to know them since the Japanese and Korean fleets ventured into our waters over the last two decades. Squid tubes can be bought cleaned and washed, but for this recipe you will need the tentacles, so buy the squids whole, one for each person. Never mind the way they look at you!

Cleaning and preparing them is a messy job but one becomes both more inured and adept with practice. Gently but firmly pull the head and tentacles away from the body. This will gut the squid. Chop off the tentacles and discard the head. Take the body sac and remove the pinkish outside skin which will strip off with gentle rubbing. Inside the resultant sac you will find a hard bony transparent piece. This is why the squid is called calmar, from the Latin *calamus*, a reed and thus a pen. Pull or cut this bone away and discard it. The resultant sac, open at both ends, should be thoroughly washed out. Chop the tentacles into half-inch pieces. Now comes the fiddly part. Thread a needle and very neatly sew up the small end of this tube. This will take a little while but is worth it for the final result. Next make the following stuffing:

> *4 tablespoons olive oil*
> *the tentacles, chopped*
> *3 chopped onions*
> *3 cloves garlic*
> *120 g breadcrumbs*
> *a little milk or white wine*
> *a tin of anchovy fillets*
> *60 g smoked bacon or speck (salted pork fat)*
> *chopped parsley*
> *salt and pepper*

This makes enough for about six medium-sized squids. Fry the onions, garlic, bacon or speck and the tentacles in the oil for about five minutes. Moisten the breadcrumbs with the milk or wine and mix them with the fried ingredients, anchovies, parsley and seasoning to taste (bearing in mind anchovies are very salty). Loosely (because it will expand) fill each squid tube with this stuffing and then, taking your needle and thread, sew up the other opening. Lay them side by side in an oven pan and pour the following sauce over and around them.

> *1 chopped onion*
> *1 clove garlic*
> *3 tablespoons olive oil*
> *375 g tomatoes, chopped*
> *1 tablespoon tomato concentrate*
> *1 glass wine or vermouth (red or white)*
> *salt, pepper, paprika*

Fry the garlic and onion in the oil and then add the tomatoes, concentrate and wine. Simmer for ten to twelve minutes and stir in the seasoning. This sauce can be used for other purposes too.

Now pour the sauce over the squids, cover the pan and cook at 190° C for 45 minutes to an hour. The squids will have swelled to plump white cushions. Spoon the sauce over them as they are served. The flavour of these squids is very strong. They need a crisp salad and bread to mop up the sauce afterwards. This is a dish I have eaten and greatly enjoyed not only in the Greek islands, but in my favourite Italian restaurant in Wellington, where it is a speciality of the house. But enough of stuffed seafood; let us proceed to the fish stew.

Fish Stews

The thought of fish stew is anathema to most New Zealanders but around the Mediterranean in particular it is an old and hallowed tradition. From thence it was carried to the Americas where it developed into a tradition of its own. Some stews contain relatively little gravy. Others are almost soups; these latter are more typical of Northern Europe. I've mentioned the water souchy, from the Dutch *waterzootje*, but there is also pepperpot. It should be confused neither with the Philadelphia dish I mentioned in the soup chapter and of the same provenance which is made with tripe and veal, nor with the Barbadoan dish which is made with chicken and cassara. Notwithstanding its appearance in the English regional cuisine (from the West Country) pepperpot is of West Indian origin. This apparent peculiarity is explained if one recollects that Bristol was, in the eighteenth century, the centre of the sugar and slave trades. The spicing of the dish actually suggests an ultimately African origin. But it also involves another traditional English combination, *viz.* lamb and crab. It's wonderful on a cold winter's night.

PEPPERPOT

700 g diced lean lamb fillet or backs lamb with the fat removed
250 g smoked bacon
1 small crab taken from the shell
½ small cabbage, shredded
1 head of chopped spinach
tablespoon chopped thyme
3 onions, chopped
3 hot chilli peppers, seeded
1 green pepper, sliced
½ teaspoon cayenne
1 teaspoon paprika
12 black peppercorns
lime juice
salt and pepper

Simmer the lamb, bacon, onions, thyme, chilli, green pepper, the black peppercorns and salt in about 1500 ml of water for about an hour. Then add the cabbage and spinach and cook for a further half-hour. Add the crab (which should weigh anywhere between 500 g and 1 kg) and continue to simmer gently. Tinned crab is rather flavourless and if you can get a fresh one you will be surprised by the difference this makes. The addition of prawns is interesting also. Finally, squeeze in the lime juice just before serving, which should be with plain boiled rice. This dish is very hot to those unused to chilli and in this regard the lime juice is crucial because it takes the heat out of the pepper without detracting from the flavour. Some dumplings cooked in it are also a nice touch. The recipe for these is to be found in the soup chapter.

The most famous of these almost soup stews is of course the *guylas*, which is the best known of all Hungarian dishes, although rarely cooked properly. It is not in fact confined to either Hungary or beef but is also very popular in Albania where the principal ingredient is white fish.

SALTFISH AND ACKEE

While we are on the subject of the West Indies (more or less), I still have a clear recollection as an adolescent of hearing Harry Belafonte sing *Jamaica Farewell* and in particular his evocation of 'ackee rice, saltfish are nice'. It was not until many years later when I was living in London and had a number of Jamaican acquaintance that I finally ate this dish. The ackee is the fruit of a tree, *Blighia sapida*, named for the much maligned William Bligh. If its large seeds are split open they will be found to contain a soft yellow edible centre — the ackee. Obviously not available fresh here, but not uncommon tinned. In fact the tins are sometimes sold off cheaply by grocers because no one knows what they are or what to do with them.

Saltfish, at least as far as I am aware, has only very recently become generally available in fishmongers here although it has been an export item for years. You will need to soak it in cold water to leach out the salt and soften it, otherwise it will be inedible.

500 g saltfish
1 large tin ackees
200 g rindless bacon, chopped
2 chopped onions
1 chopped green pepper
2 seeded chilli peppers
4 chopped spring onions
4 tomatoes, chopped
½ teaspoon thyme
salt and pepper

Simmer the soaked fish in fresh water until it is soft. Flake the fish and remove any bones and skin. Mix with the ackees and set aside. Fry the bacon in its own fat until it is crisp and mix with the fish and ackees. Take care with this; ackees are very soft and crumble up easily.

In a little butter or oil in an iron casserole, sauté the onions and green peppers, then add the chilli, spring onions, tomatoes and thyme. Continue to sauté for a few minutes, then add the fish mixture and heat through. Garnish with watercress and bring to the table in its casserole for the guests to help themselves communally. Serve with plain boiled rice.

PLAKI

There is a theory that fish, being of a delicate flavour, cannot cope with strong flavours in a dish such as that just described. This theory is nonsense; there are many quite robust fish dishes. One of the best of these, from Greece, is plaki.

This requires quite a coarse fish. Cod (or groper — even better) do very nicely.

4 tablespoons olive oil
4 chopped onions
2 cloves garlic
3 stalks celery, chopped
4 chopped tomatoes
400 g pasta
1 piece of fish for each diner
lemon juice
salt and pepper
a couple of dozen black olives

Sauté the onion, garlic, celery, tomatoes and seasoning in the oil until soft and liquid. While this is happening cook the pasta *al dente* (just done, not too soft). Drain it and put it in a buttered casserole with the sautéed vegetables on top. Add the olives and put the fish on top of that with a sprinkling of salt, pepper and lemon juice. Bake in the oven for 30 minutes or until the fish is cooked. For a dinner, unlike most other dishes, fish cooked in this way cannot be prepared in advance. This is particularly so with anything involving pasta which will turn into a solid and unpleasant mass if allowed to cool during the preparation. Consequently such dishes, which cook fairly quickly, need a certain amount of speed, juggling and confidence on the part of the cook. This comes with practice.

ZARZUELA

All around the Mediterranean they make strongly flavoured fish dishes like *plaki*. The best of these combine several different varieties of fish in the single dish and give a pleasing range not only of flavours but also of colours. Like *zarzuela* from Spain, they are sometimes named for these characteristics.

In Catalan this word also means a light opera or musical comedy. You will see why this dish is so named when you make it. It's not for every day as it is in Spain; the ingredients are too expensive here.

400 g each of several white fish
1 small cooked crayfish
24 cooked and shelled prawns
24 mussels
4 teaspoons olive oil
1 chopped onion
2 cloves garlic
3 chopped tomatoes
glass white wine
glass brandy (rougher the better)
paprika, parsley, crushed almonds
turmeric, salt and pepper

When choosing your fish, try and get varieties which are of distinctive flavours. Groper and terakihi would be a good combination, for instance. The sad fact is of course that most people have no palate for fish and are hard put to distinguish them. The fish should be boneless and cut into neat but largish pieces. Flour them. Ask your fishmonger for some groper bones also, or a fish head, and make a small stock by boiling them with half an onion, a little salt and some water. Fish heads incidentally are not so easy to come by although one would have imagined a surplus. When I enquired why, I was told that they are used to bait crayfish pots.

Remove the crayfish meat from its shell and cut into pieces. Keep the legs aside.

Heat the oil in a heavy pan and lightly fry the floured fish pieces. Put them in a warming oven to keep their heat. Fry the onions, garlic and tomatoes in the oil until they are soft and then add the wine, brandy, seasonings, spices and almonds to taste. Add a cupful or two of the strained stock and stir this until you have a smooth sauce. Put in the pieces of fish and cook them gently. Do not let them disintegrate. Add the crayfish meat, the prawns and the mussels. When all has warmed through, transfer to a serving dish surrounded by the crayfish legs. The combination of colours, textures and flavours is irresistible.

There are very few restaurants in this country serving Spanish regional food, which is a great pity, because the Iberian peninsular produces a distinctive cuisine which is neither wholly peasant nor *haute* but something unique to itself. Only one of these restaurants, at least in my experience, serves *zarzuela*, and that is in Christchurch — not a town noted by and large for its culinary delights, so eating such a dish there is all the more welcome an experience. Otherwise you will have to go to Melbourne to sample the delights of Fernando's Tablao Flamenco where they have not only excellent food but flamenco dancing too on Friday and Saturday. At least they used to and I hope they still do, even if all that stamping and glaring isn't to everyone's taste.

BOUILLABAISSE

This is one of those classic dishes which has come to be surrounded by an aura of undeserved mystery. It is simply a delicious fish stew. As Julia Child remarks in *Mastering the Art of French Cooking*: 'You can make as dramatic a production as you want out of a bouillabaisse but remember it originated as a simple Mediterranean fisherman's soup made from the day's catch or its unsaleable left-overs and flavoured with the typical condiments of the region — olive oil, garlic, leeks or onion, tomatoes and herbs.' I suspect in fact that the celebrity of bouillabaisse is reliant upon its crying up by another celebrity, Prosper Mérimée, in the time of Napoleon III. That said, it has also to be remarked that it is impossible to make this stew properly away from the Mediterranean because the fish must be very fresh and one of its ingredients is the *rascasse* or scorpion fish. This is not available in our waters; the closest you will come is a red gurnard. I have never liked eating gurnard incidentally, since I read in Aristotle that these fish can communicate with one another by grunting (a fact attested by modern marine biologists). I don't care to eat a fish that can hold a conversation with another fish.

You can prepare a very good imitation of a bouillabaisse as follows (bearing in mind that the variety of fish involved makes this a dish for a *large* dinner).

3 kg of fresh fish (gurnard, groper, eel, crayfish, mussels, prawns, hake,
    sole, mullet, terakihi, etc., at least four different)
120 ml olive oil
2 chopped onions
2 chopped leeks
12 cloves garlic
3 'beefsteak' tomatoes
4 peeled sliced potatoes
2 chilli peppers
parsley, fennel, cayenne, salt, pepper, turmeric

You will need a pot large enough to hold 3 litres of water in comfort. Put the oil, vegetables (except potatoes), herbs and seasonings to taste in the pot. Add the fish and then the potatoes. Onto this gently pour three litres of warm water and bring this to the boil. Boil it *furiously* for ten minutes. This is crucial because it blends the oil and water. The crayfish should be split lengthways and put in shell and all, and the mussels and prawns scrubbed but left in their shells. Simmer for another ten minutes, then remove the fish and potatoes to a serving dish. Boil the remaining liquid again for five minutes and strain into a tureen. The two dishes should be served separately with toast. Each guest helps himself or herself variously to the solids and liquids and then sops up the latter with the toast. This is the only fish dish I know which deserves a rosé wine. It should also be served with its famous sauce, *rouille:*

Pound 3 cloves of garlic with two red chilli peppers and two sweet red peppers. Into this beat 2 egg yolks and 100 ml of olive oil. Season with salt, pepper and a very little mustard.

You can also add a little fish stock if you like. This sauce is rather fiery but no bouillabaisse would be complete without it.

BOURRIDE

Of course in such a magical place as Provence they have invented more than one fish stew. For myself, although I like bouillabaisse well enough, I prefer their other great fish culinary triumph — bourride.

Despite my liking for it, this dish is the bane of my life because I always manage to curdle it at the end, which leads to a tantrum and the flinging away of the offending recipe book. I suspect that when they know I intend to serve bourride those invited to dinner accept with alacrity but for the tantrum rather than the food. The fish used is plain white, although a little squid does not go amiss and it is good to mix several white fish varieties.

Again this is a dish for a *large* group, perhaps eight, unless you have some gluttonous friends (which I do).

3 kg of fish cut into chunks about 7 centimetres by 5 centimetres

Put this fish to one side and make a stock as follows:

2 each carrots, onions and leeks
4 tablespoons olive oil
2 chopped tomatoes
500 g fish trimmings
2 litres water
150 ml dry white vermouth
2 bay leaves
zest of an orange
2 unpeeled but halved garlic cloves
½ teaspoon turmeric
1 tablespoon salt

Cook the vegetables gently in oil in a large iron pan until they are just at the point of browning. Add all the other ingredients and simmer for about an hour, covered. Cool and strain. Discard the vegetables and other solid residue. What you will have is a very rich fish stock. This can all be done the previous day and refrigerated if you wish. Now prepare another famous Provençal sauce, *aioli*.

crumbs from a slice of stale white bread
wine vinegar
8 garlic cloves
6 eggs yolks
600 ml olive oil (yes, that's right)
salt, cayenne, pepper

Put the crumbs in a blender and moisten them with wine vinegar. Add the garlic and mix well using the chopping blade. Add a little salt and two of the yolks and blend again. Through the top of the blender begin to add the oil *drop by drop* until the sauce is heavy and smooth and then beat in the oil in larger quantities. Set half of this aside for serving separately with the stew. Beat the other four egg yolks into the remaining sauce and set this aside too, well covered in the refrigerator. About fifteen minutes before serving bring the prepared stock to the boil and quickly (about 8 minutes) cook the fish. Take it out, put it on a platter and keep it warm.

Now comes the tricky part. Lower the heat on the broth until it is just below a simmer and very carefully trickle two or three ladles of it into the egg-enriched *aioli*, i.e. the second half. Then very carefully pour it back into the broth and stir it until it thickens. This will take about five minutes. If you let it come to a full simmer it will curdle but if unlike me you can get it right it will be a beautiful smooth ivory yellow.

Serve it immediately along with the fish, and as for bouillabaisse. If you wish you can halve the broth before adding the *aioli* and serve broth, sauce and fish separately. Lots of French bread goes well with this dish.

Both of these stews have their equivalents and variations all over the Mediterrean area. In Spain *bourrida*, in the Adriatic *caccinoco*, which contains the ink sac of a squid and is as black as — well, ink. This is a particular speciality of Trieste. Let's not imagine however that the north of Europe is so locked in culinary slumber that it has no equivalent dishes. Among a number of eighteenth-century collections of recipes are those for English fish pottages, which are just as fine.

FISH POTTAGE

This one comes from a Yorkshire collection of 1780. It is simpler than the stews already given, has no sauce, and is, I suspect, closer to the medieval roots of them all. It must be recollected that the Lenten fast and the various fish days of medieval Europe were strictly observed and enforced. There were lively debates about whether a porpoise was a fish or not (the consensus was that it was — there is a curious medieval dish called nombles of porpoise which was a great Lenten favourite). In fact about half the days of the year were meatless for one reason or another and this was a great encouragement to variety in fish dishes, at least among the rich. The poor ate salt herring or nothing. A poor cleric in the fifteenth century wrote into his manuscript daybook: 'Thou wilt not believe how weary I am of fish and how much I desire that flesh were come in again for I have ate none other but salt fish this Lent and it hath engendered so much phlegm within me that it stoppeth my pipes that I can neither speak nor breathe.'

The occurrence of mace in this recipe suggests that it is a medieval survival. The fish day custom had almost disappeared by the reign of Elizabeth Tudor, who reintroduced it for other reasons, *viz.* to revive the flagging local industry.

3 small red mullet
500 g groper or hake fillets
1 small crayfish
1 fresh crab
250 g shrimps or prawns shelled
3 onions

bouquet garni
500 ml white wine
mace, salt, pepper, turmeric
60 g butter
60 g flour

Keep the mullet whole (although gutted). Shell the crayfish and the crab and put the meat to one side. Put the shells, together with a fish head, one of the onions, quartered but unpeeled, the bouquet garni, mace (about a teaspoon) and a little salt and pepper in a litre of water and simmer this briskly for about three-quarters of an hour. Strain, and discard the solids. Add the white wine and the remaining onions, chopped. In this poach the groper and the mullet for about 30 minutes. Do this carefully so they do not disintegrate. This is where a fish kettle comes in handy because you will need to remove them to a flat serving dish and keep them warm.

When the groper has cooled a little, remove any skin and bones and flake it. Rub the butter and flour together until they are thoroughly combined and stir this into the broth to thicken it. Return the flaked groper, add the crayfish, crab, prawns and shrimps and the turmeric. Simmer for five minutes or so and then adjust the seasonings before serving.

The mullet can be served separately, or in the sauce. Originally, saffron would have been used rather than turmeric (another pointer to a medieval origin) but saffron is not only almost unprocurable but quite unbelievably expensive. Crocus stamens sold in some health food shops as saffron are *not* saffron. Proper saffron is made from the dried and powdered stamens of *Crocus sativus*; it takes 200,000 of these to make about 500 g of saffron, which explains its expense. In medieval England it was used not only for soups but for dyeing the hair of both men and women. Mostly it was grown at Saffron Walden (hence the name of the town). Sir Francis Bacon remarks: 'What made the English people sprightly was the liberal use of saffron in their broths and sweetmeats'. According to Nicholas Culpepper saffron guarded against fainting and palpitations of the heart.

A word too on the mullet. European fish tend to be smaller than ours. Depending on the number of dinner guests, one may suffice. If you cannot get mullet then any largish fish of firm flesh will do. This recipe is the English sea equivalent of a water souchy. Understandably the gourmets on the other side of the English Channel have their version and regard it as superior.

There is a recipe for such a dish in Henri de Toulouse-Lautrec's *The Art of Cuisine*. Toulouse-Lautrec enjoyed cooking very much; there is a portrait of him by Edouard Vuillard standing by his oven attired in bright orange and red. Among his several recipes for bouillabaisse is one he labels English Channel Bouillabaisse of which he says: 'This bouillabaisse is only a pale reflection of the bouillabaisse of Marseilles since it lacks rascasse the

Mediterranean rock fish which makes both its basis and its savour.' The painter's strictures notwithstanding, the dish to which he refers is best known in a version which was carried to the New World and which emerged in New England as the chowder.

Chowders

There is great debate on the subject of chowder. General consenus exists only concerning its name, which is said to derive from *chaudière,* the iron pot in which Breton fisherfolk cooked their fish stews and which they brought with them to the fishing banks off Newfoundland. From there it migrated south to Cape Cod. In the seventeenth and eighteenth centuries a chowder kettle was part of the basic household equipment which a new wife was expected to bring to her marriage as part of her dowry (along with six patchwork quilts and a feather mattress). Some people say that you should not to put milk in a 'proper' chowder. The fact is that there is *no* proper chowder. I have eaten it from Boston (at an astonishingly good fish restaurant called Legals) to Provincetown at the very tip of Cape Cod. Always it is different in some way and always it was delicious. The fish used can vary; indeed in some recipes they do not have fish at all. For instance at Sturbridge in Massachusetts at the Levi Lincoln House they serve corn chowder. At the Publick House just down the road it is made with corn and chicken. So much for the pursuits. Here are two recipes, neither of which has milk in it (but it can replace half the water or stock) and one of which has potatoes in it and the other not. Both however have tomatoes. All of these variations lead otherwise staid and respectable New Englanders to quarrel bitterly and not to speak to one another for a lifetime. To play it safe and to protect myself I clipped these recipes from the *Boston Globe* for Wednesday 12 October when I was in Massachusetts in 1983. If that isn't authentic then I don't know what is. Incidentally the first has no salt pork, which some say is an absolute requirement.

FISH CHOWDER

1 kg of white fish fillet cut into cubes
6 medium potatoes peeled and sliced thin
3 cloves garlic chopped
1 large onion sliced
2 large tomatoes chopped
salt and pepper to taste

bouquet garni
chopped zest of an orange
¹/₃ cup olive oil
6 cups boiling water
a few drops tabasco

Please note that the equivalent of 6 cups American is 48 fluid ounces, i.e. 2½ pints imperial or 2 litres metric. That will make quite a lot of chowder. You can cut down the liquid if you like and use half-and-half water and milk. Wipe a deep iron pot with olive oil and put the fish on this. Layer the potatoes on top, then the onion, garlic and tomatoes. Add the salt, pepper, bouquet, orange and tabasco, then add the olive oil and the water and milk. Simmer for twenty minutes and it should be ready. It's really as simple as that. It can be served with a *rouille* but for me the best accompaniment is Jonnycake, or in Rhode Island Johnnycake (where I have eaten it in Providence). Traditionally you need a 'spider' to make this cornbread (which was a staple in pre-revolutionary New England). A spider is a flat griddle with very long iron legs to go over an open fire. If you saw one you would know at once why it's called a spider. However, a very large iron frying pan will do.

JOHNNYCAKE

1 teaspoon salt
1 tablespoon butter
200 g coarse cornmeal
2 tablespoons lard, melted
250 ml boiling water
60 ml milk

Mix the salt, butter and cornmeal thoroughly. Bring the water to the boil and pour it over the mixture and stir it in thoroughly. Add the milk and stir it in too. Melt the lard in the pan you are going to use and make sure it greases the sides. Pour in the batter and continue to heat on the hob or stove until it bubbles at the edges. Quickly transfer it to an oven pre-heated to 230°C and when the top is crusted over reduce the heat to 180°C. Bake for a further 30 minutes. Some people eat this with maple syrup but obviously that doesn't go with fish, although I once ate breakfast every morning for three weeks in the company of New Englanders tucking into fried eggs, bacon, sausages and pancakes with maple syrup. No one seemed to find this as hair-raising as I did. On the contrary they seemed to enjoy it. As Lévi-Strauss has presciently remarked, cultures define themselves by the food they consider suitable. With a chowder, Johnnycake should be plain or with butter, but either way hot.

MUSSEL AND OKRA CHOWDER

This is an adaption of the most famous of all chowders, clam. These small shellfish are justly celebrated (by Walt Whitman in *Song of Myself* among others) but are unprocurable fresh in this country. In *Moby Dick* Ishmael records his first encounter with clam chowder at the Try Pots Inn, Nantucket, in glowing terms. I trust he would have waxed equally lyrical over this dish.

1 large chopped onion
100 g unsmoked streaky bacon (or salt pork)
3 large tomatoes, chopped
4 okra pods
2 red sweet peppers chopped and seeded
1 litre fish stock
1/3 teaspoon cayenne
1 teaspoon arrowroot
2 dozen mussels

Try to get fresh mussels if you can. There is a growing practice of selling them marinated in very strong vinegar, which destroys their delicate flavour. Fry the bacon in its own fat until it is just browning. Add the onion, tomatoes, okra and peppers. Sauté for a minute or two, then add the stock and cayenne. Simmer for twenty minutes, add the arrowroot mixed with a little water and cook for another five minutes until the dish thickens. Add the mussels with their strained liquor and serve when they are warmed through.

There is a very similar gumbo from the southern end of Chesapeake Bay. There are endless variations on these basic recipes, combining fish or shellfish, adding sweet corn or cream, serving with hot buttered toast, adding cream cracker crumbs, etc. etc. I have never tried paua in it (or abalone as the Californians insist) but it would probably be quite good too. Actually the many recipes for not only stews but all sorts of shellfish and crustaceans are a splendid main course for any dinner party. That leads naturally to some recipes for them.

Shellfish and Crustaceans

Including of course the crayfish, that famous and rapidly disappearing New Zealand delicacy. Calling it a crustacean is rather like calling a kiwi an *Apteryx*. It sounds rather silly. Anyway more of crayfish anon. First a rather unusual way to deal with mussels.

MUSSELS IN COCONUT MILK

The availability of coconut milk has added a new dimension to our cooking, allowing us to take advantage of the fact that we are a Pacific society with a significant Polynesian stream in our culture. It also allows us to relate to the Caribbean cuisine which is itself a combination of elements, both African and European, adapted to local ingredients. These are in their turn common to or cognate between the Pacific and Caribbean groups of islands.

1 large onion, chopped
60 g butter
6 tablespoons lime juice (or lemon)
½ cup lentils
a meaty ham hock
4 okra pods
600 g lightly cooked spinach
2 cloves garlic, chopped
2 cups white wine
1 cup coconut milk
400 g mussels
salt, pepper, thyme, cayenne

Get the butcher to cut the hock into three or four pieces. Soak it in several changes of water to get rid of the salt, otherwise the dish will be inedible. Sauté the onions in the butter in an iron pot until they are translucent. Stir in the lime juice, seasonings and the other ingredients except the mussels. Cover tightly and simmer for an hour and a half. Remove the hock, strip off the rind and bone and return the meat to the pot. Add the mussels and heat through. Correct the seasonings and serve. Fresh lime juice gives this dish its distinctive flavour, as with many West Indian dishes. Lemon juice is a poor substitute. Okra seems to go particularly well with mussels, as does white wine. The traditional method of cooking mussels is in fact just in white wine.

MOULES MARINIERE

Toulouse-Lautrec gives two separate recipes for this classic, one involving garlic and the other not. To the novice cook it is often a disappointment at first because there seems to be nothing to it. The reaction is to say: is that all? But several repetitions will begin to establish the subtlety of the flavours involved. Its very simplicity makes it one of the most elegant dishes I know. Strangely enough in America and England mussels are regarded as rather déclassés — poor people's food. The French would never be so foolish. If you are serving this as a main course you will need rather a lot of mussels, and get them as small as you can.

3 kg of mussels
2 large chopped onions
a bunch of spring onions, white parts, chopped
2 cloves garlic, chopped
1 tablespoon chopped parsley
300 ml dry white wine
60 g butter
salt, pepper, a grating of nutmeg

Put the onions, garlic, parsley and wine into a pan and simmer for about five minutes. Add the mussels just long enough to warm through, remove them and keep warm. Whisk in the butter, seasonings and nutmeg, pour over the mussels and serve with lots of bread to mop up the juice. Conversely, you can whisk a hollandaise into the liquid which will make it thicker — but be careful not to over-simmer it or it will curdle. It is the hint of nutmeg that is the final touch. Toulouse-Lautrec recommends it in his recipes for this dish. He was very fond of nutmeg; he always carried a little grater and a berry with him to flavour the port which was his favourite tipple. Actually if you really want to go up-market with a similar dish then, provided you do not do it too often and serve it as an entrée to a main course, this next recipe goes down very well at a dinner party. The combination of the three principal ingredients should appeal to the snob in us all.

OYSTERS IN CHAMPAGNE WITH SAUSAGES

Yes — really.

1 dozen oysters for each guest
½ bottle of champagne
1 small chopped onion
4 large egg yolks
200 g unsalted butter
300 g cream
salt and pepper
a little more white wine
2 sausages for each guest

Boil the wine and onion briskly until there is only a tiny amount of liquid left, but very redolent of onion. Let this cool. Beat the cream until it is thick but not whipped, i.e. not to the point where it forms peaks. Set aside. Beat the egg yolks into the onion and wine, warm it very gently and then add the butter piece by piece and blend gently. You will eventually have a thick hollandaise. Let this cool. In the meantime gently poach the oysters in the additional wine (which need not be champagne) and grill the sausages. Fold the cream into the hollandaise and then strain the oysters and pour the sauce over them. Serve at once. Each guest alternates mouthfuls of oyster and sausage. It needs of course very good quality sausages. Your usual supermarket variety will not do at all.

This is the sort of dish which, for any heart specialists reading this, will bring on an attack of their specialism. It is also one of those vexing dishes which require the cook to work very quickly and which can go wrong quite easily. Personally I would not recommend you to try this out for the first time on a dinner party. It needs a little practice.

There's actually something about shellfish and lobsters which brings out the demon in exponents of *haute cuisine* so I might as well get it over with and continue with two further recipes, both famous and both as rich and luxurious as that just limned.

LOBSTER THERMIDOR

For this dish you must use our crayfish, which is not of course a proper European lobster (*homard*) but a rock lobster or *langouste*. These prefer the warmer waters of Southern Europe which are similar to the coastal seas off this country. The difference between them is in the claws which are present in the lobster but not the *langouste*, and there is absolutely no difference in the taste.

Crays have been a part of my life as long as I can remember, usually simply boiled. Either passing through or staying at Kaikoura (excellent name for a town) we always bought and consumed crayfish when I was a child.

Similarly, when we holidayed at Akaroa they were equally readily available. Incredible as it seems the fishermen kept only the tails and would *give* you the bodies, which otherwise were thrown away. Such prodigality seems criminal waste now that the crayfishing has been overdone and the creatures become scarcer and more expensive with every passing year.

One of my most memorable adult experiences with crayfish was during a holiday with the lighthouse keeper at Castlepoint, where the waters off the Wairarapa coast seem especially suited to the propagation of crays. One night I was constrained to rise and find my way to the bathroom. In the pitch blackness I groped my way to the basin, turned on the tap and plunged my hands into — several large and very alive crayfish caught that day. The assistant keeper still swears that my shriek was heard in Masterton sixty kilometres away and for some years thereafter I was a little wary of live crayfish in any form. Notwithstanding, if you can get your crayfish live so much the better. You will need one between two guests.

Why Thermidor? No one seems to know except that it is served very hot from the grill. It is in essence a variation on *homard américaine* said to have been invented by the chief Pascal at the Café Brebant in 1877. Other claimants include Constance Guillot of the restaurant Bonnefoy and Pierre Fraisse at the restaurant Noel Peters. My own guess is that it was called this because it was the lobster dish *preferred*, for whatever reason, by American travellers in France in the late nineteenth century when the first well-heeled tourist influx occurred. As a method of cooking and serving, it has driven out most others. If you are interested in these I commend to you Elizabeth David's *French Provincial Cooking* which has some very interesting ideas concerning the *langouste*. Certainly they have never heard of these in Kaikoura. In essence, for our recipe Thermidor, a lobster is boiled and then served in its longitudinally split shell, in a sauce.

You will need a very large pot with a tight-fitting lid (if you do not want your crayfish to climb out). In this put:

450 ml of dry white vermouth
450 ml water
a large onion, a carrot and a celery stalk all sliced
parsley, a bay leaf, a little thyme and a sprig of tarragon

Put your crayfish in this and bring it slowly to the boil. This is the most humane method of cooking a cray, and is recommended by the RSPCA. The cray becomes dopier and dopier and then expires at about 40° C. Allow about ten minutes cooking time for each 400 g of fish. When the fish is done put it to one side and strain and reduce the liquid it was cooked in. This will be the basis of the sauce. Split the crayfish lengthways into two parts, remove and chop the meat and clean the two halves of the shell. Brush the interiors lightly with olive oil and set aside. Now for the sauce.

70 g butter
60 g flour
1 tablespoon cream

Make a roux and cook for two minutes, stirring. Remove from the heat and stir in the cream. Take the crayfish coral and blend it in a bowl with:

1 tablespoon dry mustard
2 egg yolks
pinch of cayenne
200 ml cream

Beat this into the creamed roux and bring it slowly to a simmer and cook it, stirring, for two minutes. Set it to one side and quickly sauté the chopped crayfish meat in 60 g of butter and a wine-glass of cognac. Fold two-thirds of the sauce into this so the two are well combined. Heap this into the shells. Spread with the remaining sauce.

If by now you are wondering how on earth you are going to do all this in the presence of your guests, let me set your mind at rest, since everything up to this very point can be done the day before and refrigerated. Then about twenty minutes before serving sprinkle the top with grated Gruyère, breadcrumbs and melted butter and grill in the oven for 10 to 15 minutes, and serve.

Toulouse-Lautrec gives two *américaine* recipes but none for Thermidor. In the introduction to the 1966 translation of Toulouse-Lautrec's cookbook the editors M. Dortu and P. Huisman tell a charming story. Edouard Vuillard recounts how Toulouse-Lautrec prepared *homard américaine* which involves the cutting-up of the lobster alive, a most messy business, in the drawing room of an extremely fussy bachelor acquaintance, Georges Henri-Manual, with the owner in great anguish for his furniture. Toulouse-Lautrec was '. . . wrapped in a long white apron in which his short legs kept getting entangled, brandishing a spoon as long as himself and moving saucepans about.' So adept a cook was Toulouse-Lautrec that he prepared a most memorable lobster without the slightest damage to the drawing room.

The other expensive and luxurious dish which follows is also by way of a variation.

SCALLOPS NEWBERG

The original is of course Lobster Newberg. I suppose every cook is familiar with the story of how this dish was invented at Delmonico's, New York, in the last century and named in honour of a favoured customer, Wenberg. However the proprietor and the customer quarrelled, and to spite the latter, the former changed the name to Newberg. Probably apocryphal but worth repeating. So is the sauce, which is adaptable to scallops.

The scallop is embedded deep in our European consciousness. Its fan-like shell decorated the hats of pilgrims returning from the Holy Land in medieval times (from 'Afric's coral strand'). The French call them *coquilles St-Jacques* because they were the symbol of the pilgrims who crossed Europe to the shrine of St James of Compostella in Northern Spain. The same shape graced much of the best architecture and interior furnishing of a later age and gave us the 'fan light'.

The scallops we have in this country are generally much smaller than those served in Europe or North America. This once led me to wonder what I was getting when served scallops in a delicious garlic sauce in Boston, but this was quickly cleared up in discussion with the waiter. Either way they are quite monstrously expensive here, and the fact that you will need so many may put you off. Do not despair, because this and the following recipe are just as good for a groper steak or other strong white fish.

12 scallops for each person
150 ml dry vermouth (white)
150 ml water
bouquet garni
90 g butter
80 ml cognac
150 ml madeira
250 ml cream, plus 1 tablespoon cream
salt and pepper
2 egg yolks

Simmer the vermouth, water and bouquet garni together for a few minutes and then poach the scallops in the liquid for five minutes. Remove and drain them. Melt the butter in a pan and sauté the scallops for two minutes or so, then warm the brandy, fire it and pour it over the scallops. Turn them as it burns. Add the madeira, and then the cream after a little pause. Let this gently reduce. Separately make a sauce with the egg yolks, additional cream and a little of the wine stock. Stir this into the shellfish and season to taste.

Sauces of this sort are not the property of the nineteenth-century French. There is a most unusual orange sauce in Hannah Glasse's *The Art of Cooking* published in 1747. With the mace and cloves it probably goes back much further. Even more unusually it goes very well with fish. So, incidentally, does gin as a sauce base. Fish dishes are full of surprises. Oranges are natives of China and arrived in Europe towards the end of the Roman Empire by way of Persia whence they picked up the name *narandj* meaning 'perfume within', and it is from this word that we derive our 'orange'. It took a long time for oranges to reach Northern Europe, where the severe winters killed the trees. In seventeenth-century England they were kept in heated, sunny buildings — the orangery — during the winter and were wheeled out in pots on wheels with handles into the sunshine in the summer, a sort of tree-in-a-wheelbarrow. There is a fine orangery at Kew Gardens built at the instruction of George III. I suppose he had to do something to console himself for the loss of the American colonies. In the eighteenth century most of the oranges used in cooking were Sevilles, that is, they had a sharp flavour but still very orange. This can be imitated by mixing orange and lemon juice.

12 scallops for each diner
150 ml dry white wine
150 ml water
1 tablespoon white wine vinegar
1 teaspoon mace
2 cloves
30 g butter
heaped tablespoon flour
juice of an orange and juice of a lemon, mixed
seasoning to taste

Simmer the wine, water, vinegar and spices together for about 7 to 8 minutes and season with salt and black pepper. Poach the scallops in this liquid for perhaps five minutes. Remove and keep warm. Mash the butter and flour together so that the flour is thoroughly rubbed into the butter. Use your fingers to do this because it is the key to a properly thickened sauce. Now whisk the butter and flour in pieces into the sauce, add the fruit juice, and more salt and pepper if necessary and simmer it until it thickens. Pour it over the scallops and serve. This needs lots of bread to mop it up and a plain salad. In a restaurant a couple of years ago I was astonished to be served scallops surrounded by piped mashed potato. Not at all an appropriate accompaniment. The chef was quite surprised when I remarked unfavourably on this. If you really feel the need to have something with your fish which will absorb the fish sauce and you don't want to eat a lot of bread, then the preferred solution is not mashed potato but a fish pie.

Fish Pies

Making a pie with fish filling is these days thought to be rather eccentric. It used to be very common, particularly when fish days were strictly enforced but some sort of celebration was in order. Usually an elaborate mixture of fish, shellfish, fruit, herbs and spices was used. These pies, which contained sugar and rosewater, are not much to the modern taste but some recipes which are eighteenth-century adaptions of them are very good. The cookery books of the time give much advice to those buying their fish at Billingsgate and other London markets to ensure that it was fresh. The methods used to disguise the putrefaction of fish were extraordinarily elaborate and it was a case of *caveat emptor*. Some fish were brought live overland in tanks of water in the backs of carts or were sailed up the Thames similarly swimming in specially adapted ships. Potting was also popular.

CRAYFISH PIE

This combines an eighteenth-century Cornish recipe with the famous local delicacy. You will need all the meat from two cooked crayfish which will make this a rather expensive dish — but worthwhile.

meat of two crays
300 ml cream
pepper, salt, mace
short pastry
150 g butter
6 hard-boiled eggs
a dozen oysters

Line a pie dish with pastry, leaving enough for a lid. Put in the crayfish meat and season it to your taste. Cut about half the butter into cubes and spread this on top, then the quartered eggs, the oysters in their liquor and the remainder of the butter. Put on the lid and bake for about half an hour at 190°C. Then remove the pie and very carefully prise up the lid (or make a vent in the top before cooking). Heat the cream and pour it in and return the pie to the oven for about five minutes before serving.

The prodigality with which eighteenth-century recipes use oysters seems extravagant today. Recollect however that until the mid-nineteenth century they were poor people's food. Four hundred could be had for a few shillings in the reign of Queen Anne, when they were sold from stalls in the street in association with gingerbread. Pollution and over-fishing have made them a rarity, a lesson to us in respect of other varieties of shellfish. Perhaps a more conservation-minded age will see them return in plentiful supply. A less expensive dish can be made of crab (or mussels for that matter).

CRAB TART

Line a 20 cm pie plate or flan with shortcrust pastry and blind bake it for about ten minutes at 200°C. Then make a mixture from the following:

1 kg cooked crab
salt, pepper and cayenne
1 whole egg and two yolks
300 ml cream
2 tablespoons strong grated cheddar

If you can get fresh crabmeat rather than tinned it will taste much better, although stripping out the shells and then poaching the meat is a fiddly business.

Whip the two egg whites until they are stiff and fold them into the pie filling. Pour this into the pastry case and cook in a pre-heated oven at 200° C for ten minutes. Lower the temperature to 180° C for about half an hour or a little longer. The tart is cooked when the top is crusted and the centre is just set like a custard. Serve hot. Mussels cooked in this way are particularly delicious if you add a few shelled prawns.

Another very good fish pie can be made from eels.

EEL PIE

I had never tried this dish until I went to live in England and found myself at one of those bizarre south-east coast resorts where the English go each summer to walk along the front in showers of rain and to catch pneumonia. This is known as a holiday at the seaside. One of its few redeeming features is the summer variety show on the pier (which was why I was there — I had the pleasure of meeting Arthur Askey). Another is the huge number of small stands selling whelks, jellied eels and so forth. It was at one of these that I first ate eel pie, for which I have since cultivated a taste.

2 freshwater eels, skinned, boned and cut up
6 spring onions, chopped
90 g butter
1 tablespoon fresh chopped parsley
salt, pepper and nutmeg
150 ml dry sherry
40 g flour
lemon juice
a sliced hard-boiled egg
puff pastry

Soften the onions in half the butter then, add the parsley, sherry, eel pieces and seasonings. Cover with a little water and simmer until cooked. Remove the eel to a pie dish and thicken the liquid with the remaining flour and butter rubbed together. Pour it over the eel and add the lemon juice and egg. Cover with pastry and bake at 200° C for fifteen minutes then for half an hour at 180° C, covering the crust with foil to prevent burning.

This pie can be eaten hot or cold. It is an adaption of a recipe given in *The Cook's Oracle* of 1843. At that time it was fashionable to picnic upon cold eel pie on an island in the Thames. So popular was this pastime that the island became known as Eel Pie Island, a name it retains. The island features from time to time in the notorious late-Victorian comic paper *Alley Sloper's Half*

Holiday. Of all fish pies the grandest however is a classic dish from the Russian cuisine — kulebiaka.

KULEBIAKA

I first developed a liking for this dish when I was given a large quantity of field mushrooms and was on the lookout for ways to use them up. Mushrooms are an important ingredient in Russian cuisine. Schoolchildren are taught to identify the edible varieties and there are special night excursion trains from Moscow during the appropriate time of the year to allow the city-dwellers to engage in the traditional pastime *hodit po griby* (looking for mushrooms). Pies too feature largely in traditional Russian cooking as *pirogi*. As with medieval Europe these were feast day dishes. There is an amazing description of a fish pie in Gogol's *Dead Souls*. Traditionally the pastry would have been made with rye flour and the filling flavoured with *vijaziga*, the dried spinal cord of a sturgeon. For the pastry:

450 g plain flour
240 g unsalted butter
100 g lard
1 teaspoon salt

Rub all these ingredients together and bind them with a little cold water. Divide into two and refrigerate for two hours. For the filling:

1 kg smoked fish
450 ml milk
150 ml water
125 g long grain rice or kasha
300 ml chicken stock
300 g sliced mushrooms
120 g butter
lemon juice, salt and pepper
3 chopped onions
2 teaspoons curry powder
3 chopped hard-boiled eggs

Cut the fish into pieces and simmer it in the milk and water for ten minutes or so. Strain it, flake it and discard any skin and bones. Cook the rice or kasha (buckwheat, traditional for this dish) in the chicken stock and drain it. Fry the mushrooms in butter and season them with lemon juice, salt and pepper. Soften the onion in more butter. To assemble the pie roll out the first piece of pastry to a large oblong on a baking sheet. Spread half the rice/kasha on this leaving an edge of about an inch all around. Sprinkle the curry powder over this. Spread half the egg, mushrooms and onions on top, then all the fish, then the remaining halves of everything in reverse order. Pour a little melted butter over the whole thing.

Now roll out the other pastry portion and drape it over the top, rolling the wetted edges neatly together to make a tight seal. Glaze, decorate and make a central hole. Bake at 190°C for about 40 minutes. Serve with a little sour cream heated through for each guest. It can be served cold, but is better hot.

Obtain properly smoked fish if you can, not the orange coloured outrage passed off as such in fishmongers. If you have your own smokehouse so much the better. I am obliged to rely upon a friend but as he catches and smokes large trout this is not too great an imposition. He also from time to time provides me with the wherewithal for some cold fish dishes for summer.

Cold Fish

For a summer luncheon there is nothing better than a centrepiece of cold fish served with salads and fresh bread. And of these none looks better than a fish in aspic or a mousse. Fresh salmon trout are excellent for these purposes.

TROUT IN ASPIC

1 large filleted trout
400 ml claret
600 ml aspic jelly
lemon juice, salt and pepper
120 g finely sliced, sautéed mushrooms
2 hard-boiled eggs, sliced thinly
a couple of dozen stuffed olives, halved
small tin of anchovies, drained

Poach the fillets in the red wine and allow to cool. You will need a mould or smallish soufflé dish for each person. Using the wine from the fish poaching, make up the aspic jelly, adding water to bring it up to quantity. Add lemon juice and seasoning, bearing in mind that cold dishes need more flavouring than hot. Rinse the moulds, and when the jelly is almost set pour a little into the bottom of each. When this has set, lay a slice of egg, mushroom and olive on top and then carefully roll the fillets of trout around the inside edge of each mould. Fill the internal space this creates with the other ingredients, and then fill the moulds with the remaining jelly. This may have set by now, so warm slightly to reliquefy. Allow to set firmly in the refrigerator and turn out for serving on a central dish surrounded by salad greens, and with a cold sauce such as horseradish. This is one of the few occasions when an avocado salad is justified, because of the combination of flavours. Conversely, you might like to make a mousse with your trout.

TROUT MOUSSE

This dish is equally good with fresh salmon if you can get it.

500 g cooked trout
4 egg whites
lemon juice
100 ml brandy
30 g butter
450 ml cream
salt and pepper

Mince the trout in a blender with the salt, pepper and two of the egg whites.
Add the lemon juice and brandy and blend to a smooth mixture. Put this to
cool in the refrigerator. Beat the cream and the two remaining egg whites
separately until stiff and fold these into the blended mixture. Poach it in a
bain-marie at 160°C for an hour. Let it cool for a few minutes before turning
it out to serve. Cucumber salads go very well with fish in this form, as does
horseradish sauce.

GALANTINE OF EEL

I have already mentioned jellied eels. This is a somewhat more up-market
version of the same dish. You will need about 2 kg of eel skinned and boned
and cut into chunks. Skinning an eel is not too difficult. Cut the head off a live
eel by a single sharp chop. If the eel is wriggling about this will not be easy so
slow it up by putting it in a deep freeze for an hour. This may sound cruel but
isn't. Cut a line all around the decapitated eel with a sharp knife between the
flesh and the skin and then grasp the skin firmly and peel it off. If the eel is
hanging up this will be easier. Cut down the belly and clean the inside, then
turn the fish over and hit it firmly all along the backbone with a heavy blunt
instrument. When you turn it back over, the bones should be sticking up and
easy enough to pick out. If all this makes you feel a bit squeamish you will
never be a successful cook. Marinate your chunks of eel in the following
mixture for about an hour:

1 glass brandy
1 glass white port
juice of a lemon
2 chopped carrots
1 chopped onion
2 chopped cloves garlic
parsley, bay leaf, thyme

Strain the marinade and add to enough liquid aspic to make up about a litre.
Poach the eel meat in this for about an hour. Drain it and set to one side.
Reduce the jelly liquid by about a quarter and skim off any fat. Pour the liquid

into a wetted mould, with layers of fish and fresh parsley or watercress between each jelly layer. Let it set and turn it out onto a serving dish surrounded by a green salad. A few drops of green food colouring added to the jelly before it sets enhances this dish. Like the two preceding dishes this should of course be served with a cold sauce. Horseradish is the best for this purpose, in my view, although gooseberry is also good.

HORSERADISH SAUCE WITH WALNUTS

Whenever I go to Palmerston North, which is about three times a year, my friend Alan takes me to the Sunday open market. There I can invariably buy cheap produce of one sort or another; strings of garlic, onions, carrots, etc. But what I always look for is shelled walnuts, which I then use for this sauce. The recipe comes from an account by Escoffier of a country house weekend he spent in Haute-Savoie around the turn of the century, when the sauce was served as an accompaniment to cold poached char for lunch one day. It goes particularly well with trout but will complement any cold fish dish. All you need to do is blend the following ingredients to a smooth paste:

200 g shelled walnuts
1 teaspoon sugar
2 tablespoons breadcrumbs
150 ml cream
1 tablespoon lemon juice
salt
200 g grated horseradish

If you have no fresh horseradish then buy a prepared quantity. The trick with this sauce is to make it immediately before use, or the tannin in the walnut skins will darken it unattractively. You could of course skin the walnuts but that's a lengthy and frustrating proceeding which I do not recommend. There are many sauces and mayonnaises for cold fish but none I have had so far has matched this one. It is also most suitable to go with the cold fish mentioned in the next chapter.

Entrées & Appetisers

The main trouble with them (appetisers) is that if they are enjoyed to the full hilt, the meal that follows is, can be, and usually must be more or less ignored — except by real trenchermen that is. The variety, the tempting spicy smells, the clashing flavours, all lead even jaded appetites to a surfeit that destroys what is to follow, no matter how simple or how Lucullan.
— M.K.R. Fisher, *An Alphabet for Gourmets*

IN TRADITIONAL EUROPEAN cuisine the menu consists of four courses, i.e. soup, fish, meat and dessert. Sometimes however a fifth manages to squeeze itself in between the fish and the meat. The French call this the entrée, appropriately, since it is the entry into the main course. Now in my view three courses for a meal are certainly too few, because then the meal is over too soon, but on the other hand five is really too many. Despite a tendency to gluttony among us all, even among those who make a fetish of fastidiousness, with five courses I have noticed my dinner companions becoming a little glazed before they arrive at the dessert.

Four courses, like baby bear's porridge, seem just right. They manage to impart the necessary element of leisure to a meal. By the time we arrive at the main course, the first course is already half forgotten. The entrée provides that something in between. And there is another reason for the entrée — the cook may need to put the finishing touch to the main course and while that mystery is being performed, why, the guests can just regale themselves with a little snack and some conversation in the pause. What happens in that little interval is purely arbitrary.

Digby Law in his excellent *Entrée Cookbook* states better than I am able to do this general rule of flexibility: 'An entrée can be simple or elaborate, depending on your personal style, or on the style of dinner you have chosen; it can also be influenced by foods in season, or those which you have on hand. Perhaps someone has given you a bunch of watercress or some smoked salmon, so you seize the chance to plan your meal around these; or overseas guests may dictate a meal based on the best of New Zealand produce; or then again you may be overcome by a whim to use something like chicken livers. Some cooks plan their meal around the main course, which they select first, so that the entrée is then planned to complement it.'

In other words the rule is that there is no rule, except appropriateness and circumstance. Digby Law goes on to remark that although most cuisines have a tradition of an appetiser, this can take many forms. In Greece for example there is the tradition of the *mezethakia* or *oretika*, to open the entire meal with something to drink. My experience has been that this can go on for at least an hour before anybody even begins to think of ordering the meal proper and it continues while this latter is being cooked. It is often a complex combination of olives, nuts and cold fish. It is similar to the more familiar *antipasto* in Italy. Its savour is of course conversation.

It is so also with the Spanish where the dish is known as the *tapa* which is more appropriate as a snack with wine but which shades imperceptibly into the *entremeses* which is the more formal equivalent of our entrée. When you eat which, really depends upon what time of day it happens to be — I would suggest the latter at lunch, that is at about 2 pm, and the former after siesta, that is, any time after 5 pm.

But the cuisine which really raises the entrée to a fine art is the Russian. Their *zakuski* even astonished the much travelled Karl Baedeker who records in his Russian guide for 1914: 'A peculiarity of the Russian cuisine is the so-called *zakuska* resembling the Finnish *smorgasbord*. In the larger restaurants there is always a sideboard or even a separate room for the *zakuska*, which consists of caviar, different kinds of fish, patties (piroshki), pickled cucumbers and mushrooms, and so forth, along with vodka and other spirits.' I can vouch personally for the persistence of this eating habit under the present regime. Its introduction is attributed to Czar Peter the Great. Personally I baulk at having a separate room in my house in which to eat the entrée. That seems to me a little over refined. But there is nothing whatever the matter with a cold entrée borne in on a large platter. Of what, however, should this entrée be comprised?

Possibly you will have a little wine left from the one drunk with the soup. Not everyone drinks at the same rate and there may be a change of wines. If so, the entrée needs to be something which can bridge the gap between these wines. That is to say something which is suitable to, at two extremes, a chablis or a shiraz. But more important it should also bridge any gap between food courses. If the soup has been particularly rich and heavy, then obviously something light such as a soufflé is needed; if the soup itself has been light then the entrée need not be. It should never be of such substance as to make the next course unbearable. And it should not be fussy to prepare. That would defeat the whole purpose.

The choice is almost unlimited. It might be almost any of the stuffed fish or shellfish dishes in the fish section. Even better it might be some cold smoked fish such as eel, an entirely neglected dish in this country, although one of our great delicacies. If it is served with the horseradish sauce described in the last chapter, it is really quite magnificent. The same is true of smoked mussels or oysters, or a platter of all three. That would be a very Greek way of handling the entrée. The Greeks have also retained the habit of eating the smoked roe of fish. This is their famous *taramasalata*. Such a dish is not as it happens out of place in this book either. Until the end of the eighteenth century a familiar English snack food was botargo, the salted and dried roe of the grey mullet. In France it is still widely eaten as *poutargue* with pepper, olive oil and lemon.

In his diary for 5 June 1661, Samuel Pepys records a charming incident. He and Sir William Penn, father of the founder of Pennsylvania, had been out dining with friends and walked home in the summer evening together. It was too hot to go to bed so one invited the other in and they sat in the garden 'talking and singing and drinking great draughts of claret and eating botargo and bread and butter till 12 at night, it being moonshine.' Sir William with his coat off and Pepys playing his flute. The next day, Pepys records, he had a frightful hangover.

I first ate *taramasalata* at Anemos, a well-known Greek restaurant in London, but it was not until I got to the Greek islands that I was able to eat it in all its glory.

TARAMASALATA

You may have a little trouble getting *tarama* although my local Greek fishmonger has it. Remember that the hard accent is on the last vowel or, like me, you may be reproved for incorrect pronunciation. If you cannot get *tarama* then smoked cod roe with the skin removed will do as well. Making the dish is simplicity itself.

150 g tarama
1 thick slice of bread
2 cloves crushed garlic
300 ml of olive oil
juice of two lemons
black olives

Cut the crusts off the bread and moisten it with just a dribble of water. In a blender combine it with the *tarama* and garlic and a little of the oil. Blend it and slowly add the remaining oil and the lemon juice until it is thoroughly mixed. Some recipes I have seen also add an egg yolk. This gives a stiffer consistency. It should be served with *pita* bread or thin toasts and garnished with the black olives. The taste is strong and slightly bitter but easily acquired. Of course the botargo can be eaten just spread on bread as Pepys' was but if you are going to do that you might as well eat caviare.

CAVIARE

This is one of those mysterious foods like truffles which have such a reputation that eating them for the first time is a disappointment. With caviare I did it properly and went to Russia for the experience. I should like to grandly pretend that that was the sole purpose of my visit but alas that would be to stretch the truth rather more than its elasticity would allow. And anyway, it isn't a specifically Russian delicacy. The Russians actually call it *ikra* and the word we use is of Turkish-cum-Venetian origin. Whatever it is called, people have been eating it since classical times. The Genoese had the medieval monopoly until the Turks captured Kaffa on the Black Sea in the fifteenth century. The Chinese also enjoyed it at least as early as the tenth century according to the *T'ai ping huan yu chi*.

Of course down the centuries caviare has suffered from one disadvantage. If you want to eat proper beluga in sufficient quantities, and not insult your guests by making them spread it on individual cornflakes, you must first take out a bank loan. It needs at least an ounce for each person and should be served on ice in a bowl. With it a little vodka (although some say without) you can take it in a gulp in the Russian fashion, freezing cold from tiny glasses. And above all make sure that you also serve *blini*, that's to say buckwheat pancakes.

BLINI

350 g buckwheat flour
a little active yeast (say 15 g)
250 g plain flour
300 ml warm milk

Beat this batter smooth and leave to prove for two or three hours. Add a further *60 g buckwheat flour* and leave another two hours. Take:

3 large egg yolks
½ teaspoon salt
120 g melted butter
a little sour cream
3 stiffly beaten egg whites

Add the first four ingredients, then fold in the egg whites. These pancakes should be cooked in the usual way and served with sour cream. If you can't afford Beluga then lumpfish caviare will do, the roe of the lumpsucker fish. It's the male of the species, incidentally, which guards the eggs for weeks after spawning until they hatch, and I have never yet met one of those people who believes that female nurturing of young is biological, who can explain this away.

Blini are also good with smoked salmon. In that case there are a range of butters and sauces to go with them apart from sour cream. Excellent ones can be made from watercress, sorrel, gooseberry or cucumber, but the one I like best is made from avocado.

2 ripe avocados, peeled and pitted
tablespoon lemon juice
1 clove garlic, crushed
300 ml sour cream
salt and pepper
2 chopped spring onions

Bring all the ingredients together in a blender and blend smooth. This sauce can also be served hot by bringing it to a simmer in a double boiler but I prefer it cold.

RAW SEAFOOD

Of course oysters or mussels served raw are excellent as an entrée. The Japanese habit of eating *sashimi* or raw fish has never much caught on here, more's the pity, although I know of at least one restaurant in Christchurch where raw squid is a standard item on the menu. If you want to eat raw fish it must be absolutely fresh. Make a dipping sauce of soy and grated fresh ginger root or *daikon* radish. The fish should be cut into bite-sized cubes. There should be a bowl of watercress on the table. Not quite a European staple in the time of Pepys or since of course. More in that tradition is the terrine.

Terrines, Pâtés, Galantines and Pots

The distinction between a terrine and a pâté is now largely buried in the mists of antiquity, although originally it was a matter of the distinction between a meat loaf and a pie. The available recipes are almost infinite and those which follow are simply some of my favourites. Two points: it would be useful if you were to obtain a proper lidded terrine dish in either cast iron and enamel or ceramic; and *never* deep-freeze a pâté. Not only do they not thaw very readily (I was once served pâté in a restaurant still icy in the middle — I sent it back remarking to the waiter that when I wanted meat ice cream I'd send for it) but the freezing seems to turn the flavour insipid and the interior of the terrine damp.

RABBIT PÂTÉ

This pâté can be served either hot or cold but is better cold in my view. If you are planning to serve a pâté cold then you will need to add a little more of the spices and salt than would normally be the case. In her book *Game Cooking*, Lilli Gore tells the following story: 'In the Quai Stalingrad in Toulon there are, or were, many restaurants, some bad, some good, but in one of them I ate a terrine of rabbit. It was on my first visit to the South of France without an adult. I think it must have been that terrine that started my conscious interest in cooking. I remarked to the waiter that the terrine was delicious. Before we left the restaurant the chef who was also the owner gave me the recipe; I think it was mainly from curiosity to see a young English girl who was impressed with his cooking.' The recipe has now found its way to the antipodes and I must say that I am as impressed as was Lilli Gore.

700 g rabbit
450 g belly pork
4 rashers bacon
3 cloves garlic
zest of a lemon
4 juniper berries
½ teaspoon dried thyme
½ teaspoon ground mace
pepper and salt
small glass cognac
2 bay leaves

Simmer the rabbit in salted water for about 45 minutes, drain and cool. Strip the meat off the bones and cut into strips and cubes. Mince the pork coarsely. Chop the garlic and crush the juniper and add these to the meats together with the zest, pepper, salt, mace and thyme. Mix thoroughly. Stir in the cognac. Cover the bottom of the terrine with two of the bacon strips. Fill the terrine with the mixture, place the bay leaves on top and then the two remaining bacon strips. Cover and cook in a water bath in an oven at 180°C for about an hour and a half. This pâté keeps well for several days in the refrigerator so it can be made in advance. Remove it from the terrine and sprinkle it with chopped parsley before serving. Instead of brandy you can use gin. Most people never think of that particular spirit as an appropriate addition to cooking. Shades of Hogarth I suppose. It actually adds a delicious flavour of juniper and in this instance enhances the berries themselves. Brown bread and butter or thin toast goes best with this pâté as with most others. This also can be done with pigeon although I haven't tried that myself. Pigeon comes my way rarely and I have other uses for it.

HARE PÂTÉ

The recipe above for rabbit is more or less the standard way of cooking a pâté. This hare variation is in two parts. A large hare used in its entirety for this dish would make a vast pâté, even although hare shrinks rather a lot in cooking. Probably some leg joints or a saddle would be sufficient.

Stage One:
    about a kilo of hare
    ½ a bottle (350 ml) burgundy
    2 onions
    3 garlic cloves
    1 bay leaf
    1 teaspoon oregano
    250 g unsmoked bacon, diced

Put the meat into a casserole with the other ingredients, cover and cook for an hour at 180° C. Strain off the liquid and reserve. Cool the hare and strip the meat from the bones.

Stage Two:
    1 teaspoon marjoram
    1 crushed garlic clove
    pepper, salt, nutmeg
    6 rashers unsmoked bacon

Add the herbs, spices and seasoning to the meat. Layer the bottom of a terrine with bacon and then alternate layers of meat and bacon finishing with bacon. Pour as much of the reserved liquid over the top as you need to have the meat moist without it swimming. Cook for two hours, covered, in a water bath at 180°C. Cool, store and serve. The same pâté can be made with venison remnants. Sometimes too the inclusion of vegetables in the pâté mixture can be most effective. With game, for instance, a little chopped celery would enhance the flavour.

PORK AND SPINACH TERRINE

Elizabeth David attributes this recipe to Orange in Upper Provence.

450 g uncooked spinach
450 g minced belly pork
salt, pepper, mixed spices (mace, cloves, allspice)

Cook and drain the spinach. Chop it roughly. Mix all the ingredients thoroughly together and cook in a terrine in a water bath for a scant 45 minutes at 170°C. Any longer and it will dry out. This is a very suitable pâté to serve between some rich soup and an equally heavy main course.

It may surprise you to have noticed that so far there has been no mention of liver. That is the pâté with which most people commence, although I don't know why, particularly, as it is not so easy to get the flavour right.

The first time I ever ate pâté it was made of chicken livers and I liked it so much I made myself ill eating it. This, I told myself afterwards, was all the fault of the hostess who made so much of it. It was to celebrate the wedding of two friends of mine. The marriage ended three days later in mutual acrimony but this was not, I think, attributable to the pâté. The recipe which follows is for a mixture of livers.

PÂTÉ DE FOIE

240 g poultry livers
120 g pig liver
4 bacon rashers
sherry, salt, pepper, brandy

Clean and trim the livers and simmer them gently in water with a little sherry for twenty minutes. Drain, cool and grind finely in a blender. Season with salt and pepper and brandy sufficient to keep the meat moist. Line a terrine with bacon, fill with the liver mixture, cover with more bacon and cook in the usual way for one hour. Serve cold. If you can get the liver of a deer this may be substituted for the pig.

In France, pâtés are preserved in the same way as we preserve fruit, by sealing them in jars using vacuum methods. I do not recommend this unless you know what you are doing. Fatal ptomaine poisoning is sometimes the consequence of preserving meat at home. Of course pâtés need not always be made of meat, as the following recipe illustrates.

EGG PSEUDO-PÂTÉS

4 hard-boiled eggs
200 g cream cheese
½ teaspoon ground mace
1 onion, finely chopped
salt and pepper

This dish is strictly speaking, I suppose, not a pâté at all but I can vouch for its flavour. Simply purée all the ingredients in a blender and press into a largish ramekin. Sprinkle with chopped parsley and chill before serving. This is an excellent standby if guests turn up unexpectedly.

PÂTÉS EN CROÛTE

There is something very grand about serving your pâté in a pastry case. Any of the meat terrines so far mentioned will do for this. They should be made in advance of the pastry and kept for a couple of days in the refrigerator to develop a 'taste'. You will also need a pâté mould, which is essentially a hinged fence with a pin holding it together. Some are decorated and imprint a pattern on the pastry, which is very attractive. A small pavlova mould will usually serve as well. There are numerous recipes for the dough of pâté en croûte. The suet pastry given later for the hare pie is very successful. If you prefer an alternative you might care to try this:

111

Pastry:
  300 g flour
  180 g unsalted butter
  2 egg yolks
  salt
  3 tablespoons water

Beat the yolks into the softened butter. Add the water and a pinch of salt and then slowly mix in the flour to avoid lumps. Chill before rolling into shape.

To make the mould:
Grease your baking tray and the interior of the mould. Fill the bottom space with an even layer of rolled pastry, about a millimetre thick. Roll out a strip to fit the interior sides and press it firmly into place, allowing a small overhang, paint the join at the bottom with a little water and press it together. This will seal the bottom and sides. Now place a thin sheet of pork fat or fat bacon on the bottom of the mould. As well as your pâté you should have handy some strips of cooked chicken, rabbit, veal or venison. These are not strictly necessary but they add an interesting touch. You should fill the pastry mould with alternate layers of pâté and the meat strips, finishing with pâté, a bay leaf and another thin sheet of pork fat. This should then be covered with pastry, the overhang folded in and an edge formed. Decorate the top with cutouts of pastry — stars, leaves, whatever you fancy. The edge seals best if pressed down with the back of a fork. Make two small holes in the top to allow steam to escape and glaze with egg or milk. Bake in an oven preheated to 190°C for just under two hours.

It is possible that a certain amount of fat will bubble out. If this gets on the oven element, it will smoke. Avoid this by setting your pâté in a wide flat dish to cook, rather than a baking tray.

Remove the pâté and let it cool. During the cooking the meat will shrink and you can fill this space with aspic jelly by funnelling it in through the ventilation holes. When thoroughly set, remove the mould and lift from the baking tray or dish to serve.

Galantines are really a variation on the pâté en croûte, but a very interesting one. They are very old dishes going back, at least in some of their manifestations, to the Romans. Essentially they comprise a bird or part of a beast, for example the head, stuffed and served cold in aspic or pastry or both. In medieval times they were very popular at feasts and there were quite elaborate variations. One favourite was a goose stuffed with a chicken stuffed with tiny game birds, the goose and chicken boned of course. Chaucer mentions these.

In the nineteenth century it was not unusual to serve a boned turkey stuffed with quail. That would be far too much for a second course! The two that follow would, however, each be suitable. One is a proper galantine while the other is not, but both are interesting and neither entirely conforms to the definition I have already given. Which just goes to show that there are no final definitions in cooking.

CANARD EN CROÛTE

You will need to bone the duck for this. Follow the method set out in the chapter on poultry. I usually bone and stuff a duck to cook it, otherwise I find that there's too little substance to it. The carcass makes good stock.

a duck, boned (about 2-3 kg unboned)
150 ml port
200 g each minced pork, veal, pork fat
2 eggs
clove garlic
salt, pepper, allspice
2 chopped onions
butter

Soften the onion in the butter and mix together in a bowl with the port, mince, the two eggs beaten, the garlic and salt and pepper to taste. Mix in one teaspoon of allspice. This is your stuffing. Fill the boned duck with this and neatly sew up the opening, after folding the duck over so that the stuffing is entirely enveloped. Then truss the duck as if for roasting so that you have a neat cylindrical parcel. Brown it in a little more butter.

When it has cooled, enclose it entirely in pastry. Decorate the pastry, glaze and make a steam vent. Bake in a preheated oven at 180°C for about 2 hours. Serve when cold.

MOULDED TONGUE

This is one of those dishes which is rather fiddly to do but looks magnificent when brought to the table. It is closer to the medieval galantine than the duck en croûte but doesn't involve any stuffing.

3 carrots
small peeled cucumber
small packet frozen French beans
1 ox tongue
1 onion
bouquet garni
prepared aspic
2 tablespoons madeira or port
salt and pepper

First prepare the tongue, by soaking it in clean water for a couple of hours. This will be particularly necessary if it has been pickled. Drain it and simmer it in fresh water to which you have added a chopped carrot, the onion and the bouquet and seasonings. When it is cooked peel it and remove any small bones from the base. Set aside.

Julienne the remaining carrots (that is, cut them into small strips) and blanch them and the beans. Drain. Prepare the aspic and add the fortified wine. Make sure that you use a little more salt than usual. Put a thin layer of aspic in the bowl you will be using as a mould. When this has set, lay out a decorative pattern of carrots and beans on top of it and pour a little more of the melted aspic on top. There is a technique to this. If the aspic is too hot it will melt everything. If there is too much, everything will float. Practice makes perfect.

When that has set, pour a little more aspic into the bowl and rotate it around the sides so that these are well covered. Then peel very thin strips of cucumber, dip them in aspic and set them in a continuous line around the sides of the bowl. Again, chill to set.

Now take the tongue, fold it into a circle and carefully set it in the bowl. Again, add sufficient cooked but liquid aspic to cover and weight the tongue down. This is best done by wrapping a scales weight in plastic film and sitting it on top of the tongue. You'll need to take this out again later, which will make a hole which also needs to be filled with stock. Leave the whole thing to chill overnight in the refrigerator.

Insert a very sharp knife carefully around the rim of the bowl to loosen it. Immerse it for a few seconds in a basin of hot water and then put the serving plate over the top and carefully turn it over. The complete mould should then turn out on the plate. It is very good served with a sharp sauce such as that made with gooseberries. The pig's head brawn described in the meat section is also a very good galantine for a second course.

Now we come to *potted meats and fish*. What is the difference between a potted dish and a pâté? Well, as my old form master used to say, hefting his cane, it's all in the flick of the wrist. Whereas one is archetypically French, the other is quintessentially English. Potted foods in general are much more finely minced than pâtés which can be made of quite roughly chopped meats. In the days before refrigeration, meats were potted and then sealed under a layer of clarified butter. They will keep fresh for quite a long time in this state and were a great standby, particularly for long sea voyages (for the cabin passengers only, though — down in the steerage they lived on salt pork and biscuit).

Keeping food under fat is one of the most ancient of all preserving methods, still practised in respect of that renowned Maori delicacy the muttonbird. Eating the chick of the sooty shearwater is not of course to everyone's taste but it is certainly to mine. I find the meat delectable, although both salty and oily, rather like a pigeon. I have often thought it would make an excellent potted meat but I have never got around to trying it. I have rather more conventionally stuck to game and, of course, that great English delicacy, fish in a pot. It must have been hell making these things in the days before mincers and blenders when the meat had to be ground in a vast pestle and mortar. Doubtless generations of kitchen boys and maids cursed the notion of potted foods, particularly as they almost certainly rarely got to taste the finished product.

POTTED RABBIT

When I took up cooking in earnest one of the first books to which I turned was *The Farmhouse Kitchen* by Mary Norwak. It is a treasure trove of traditional English country dishes, many of them familiar to my grandmother. It is from that book that this recipe is adapted.

4 rabbit pieces
50 g butter
teaspoon sugar
1 onion
12 cloves
12 allspice (whole)
6 peppercorns
ground nutmeg, salt and pepper
200 g butter
2 teaspoons Worcestershire sauce

Soak the rabbit joints in salted water for a couple of hours, drain and pat dry. Put them in a casserole with a lid with the 50 g of butter, the sugar, the onion stuck with cloves and the other spices and seasonings to taste. Cook for 3 hours at 150°C. Cool. Remove the meat from the bones and put it through the mincer *twice*. Then mix it with the juices from the casserole, the 200 g of butter melted and the Worcestershire sauce. Leave to set. This will keep in the refrigerator for some days.

Bring it out of the refrigerator and let it soften for a couple of hours before serving with bread, otherwise it will not spread. This makes quite a quantity. I usually pot it in several small earthenware containers and there's some left over for snacks on succeeding days. Nutmeg and cloves really bring out the flavour of rabbit.

In the same section of her book, Mary Norwak gives a recipe for potted stilton. Potted cheeses are not as eccentric as they sound. They were originally simply a thrifty way of storing farmhouse cheeses, and in the eighteenth century they were very common. In her celebrated work of 1747, *The Art of Cookery Made Plain and Easy*, Hannah Glasse recommends a mixture of cheddar, butter and canary wine with mace. These were the original 'cream cheeses', entirely different to the stuff sold in supermarkets today. Hannah Glasse's book was one of the most popular of the eighteenth century. By 1803 it had gone through 17 editions, although it was largely a compilation drawn from contemporary works. No less a quick-tempered old grouch than Samuel Johnson thoroughly approved of it, probably because it excoriated the eating habits of the French. As an innovative cook, Hannah was among the first to use butter as a substitute for suet or lard, a habit now all but universal. In her day this was a wanton extravagance; butter was twice the price of meat! A fine facsimile edition of her first printing has recently been done by Prospect Books.

POTTED CHEESE

There are a number of schools of thought as to which cheese is best potted and what proportions of cheese and butter there should be. This recipe is drawn from *Pottery*, published in 1946 by the Wine and Food Society and written by Cyril Connolly's father, who was a noted gourmet. It calls for:

225 g grated Cheshire cheese
90 g unsalted butter
2 tablespoons brown sherry
¼ teaspoon cayenne

These should be blended to a paste and decorated with walnut halves. Rochefort should be flavoured with chives and Stilton with port, says Connolly *père*. No, no, says Elizabeth David. It is a mistake. 'Port is, as we know, an excellent wine to drink with cheese. In the cheese it is overpowering — and produces an unappetising purplish tinge.' Proof positive that one person's meat is another person's poison. Or, as the next recipe illustrates, *poisson*.

POTTED SHRIMP

When I was a very small child my mother used to buy fish paste in tiny glass pots. She used to spread it on toast for me for lunch. I have not seen it on sale for years. Probably, like all good things, it is no longer available, driven out of production by the inexorable mechanism of a sort of culinary Gresham's Law. This dish is however a passable substitute, being an eighteenth-century recipe from a Suffolk manor. Crayfish, crab or prawns can be dealt with in like manner.

500 g shelled shrimps
250 g butter
1 teaspoon mace

½ teaspoon ginger
salt and cayenne

Chop half the shrimps and leave the rest whole. Mix with the mace and ginger. Melt 180 g of the butter and cook the shellfish in it with a pinch of salt and cayenne to taste until the butter is absorbed. Mix with the rest of the butter softened and press into a pot. Refrigerate before serving. This may be cut in slices and served on toast. There is a similar recipe in Dorothy Hartley's *Food in England* which combines the shellfish with white fish. I have also tried the crayfish variant, which is excellent.

Most meats can be potted — venison, beef, pork and so forth. The next dish is something rarely seen but truly delicious.

POTTED TONGUE

This recipe is from a now almost forgotten book *The London Art of Cookery* published in 1783. Its author, John Farley, was the keeper of the London Tavern, a famous eighteenth-century house, now alas long gone. If you want to have some idea of what these eighteenth-century inns were like and you happen to be in London, try The Windmill on Clapham Common. Farley's book went through many editions and was even translated into French, the ultimate culinary compliment. The recipe Farley gives is simplicity itself: a smoked and peeled ox tongue is blended with two-thirds its weight of softened clarified butter, and a little ground mace and some freshly ground black pepper. Pack it into a pot and let it mature for a day or so. Serve with toast.

On the other hand, if you really want to do something with some chicken livers to impress your guests then you can prepare this dish which has one of the longest names in cookery.

GÂTEAU DE FOIE BLOND DE POULARDE DE BRESSE AU COULIS DE QUENELLES D'ÉCREVISSES

This comes from a book by Lucien Tendret published in 1892, *La Cuisine au pays de Brillat Savarin.*

300 g chicken livers
50 ml strong beef stock
50 ml milk
2 eggs
2 egg yolks
clove garlic, pepper and salt

Put all the ingredients in a blender and make a smooth paste. Transfer to one large or several small ramekins, leaving room for rising. Put in a water bath in an oven at 150° C for about an hour and a half with a sheet of foil over the top. Serve hot with the following sauce:

300 g cooked shrimps
120 ml butter
150 ml cream
2 egg yolks
150 ml chopped fried mushrooms

Blend the first four ingredients. Cook them very gently in a double boiler for ten minutes or so. Don't let this sauce get too hot or it will curdle. Just before serving, stir in the mushrooms. It can then be poured over the turned-out gâteau of liver. This is quite an impressive dish but requires a degree of fiddling at the last moment, so I don't cook it very often. If you don't feel able to manage the sauce, the liver gâteau on its own is very interesting. The French word *coulis* meaning a sauce had its equivalent in medieval English — cullis, from which I am told derives another obsolete word — cully, meaning 'a saucy fellow'. Interesting, but nothing to do with cooking.

Hot Fish Dishes

Let's just go back to fish for a moment, but by rather a roundabout route. Most writers will tell you two things about their craft. The first of these is to do with being unable to make a living at it, so that it becomes a part-time activity and thus of necessity a highly disciplined one. Time must be firmly set aside for it and not only strictly observed by the writer but respected by the writer's friends. Secondly, and related to that, is the ritualisation of the period spent writing. This latter may involve all sorts of peculiar things. One of my fellows has to use foolscap paper and a pencil; another requires classical music as a background. If these conditions are not met then no writing happens. My writing day is Sunday and one of my rituals is coffee at eleven. Not at my house, but at the house of some near neighbours. If you are a member of the Council of the Rugby Football Union you are about to begin gnashing your teeth because one of these neighbours is Trevor Richards —who just happens to be a superb cook. If it had not been for the many cups of coffee that he and his friend Patti (also a good cook) have given me, this book could not have been written. And so, in recognition of that I have asked Trevor to include his favourite entrée recipe. Here it is in his own words.

HOT CRACKER CRAB

When I was about eighteen I bought my first cookery book which I still have. It opened up wonderful new horizons for tastebuds which were not a prisoner to more traditional kiwi fare. It contains a recipe for Hot Cracker Crab which I would highly recommend for its versatility, taste and general success with guests. It can be served at almost any time — for lunch with a salad, as a dinner entrée, as part of a buffet dinner, as an after the movies snack or with the rugby at 3.00 am. Its versatility also extends to its ingredients. Although I have cooked it dozens of times, never have I constructed it the same way. The occasion, the state of the pantry and my pocket all help determine its variations.

230 g crabmeat, cooked
60 g celery
60 g green pepper
60 g shallots
30 g parsley
85 g water biscuits
salt, dry mustard
¼ teaspoon cayenne
115 g clarified butter
60 ml cream
butter

Cook the crabmeat lightly and slice very finely the celery, shallots and green pepper; finely chop the parsley; crush the water biscuits roughly; melt butter to brush, and preheat oven to 180°C. Melt 60 g clarified butter in a saucepan, add shallots, green pepper, celery, sliced crabmeat. Season with salt, mustard, cayenne. Stir in 85 g cracker crumbs, cream and parsley. Place in shallow casserole or baking dish. Top with remaining crumbs, brush with remaining melted butter. Bake at 180°C for 25 minutes.

For crabmeat I often substitute shrimps (much cheaper and, depending upon your taste, just as good). If you are short of cash there is no harm in reducing the amount of crab/shrimps whatever. If you are feeling extravagant, use fresh prawns. I used them in the dish once and they were not wasted on it. (A word of caution: if using tinned seafood, check for saltiness — some are very salty and as a consequence little if any additional salt needs to be added.)

The vegetables can be varied to suit taste and seasonal availability. I don't care for celery so it is usually omitted or the amount reduced when I cook. Onions are a good substitute for the spring onions. The heat of the dish can be varied by the amount of cayenne used, and it is a good dish with none. For those just learning to cope with vaguely hot foods, it is a good dish to encourage you to extend your threshold.

KIPPER FLAN

Kippers are a great delicacy in England which I never truly appreciated until I went to live there. The kipper is a relative newcomer to English cuisine, which is strange when you consider that in pre-refrigeration days the rough smoking of herrings was one of the major industries of Europe. It appears however that kippering was invented in the 1840s by John Woodger of Northumberland.

The herring is split and folded out, gutted, soaked briefly in brine and then smoked over oak for about eighteen hours. Kippers don't travel terribly well but they can sometimes be bought in delicatessens. Frozen or tinned ones should be avoided like the plague. If they've been properly smoked they don't need other means of preservation. I don't, as a rule, eat breakfast but when I lived in England I made an exception when I travelled by British Rail which serves a marvellous traditional English breakfast. While I was there BR tried to remove the kipper from their breakfast menu, causing a public controversy which prompted a letter in *The Times* from no less a luminary than Lord Olivier. There was such an uproar British Rail were obliged to reinstate kippers, although I understand they have been trying to do away with them by stealth since.

short pastry
pair of kippers

120 ml cream
3 eggs
tablespoon French mustard
salt and pepper
juice of a lemon

Line a tart tin or flan with the pastry and bake it blind for about 7 or 8 minutes. Jug the kippers: this involves standing the fish upright in a ceramic jug, pouring boiling water over them and letting them stand for a few minutes, which gets out some salt and softens the fish so you can then pick out the bones and skin. When you have done this, put the fish in the pastry shell.

Beat together the cream, eggs and mustard, add pepper and salt to taste (take care with the salt) and pour over the fish. Bake at 180°C until the filling browns and puffs up, about 40 minutes. The flan can be eaten hot or cold. Squeeze the lemon juice over it just before serving.

Cold Entrées

FISH MOUSSE

1 litre fish stock
200 g skinned boneless terakihi
bouquet garni
250 g mushrooms, diced
15 g gelatine softened in 50 ml dry vermouth
150 ml cream
salt and pepper

Simmer the fish in about half the stock with the bouquet until it is just about cooked, perhaps 10 minutes. Remove the fish to cool, discard the bouquet and cook the mushrooms in the stock for about ten minutes. Strain and set aside. Now stir the gelatine into half the stock and blend it thoroughly. (Set the other stock aside.) Cool the first half of the stock a little and then liquidise it in a blender with the cooled fish. Season carefully and add the mushrooms. Set aside to cool. When the stock is almost set, lightly beat the cream and fold it into the mixture. Pour into a mould and chill. When you are ready to unmould it, serve it with the following cold sauce:

fish stock remaining from the recipe above
300 ml cream
½ teaspoon tarragon
15 g gelatine softened in vermouth
350 ml cooked crab or shrimp

Simmer the stock, cream and tarragon until it is reduced a little, then blend in the gelatine. Warm the cooked shellfish in a little vermouth and season it, then separately chill this mixture and the stock and cream. Fold the sauce into the shellfish and when the resulting sauce is almost set, coat the unmoulded mousse with it and chill again for serving. You can decorate with raw vegetables, mushrooms, etc.

This dish also makes a very good main course for a summer lunch, although you'll need to double the ingredients. There are a number of mousses which make very good second courses if you combine the right flavours. There is a technique to using gelatine however. Most people use too little the first time and their mousse runs everywhere. The next time they compensate and use too much. Their dish then is suitable only for the missile in squash racquets. Gelatine is a difficult substance because its consistency varies. Practice makes for perfection — which consists in something which looks as if it is about to flow away but doesn't and stays firm instead.

PEAR AND CHEESE MOUSSE

This combination of fruit and cheese is a particularly attractive one. I make it in late summer when the pears on my tree ripen.

3 large pears, peeled, cored and cooked
250 g cream cheese
1 teaspoon onion juice
salt and white pepper
150 ml chicken stock
15 g gelatine soaked in vermouth
2 tablespoons wine vinegar
1 tablespoon caster sugar
¼ teaspoon mace
150 ml cream

Dice the pears. Blend the cheese, onion juice and seasonings. Heat the stock and dissolve the gelatine in it then add the cheese. Lightly beat the cream. Combine the pears, vinegar, sugar and mace. When the cheese mixture is cold, mix it with the spiced pears and fold in the cream. Set in a mould. This should be garnished with watercress and slices of red and green pepper. A blue cheese can also be used, but this makes a mousse which is too strong in flavour for my taste.

A combination of pears, Stilton and black pepper heated on toast is served at Locket's restaurant in London or at least used to be. Probably people have been eating fruit with cheese since the dawn of time. The pear as we know it, however, was developed in France firstly in the fifteenth century by Saint Francois de Paul (le bon chrétien) and again in the seventeenth century by one of those great unsung heroes of cuisine, de la Quintinie, orchardist and kitchen gardener to Louis XIV. Finally, the great work of creating the pear was completed in the nineteenth century at Angers. There in 1850 Miller de la Turtandière of the Comice Horticole and his gardener Hillaire Dhomme brought the pear to the peak at which we now enjoy it. Next time you eat a pear, spare a thought for the gardener Dhomme. Pears also make a good salad ingredient. This same mousse, incidentally, can be made with cucumber.

TOMATO MOUSSE

This is the most surprising of all the mousses I have made.

250 ml tomatoes, chopped and sieved
175 ml tomato juice
15 g gelatine
4 tablespoons vermouth
salt, Worcestershire sauce, pepper, sugar
300 ml cream

Dissolve the gelatine in the vermouth and then very gently heat the tomato juice and blend in the gelatine. When it is well blended remove from the heat and stir in the tomatoes. Season with the sugar, salt, sauce and pepper. When it is cold, fold in the lightly whipped cream and leave to set in a mould. Chill.

This dish, when unmoulded, will be found to have a superb rose colour. Surrounded by halved eggs, slices of peppers, etc. it looks magnificent brought to the table on a white plate.

Eggs and tomatoes actually go very well together, as the following recipe illustrates.

EGG AND TOMATO IN ASPIC

The Victorians, who were very fond of all manner of fancies with aspic, had this as a favourite summer luncheon dish.

1 hard-boiled egg for each person
1 very large tomato for each person
300 ml aspic jelly
mayonnaise
pepper and salt
watercress

The trick is to find those *extremely* large tomatoes that are not often sold in the shops 'because the customers don't want them'. You may have to speak nicely to your greengrocer or even go to a supplier in the country to get

123

them. Carefully blanch each tomato and cut off the top. Remove the inside, season with salt and pepper, pour in a little aspic and then put the shelled egg on top. Fill up with aspic. The best aspic jelly for this can be made of half white wine and half chicken stock with enough gelatine to just set. It needs to be well seasoned. Chill and serve on a bed of watercress with a separate mayonnaise.

There are many mayonnaises. But all have this in common: an egg yolk must absorb an oil. This happens best with the egg at room temperature and the oil slightly tepid. A large egg yolk absorbs oil slowly, so the oil must be added drop by drop until the emulsifying process begins and there is a change to a thick cream. Then the oil can be added more quickly, but it is still something not to be rushed. A single yolk cannot absorb more than about 150 ml of oil, and if you go beyond this the yolk breaks down and the sauce curdles. The trick is to beat continuously until the thickening occurs. As you beat the yolks and oil together add a little salt, lemon juice and if you like some mustard.

At the very end add four tablespoons of boiling water. This increases the keeping property. This sauce will keep for a couple of days in a refrigerator if it is closely covered. It is a basic sauce and may then be incorporated with other ingredients such as herbs, or onions, or even capers and anchovies. But I like it best in its pristine state.

It is also pleasing to see watercress becoming more readily available. In fact, blended into a mayonnaise with anchovies and capers it becomes *beurre montpellier*. Watercress is actually a variety of nasturtium and has been grown commercially in Europe since the eighteenth century, but was eaten long before that. Culpepper, the seventeenth-century herbalist, recommended it as a blood purifier and it was known to be particularly good as a counter to scurvy. In twelfth century Ireland it was hymned by poets. Victor Hugo did the same seven centuries later so it must have something going for it. John Evelyn mentions it in his salad calendar for February, July and November. In this country it is available all year round and requires only a continuous supply of clean running water for its cultivation. It is best however in the summer. Smoked eel on a bed of watercress always seems particularly apt to me.

A Winter Entrée

I have spoken so much about cold entrées for summer that winter has been quite neglected. In that season my favourite is the leek, neglected unjustly because too humble.

LEEK TARTS

These tarts are easily made in advance and can be left in a patty pan. Then pop them in the oven while you serve the soup and in twenty minutes they are ready.

800 g trimmed leeks
2 tablespoons butter
5 tablespoons cream
salt and pepper
puff pastry
cheddar cheese

Wash and chop the leeks. Melt the butter in a heavy casserole with a lid, tip in the leeks, put on the lid and let them stew for thirty minutes, stirring now and then so they don't stick. Season them and liquidise them with the cream in a blender. Cut out the pastry to fit the patty pans and put some filling in each. Grate a little cheddar over the top and then cover with a pastry lid, pinching the edges together. Glaze with beaten egg and cook at 220°C for 20 minutes until they are lightly brown. They taste quite delicious brought to the table hot and are not too filling if eaten in moderation. The trouble is they can't be eaten in moderation. I always think that there will be a few left for lunch the next day. Strangely, there never are.

If however you would like a hot dish which is not heavy then the best thing to serve is a soufflé. This will be something of a test of your skill as a cook but even more of your patience. Soufflés are unpredictable and no matter how many times you have made them perfectly they still have a distressing tendency to come out not light and airy as a feather but as the proverbial lead balloon.

Soufflés

Reduced to its simplest terms a soufflé is a sauce with flavouring into which have been folded stiffly beaten egg whites. When this is placed in the oven the egg whites expand and this lifts the whole dish into a light and airy puff. That at least is the theory, but some soufflés are not familiar with this theory. The failure of a soufflé is usually a failure in the beating of the whites of egg. They must be stiff (they are stiff enough if they will support a whole egg placed on top).

Egg whites will not whip if they contain the slightest particle of yolk. They will also stiffen better if they are slightly acidified, so some recipes recommend a pinch of cream of tartar or a teaspoon of vinegar. Actually you can achieve the same effect by beating the egg white in a copper bowl. It is also a curiosity that you get a better result, although a very tired arm, with a hand balloon whisk than you do with a mechanical beater. Three minutes is usually sufficient by hand, whereas it can take up to eight minutes with a hand-held electric beater.

There is also a certain technique to 'folding in'. The trick here is to mix thoroughly, but not so as to drive all the air out again. If you use a rubber spatula and turn the sauce over onto the egg this will usually achieve the desired effect after about a minute of fairly rapid turning.

CHEESE SOUFFLÉ

This is the classic I guess, although as with most classic dishes there are a number of different recipes. The first is French.

60 g butter
50 g flour
300 ml milk heated to boiling
salt, pepper, cayenne, nutmeg
4 egg yolks
5 egg whites
100 g grated Parmesan cheese

Make a roux of the butter and flour. Cook it for a couple of minutes but don't brown it. Remove from the heat and beat in the boiling milk. Then beat in the seasonings and return to the heat to simmer and thicken. Remove from the heat again and beat in the egg yolks. Beat the egg whites until really stiff and fold into the sauce. Gently stir in the Parmesan.

Turn into a buttered soufflé dish. Have your oven preheated to 200°C and put the soufflé in the middle. Immediately turn it to 190°C and cook for 35 minutes, by which stage it should have puffed and browned nicely. Take it straight to the table for serving.

This alternative recipe is American. I came across it in Eleanor Early's *New England Cookbook*. She claims it to be infallible. I refuse to believe it but it hasn't let me down yet. What attracted me most to it was a charming story Ms Early tells about her friend Stanley who wanted to buy a piano, and who raised the entire price by cooking this soufflé for his friends at a dollar a head (this was 1954). In fact he was so successful with his soufflé that he became a well-known Boston restaurant owner (and part-time pianist). This is Stanley's recipe:

3 tablespoons butter
¹/₃ cup of flour (well it is an American recipe — 60 g to you)
1 tin evaporated milk
equal quantity water
salt
½ teaspoon dried mustard
1 medium onion
200 g grated cheddar
6 eggs separated

Put all the ingredients in a blender except the egg whites and blend thoroughly. Beat the whites stiff and fold them into the sauce in a bowl. Transfer to a soufflé mould and cook at 150°C for one and a half hours. The curiosity of this is that the result is almost exactly the same as the French recipe despite the extraordinary difference in cooking times.

When you have achieved command of this master recipe you are ready for any soufflé. To make, say, a spinach soufflé, use the French recipe. Cook some chopped spinach in butter for a few minutes and stir it into the sauce immediately after adding the egg yolks. Then simply proceed. Or do the same with diced ham, or sliced mushrooms, or asparagus or artichokes or just about anything which takes your fancy, including 300 g tinned salmon or some boiled and flaked fish. There are many variations on this theme —unmoulded soufflés, soufflé with egg whites only and of course sweet or fruit soufflés but these last belong with desserts. Essentially they are all the same soufflé.

Sorbets

Finally there are sorbets. Like soufflés these can be either entrées or desserts, depending upon the flavour. I shall be remarking upon them again in the chapter on desserts. If you are having a rather heavy or strongly flavoured soup followed by a main course of equally strong but quite distinct flavour, then a sorbet is ideal to separate the two for two reasons. Firstly it is light, being mainly flavoured ice. But secondly of course it has a very fine palate-cleansing effect and thereby the flavour of one dish will not carry over into the other. As an entrée a sorbet needs to be of a very sharp flavour. Citric sorbets are excellent for this purpose, grapefruit in particular. But mint is also good and there are some very fine wine sorbets. The chef at one of my favourite Wellington restaurants makes superb sorbets. I asked him once to tell me how he got his sorbets so perfect. 'I don't know', he replied, 'I just put the mixture into the sorbet making machine and it comes out the way I serve it.' The ones given here are a selection which I have found particularly suitable between the soup and the main course on appropriate occasions.

BASIC SORBET RECIPE

A sorbet is a syrup, a flavour and beaten egg white, combined and frozen. The changes which can be rung on that theme are virtually endless. To make the syrup, dissolve 150 g caster sugar in 500 ml of water and boil it furiously for about five minutes, by which time it should have thickened. Into this mix about 200 ml of the juice of citrus fruit and when it has cooled set it to freeze. When it is frozen around the edges but still liquid in the middle, beat it in batches in a blender until it is smooth and free from icy granules. You should add any appropriate alcohol at this point, as well as two whites of egg beaten until firm. This can then be frozen until you need it.

A finished sorbet should be nice and creamy. If kept for too long it will crystallise again but that can be fixed by giving it another beating. When it comes to eating there are two schools. Some say it should be served frozen and others say it should be thawed a little first so it is soft. I belong to the former.

The alcohol you use depends on what you are making. With lemon, lime or grapefruit a jigger of gin goes quite well. With the last-named, grate and add the zest of two large fruit. A very good mint sorbet can be made by blending the syrup with a handful of mint leaves, straining the result, and adding the juice of a couple of lemons. But if you really want a touch of luxury you should make *Champagne Charley*. When you make your syrup use 150 g sugar to 125 ml of water. Add the juice of two lemons and two oranges and the grated zest of the latter. Mix this thoroughly with about 600 ml of dry sparkling white wine. Then proceed as usual, using a jigger of cognac.

Main Course: Meat

Here a little child I stand,
Heaving up my either hand;
Cold as paddocks though they be,
Here I lift them up to Thee,
For a benison to fall,
On our meat, and on us all. Amen.
— Robert Herrick 'Grace For A Child'

ROBERT HERRICK (1591-1674), author of the famous *Cherry Ripe,* was using 'meat' in the now obsolete sense of any principal food dish, and not just cooked animal protein. That the word has come to change its meaning in this way is an interesting social commentary on the changing culinary habits of our European forebears and contemporary relations. Our dining habits would surprise even these latter I suspect. (Paddocks, incidentally, are frogs; 'cold as a little frog' as my mother would have said in a like circumstance.)

There is no doubt that we eat far more meat than we need. I was not aware of just how much we do tuck away until I went to live in Europe (where meat has always been very expensive) and there got into the habit of eating it only two or three times a week.

That is not to say, of course, that meat wasn't in the past important in English cooking. On the contrary, European visitors were often scandalised at the amount of meat eaten in England, even among the lower orders. The French traveller, Misson, wrote disapprovingly in the 1690s that 'among the middling sort of people they have ten or twelve sorts of common meats which infallibly take their turns at their tables and two dishes at their

129

dinners: a pudding for instance, and a piece of roast beef.' Half a century later his Swedish counterpart, Per Kalm, also commented in some wonder on the habit. 'Roast meat is the Englishman's *délice* and principal dish.' This habit we inherit.

People have been eating meat in Britain for a very long time. Excavations at Star Carr in Yorkshire reveal that as early as 5000 BC meat, usually game, was being hung and spit-roasted. The gut was also being used to make a form of haggis. Sheep, goats and cattle were all being herded in neolithic times. The Celts roasted both mutton and pork; the remains of the cooked joints of these animals have been found in the graves of chieftains killed in the capture of Maiden Castle by the Romans in 70 BC, presumably intended as sustenance in the afterlife. They evidently boiled meat also; large troughs of water were heated with red-hot stones and joints of meat wrapped in plaited straw were cooked in them. Recent experiments based on medieval Irish descriptions have confirmed the use of this technique as recently as a thousand years ago. By Roman times most people, even the poorest, used iron cauldrons for boiling meat. For centuries, however, the pattern of meat-eating in Europe was of necessity very different from that to which we are used.

Until the eighteenth-century development of high-yield fodder crops, part or all of farmed livestock had to be slaughtered in the autumn. It was then eaten or preserved either by smoking or salting. In 1557 Thomas Tusser wrote in his *A Hundreth Good Pointes of Husbandrie:*

> At Hallowmas slaughter time soon cometh in,
> And then doth the husbandman's feasting begin.
> From that time to Candlemas weekly kill some.
> Their offal for household the better shall come.

Hallowmas fell on 1 November and Candlemas on 2 February. The habit of feasting at Christmas long predates Christianity and was a severely practical consequence of the techniques of animal husbandry. It was almost certainly accompanied by religious rituals, which the early Church took over. As we shall see it is one of the curiosities of such festivals that their cuisine is very conservative, and quite ancient dishes survive at Christmas time when they have long fallen from use at other times of the year.

When I first returned from Europe I found the habit of eating large quantities of meat at every meal to be slightly nauseating; I have now again grown used to others doing so but it's something to which I still can't quite get used for myself. Particularly in the summer I prefer vegetables or fish as a main course.

Quite aside from the unhealthy consequences of too much meat, like obesity, there are other results, one of which is boredom. Familiarity breeds contempt, and most of us eat only lamb or beef, and that in a very narrow range of ways. If we eat poultry at all it is either a roasted chicken or, at Christmas, a turkey. We rarely eat game or the more unusual cuts. This dull situation needs to be remedied. One answer can be to restrict the intake of meat, in order to heighten the pleasure when it is eaten. Another is to explore more unusual ways of cooking it. For a dinner with friends, in particular, one wants to expend a little energy and imagination on the main dish. It is the centrepiece of the meal after all.

Lamb and Mutton

We should perhaps begin our exploration with this most commonplace of all our meats, although mutton is actually quite hard to get these days. Sometimes what we do with lamb and mutton beggars description. 'I have seen their admirable mutton brought to the table in such miserable shape that the hogget — so they call a sheep of uncertain age — appeared to have been killed by a bomb and the fragments of its carcase incinerated in the resultant fire.' Such was the harsh judgement of Eric Linklater, who perhaps went too far. Nevertheless it is true that our traditional manner of dressing lamb, by roasting in the oven, leaves a good deal to be desired. This is partly because the way in which the animal is raised leaves it far too fat. It was not until I ate decent lamb in southern Europe that I appreciated the advantage of lean sheepmeat. Nor will New Zealanders use traditional herbs such as garlic or rosemary to advantage. Garlic has a bad name and this prejudice I am sorry to say we inherit from our English tradition. From Naples in December 1818, Shelley wrote: 'What do you think? Young women of rank actually eat — you will never guess what — garlic.' And Mrs Beeton, staring down her nose, was more than definite: 'The smell of this plant is generally considered offensive and it is the most acrimonious in its taste.' Between them they helped to establish a most regrettable taboo. In fact garlic (*Allicum sativum*) has been known and enjoyed for thousands of years. Biblical scholars will know that one of the list of complaints the Jews brought to Moses in the wilderness was that there was no garlic available during their wanderings.

It has to be agreed of course that garlic has a strong smell but that cannot be helped: it should still be a standard accompaniment to lamb.

We export our best lamb, thus the French get our fillet and we get the chops. The French also know that even lamb should not be eaten too fresh. A leg, for instance, should be purchased several days in advance of cooking and kept in the refrigerator wrapped in plastic film until it is needed. When the time comes to cook it, it should be trimmed of all fat and preferably boned and stuffed.

Boning a leg of lamb is quite easy. It involves cutting down through the meat to remove the shank bone. If you don't feel confident enough to do this your butcher will usually do it for you. Boning creates a small cavity which can then be stuffed with whatever you might like. The joint can then be skewered up and laced for cooking and the skewers removed just before serving. This certainly makes it very much easier to carve. Some recipes recommend sewing up the cavity before cooking but I don't think that this is a good idea. The stitches are almost impossible to remove and your guests are liable to get a mouthful of thread.

Of all meats, lamb responds best to slow cooking. This involves using the oven at a low temperature (100°C) and cooking for at least eight hours and possibly more, covered, on a bed of chopped vegetables. I use celery, carrots and onions supplemented with a little white wine or vermouth. Towards the end the cover is removed and the temperature increased to 180°-190°C for about half an hour, for browning. The vegetables may either be transferred to the serving dish, and the finished joint replaced on them, or they may be discarded and the strained juices used for a gravy.

This method of cooking lamb has two great advantages. First, it is very flexible and gives you the freedom to work on something else. Second, it suits the meat, since lamb can be cooked almost indefinitely without burning, and comes out so succulent and tender that once you have tried it you will rarely cook it any other way. The method is almost as good with pork, but does not really suit beef, game or poultry: beef dries up; game shrinks; and poultry cooked in this way becomes *too* tender and falls to pieces.

The following recipes for lamb all use the slow cooking method.

LAMB STUFFED WITH CRAB

A combination of seafood and meat is a very old tradition in English cookery. It has now, alas, almost entirely died out. Its last survivors are steak and kidney pudding with oysters and that Texan monstrosity the carpetbag steak. As a combination of flavours it is excellent and there are one or two extant recipes. This is one of them, adapted from the 1811 edition of John Farley's *The London Art of Cookery*.

1 large leg of lamb
salt, pepper
carrots, onions, celery, chopped or diced
300 ml dry white wine
300 ml lamb stock
150 ml cream
1 teaspoon curry powder

Stuffing:
1 boiled crab, about 750 g
½ teaspoon curry powder
1 tablespoon chopped mint
3 egg yolks
salt and pepper

To obtain stock, if you don't have any stock on hand, boil the bone and the trimmings from the leg, for a couple of hours with mixed vegetables. The leg should be seasoned both on the outside and within the cavity. Mix the stuffing ingredients together. Getting the meat out of a crab (if you can get one) is a rather fiddly job but well worth doing. You can buy tinned crabmeat if you have to (about 250 g) but it will be almost tasteless because of some nameless and unknown thing that those preparing it seem to do with it. Strangely enough a cooked whole crab can usually be bought cheaply because crabs are not highly regarded, whereas imported tinned crabmeat is quite expensive.

Stuff the interior of the lamb with the mixture and skewer it up. It should then be cooked on a bed of vegetables as already described. Transfer it to a metal serving plate and replace in the oven to brown, and leave the vegetables in the cooking pan. Pour the wine and stock over them and bring this to the boil on top of the stove. Simmer it for five or ten minutes and strain it into a saucepan. Skim off the fat and add the curry powder and cream. Keep it hot over a low heat and pour it into a warm sauceboat for serving.

This recipe, despite my earlier strictures, contains neither rosemary nor garlic. The next makes up for that.

ARNAKI YEMISTO: STUFFED EASTER LAMB, DODECANESE STYLE

The best time to be in the Greek islands is during the Orthodox Easter which is a little later than ours. It is then that they serve the pascal lamb.

133

This recipe is also excellent for a young kid which can sometimes be obtained in specialist butcher shops. My butcher tells me that a small abbatoir near Levin annually dresses goat meat.

1 leg of lamb (or kid)
500 g minced back mutton
2 kidneys and a lamb liver
300 g rice
170 g butter
2 large chopped onions
2 chopped cloves of garlic
3 large lemons
2 tablespoons chopped fresh rosemary or 1 teaspoon dried
small piece of cinnamon
salt and pepper

Bone the lamb and rub both the inside and out with salt and pepper, half the butter and the juice from the lemons. Chop the liver and kidneys, mix with the mince and fry this in a dry pan for about ten minutes, stirring to avoid catching. Then add the remaining butter, the onions, garlic, rice, ground cinnamon and more salt and pepper. Cook for five minutes and add the rosemary. Cook for a further ten and allow this to cool a little.

Stuff the boned leg loosely, and skewer. Shape any remaining mixture into small balls. Place the stuffed leg on a bed of vegetables with the balls of stuffing around and pour over two cups of water. Cover and slow cook at 100°C for eight hours, removing the lid towards the end to brown. Serve on the bed of cooked vegetables surrounded by the stuffing balls and with the skewers removed.

Many legends surround the herb rosemary, most of which associate it with the Christchild. It is reputed to have been the bush on which the Virgin draped the newly-washed clothes of the holy family during the flight from Egypt. Botanically *Rosmarinus officinalis*, it's sometimes also known as 'dew of the sea' and is reputed to flourish best near the coast. It was believed in medieval times to be a restorative of memory. It appears in one of the earliest herbals, the Saxon *Leech Book of Bald*, as proof against the evil eye. Brides carried a sprig on their wedding day for this reason in Tudor times.

Other vegetables can be used when cooking lamb by the slow method. In France it is often done with haricot beans as *Gigot ou Epaule de Pré-Salé Braisé aux Haricots*. The lamb is cooked in the usual way, stuffed or not as preferred, but with rather more liquid, and the strained liquid and lamb returned to the dish without the vegetables before the browning, placed on a bed of previously soaked and cooked white haricots which, during the final thirty minutes of cooking, absorb the pan liquid. Beans and lamb are then served together. Lamb navarin, that is, with turnips, is also very good.

Lamb may be cooked to advantage with fruit. In my garden is an ancient plum tree, and every year about the beginning of February when the plums are ripe I make the following dish.

LAMB WITH PLUMS

a leg of lamb sufficient for six
butter
two glasses of dry white vermouth
a jigger of slivovicz
about twenty large plums
1 clove of garlic, chopped
1 medium onion, chopped
½ teaspoon each of ground cinnamon and allspice or nutmeg
1 teaspoon sugar

Cut away as much of the fat as you can from the leg, which can be boned or not as you want. Brown it all over in butter and put it into a deep casserole with all the other ingredients. Cook covered for eight hours at 100°C, removing for the last half hour for browning at 180°-190°C. Skim and strain the juices into a saucepan, add more spices if you think necessary and keep hot. Pour a little over the meat when serving and serve the remainder in a sauceboat. This dish goes well with plain boiled potatoes.

PERSIAN LAMB

When it comes to cooking meat with fruit, other culinary traditions are much more adventurous than our own. The Middle Eastern *khoresh* is the best of these in my estimation. Essentially it is a lamb stew, cooked with fruit and sometimes with vegetables also. In Persia lamb is similarly cooked, not only with peaches or with apples but with spinach and prunes, or apple and aubergine in combination. If you want to try it proceed as follows.

In a little oil, brown a finely chopped onion and about 500 g of lamb fillet cut into cubes. Season with salt and pepper and a teaspoon of ground cinnamon. Cover it with about a pint of water, bring it to the boil and simmer for an hour. If you want a really rich texture put a couple of tablespoons of dried split peas in as well. Fry a cubed aubergine and two peeled, cored and sliced apples and at the end of the hour add these together with the juice of a lemon. Continue simmering until the aubergine is cooked. The same dish can be made with boned chicken. You can add some chopped tomato and garlic if you like, or some cumin instead of the cinnamon.

LAMB WITH AUBERGINES

Lamb is very good with aubergines, as the Greeks discovered when they invented moussaka. It can also be prepared as a mould. Line a mould dish with the skins of baked aubergines and fill with a combination of mushrooms, spring onions, oil, minced cooked lamb, the diced cooked flesh of the aubergines, salt, pepper, rosemary, thyme and garlic. Bake this covered in foil at 180°C for about an hour and a half.

All of that takes us a long way from lamb in the European tradition.

One of the things the English do very well in their cooking is the rather grand dish for a special occasion. They manage not to get fussy about it, unlike the French, whose metropolitan cooking can be all of a pother about sauces. The following dish, which is admirable of that category, is clearly a survival from medieval cooking techniques, as its cooking method shows. The recipe upon which this one is based comes from Hannah Glasse's *The Art of Cookery Made Plain and Easy* published in 1747, one of the best known of all cookery books of the eighteenth century. Its first edition has recently been republished in facsimile. The author, natural daughter of a military officer, did much to rescue the native English tradition from one of the regular and continuing French culinary invasions.

LEG OF LAMB A LA ROYALE

You will need a largish kettle with a lid, as this dish is cooked on the top of the stove.

1 large leg of lamb
1 leg piece of rump of beef, tied to roast (between 800 g and 1 kg)
2 bouquets garnis
1 large onion, stuck with 12 cloves
1 teaspoon mace
12 peppercorns
salt
100 g butter
1 tablespoon flour

Flour the lamb and the beef and brown each separately all over in butter. Transfer them both to the large kettle, add the other ingredients, cover with three litres of water and simmer very gently, closely covered, for at least two hours. Those are the basic ingredients but you will also need:

6 lamb kidneys
350 g mushrooms
125 ml red wine
120 g flour
two tins asparagus
2 tablespoons chopped parsley
1 tablespoon drained capers
salt and pepper and a little lemon juice

After the meat has been cooking for about an hour and a half, start to prepare the gravy and garnish. Skin and slice the kidneys and fry them in butter in a separate pot or casserole. Remove. Slice and fry the mushrooms and then return the kidneys to the pot along with the wine. Take about half a litre of the meat stock from the kettle and add this also. Gently stew this mixture for about fifteen minutes. While that is happening heat the asparagus, drain and wrap it in foil with a knob of butter. Pop it in a preheated oven at 125°-150°C. This is a handy trick which will keep the asparagus hot and tender until you need it.

Now mix the 120 g of flour to a smooth paste with cold water and pour half the boiling gravy into it. If you try to add the flour directly to the gravy it will go lumpy, which is devilish to do anything about in a hurry. Return this, well stirred, to the casserole and keep stirring in further liquid from the kettle in small amounts until you have a creamy consistency. Add the lemon juice and more salt and pepper if necessary. Let it simmer very gently.

Lift the mutton and keep it hot in the oven. Likewise lift the beef and carve it quickly into slices and position around the mutton. Pour the hot kidney and mushroom sauce over the beef and position the spears of asparagus around the dish. Sprinkle with the parsley and capers and bear it in triumph to the dining table.

This dish is a sure-fire hit. Some friends to whom I served it years ago are still talking about it. The last steps sound like a cook's nightmare but if you do as much as possible in advance and work fairly quickly in the order given it is manageable. Obviously you don't want to be preparing an elaborate vegetable dish at the same time. Plain boiled green peas are ideal. If the beef has cooled too much while carving, put it into the oven for a few minutes to warm before adding the gravy.

The cauldron cooking of this dish does point to a medieval origin, and another clue is provided by cloves which are an important constituent in many late medieval meat dishes. The Genoese and Venetians used to guard their monopoly of the spice trade jealously; when an Englishman, Robert Sturmy, tried to deal directly with the Arab merchants in 1458 the Genoese waylaid him off Malta and dumped his cargo in the sea. It was this sort of thing which stimulated the search for a passage around Africa. As early as 1316 cloves are mentioned in an ordinance of the Guild of Pepperers, who imported and retailed most of the spices in medieval London. Cloves were quite expensive and therefore not usually available to the poor, unlike pepper, which was relatively cheap.

Cloves are the dried flower buds of the evergreen clove tree native to the Molucca Islands, and the pungent odour made cloves a suitable ingredient in preparations to kill bad odours in earlier times, when the drains could be fairly noisome, especially in high summer. An orange studded with cloves was sometimes carried by individuals for similar reasons in an age when few bathed regularly; it's said Cardinal Wolsey usually had one with him.

Nowadays cloves are not much used in meat dishes, with the exception of Christmas hams (I mentioned festive conservatism earlier) and are more usually found in combination with fruits, especially apple.

Another tradition we have chosen to abandon to our disadvantage is that of the savoury pie as a principal dish for a special meal. Commercially meat pies linger on only as disgusting objects, overcooked and without perceptible meat filling, which serve as fast food in lunch bars or at sports fixtures. The following recipe, despite its name, may serve to help rehabilitate the meat pie.

KATT PIE

This is a grand raised pie made of fillet of mutton or lamb. No one seems to know the origin of the name except that it's Welsh and has nothing to do with *Felix domesticia*. The pie has traditionally been eaten hot on Templeton Fair Day (12 November) for at least two hundred years. A very similar pie from the southeast of England is called Squab Pie and is in its turn very similar to the mutton and turnip pie of neighbouring Cornwall. The combination of meat and fruit gives away its medieval origins, particularly the use of currants. In fact there's a lamb pie from Westmorland which goes much further and contains not only apples and currants but raisins, sultanas, chopped peel and orange and lemon juice as well. That's altogether *too* medieval for my taste!

The tradition of the savoury pie is a very old one in English cooking and one of its great delights, and in earlier times there was no distinction such as we draw between sweet and savoury. A seventeenth-century writer on food, Gervase Markham, has an extraordinary recipe in his *The English Hus-wife* (1615) for a herring pie which includes not only pickled fish but raisins, dates, pears, sugar, cinnamon and unfermented grape juice. Others again include rosewater. By the beginning of the eighteenth century the present distinction between savoury and sweet pies had appeared.

The basis of these pies is the pastry case (or coffin as it was sometimes known), which holds and absorbs the juices exuded during the cooking. Potato is now often used for that purpose. In a pre-foil era, the lid not only sealed in the juices but prevented burning. To do the dish properly you need to make your own pastry. Traditionally this was made with melted butter, suet or lard, and hot water combined with flour. Today we are more inclined to use a short pastry. The earliest reference I know to this latter is to be found in an unusual cookery book of 1669, *The Closet of the Eminently Learned Sir Kenelm Digby Knight Opened.* Sir Kenelm was a prominent member of parliament, who played a leading role in the events of the English Civil War and the general political brouhaha of the mid-seventeenth century. His father, Sir Everard, who according to John Aubrey 'was accounted the handsomest gentleman in England' was one of the Gunpowder Plot conspirators and ended on the scaffold. Sir Kenelm was a successful admiral (in 1627 he defeated a combined French and Venetian fleet in the Mediterranean) and unlike his father was a royalist which got *him* locked up for his trouble by parliament. When Sir Kenelm died his son went through his papers, discovered that he had been interested in cooking and had a collection of his recipes published. Whether, like Sir Kenelm, you prefer a short pastry, or the more traditional raised pie pastry, is a matter of personal taste. I prefer the latter, hence the recipe which follows.

450 g plain flour
225 g shredded suet
pinch of salt
500 g minced lamb fillet
225 g currants
225 g brown sugar
3 cooking apples, peeled, cored and chopped
seasoning to taste

Put the suet in 125 ml of water and bring it to the boil. Let it boil for two minutes and then mix it into the flour with the salt. When it has cooled,

139

press it into a pie mould leaving enough for a lid. Combine the other ingredients and fill the case, seasoning it well. Put on the lid. Now leave it in the refrigerator for at least two hours to really stiffen up the pastry. Bake it in a hot oven 215°C for 30-40 minutes, covering the top with a piece of foil if it looks as if it is getting too brown. This pie should be eaten hot. You will find its sweetness unusual in a main course dish. If you can't cope with that then serve it as a dessert, for which you will find it will do just as well; it will also surprise your guests.

Lamb fillet isn't always available. Backs mutton or lamb will do as well and is cheaper besides. It is rather fiddly however as you will need to strip the meat from the fatty gristle before mincing it. You can also use small lamb chops if you prefer, one for each person, but be sure to trim them carefully of all the fat they invariably have on them. Actually it always rather irritates me having to pay by weight for that fat only to discard it.

Of course there is much you can do with the other parts of a sheep or lamb, particularly the kidneys and the tongue, both of which are sold very cheaply. To my disgust some of my friends buy lamb tongues for their pets. They were surprised when I told them how delicious tongues are when cooked in a crumble.

TONGUE AND MUSHROOM CRUMBLE

750 g pickled lamb tongues
1 large carrot, chopped
2 large onions, chopped
bouquet garni
300 ml dry cider
125 g butter
200 g mushrooms
rounded dessertspoon flour
6 tablespoons dry white wine
50 g breadcrumbs
salt and pepper

Soak the tongues overnight to get out the salt, and drain. Simmer them in a pan with the carrot and one of the onions, the bouquet, the cider and enough water to cover. It will be an hour to an hour and a half before they are ready. Strain off the stock and retain, and discard the bouquet and vegetables. Let the tongues cool and then chop them coarsely and place in a well-greased casserole.

Cook the sliced mushrooms lightly in half the butter and tip them over the tongue. In the same pan fry the other onion in a little more butter and when it is just browned add the flour and cook for two minutes. Then add the wine and a little of the stock. Let it cook until it has thickened and also tip this into the casserole.

Melt the last of the butter and mix it with the breadcrumbs. Spread this over the top of the dish. Avoid the temptation to add water to moisten it further; if you do the dish will not work. Cook at 190°-200°C until the crumbs have browned and the sauce is bubbling through the crust. This is one of those useful dishes which can be done mostly in advance and heated up in the last half hour or so before serving.

LAMB KIDNEY CURRY — GURDAKUPURA TURRCARRI

I make no apology for including a curry in a book concerning English-based cuisine. On the contrary it would be incomplete without one. In traditional Indian cooking a curry is the result of aromatised meat, which is tenderised by the long cooking and forms a thick sauce. The colonisers and adventurers who went out to India in the eighteenth century found curries there and made them their own. Through these colonials, the curry entered English cuisine.

It is still traditional on the surviving English passenger liners to serve curry for breakfast, a reminder of the days when P & O carried mustachioed sahibs and their mems to rule the Empire and brought them safely home again with a taste for the exotic in food.

As early as 1747 a recipe for a curry had appeared in Hannah Glasse's *The Art of Cookery*. Unfortunately many people have been put off curry for life by being served in their childhood a revolting paste, coloured brilliant yellow, as hot as the furnaces of Hell, and in which hapless sausages had been done to death. Any resemblance between this monstrosity and a real curry is purely coincidental.

With rare exceptions, prepared curry powders are to be avoided, a fact well known to a remarkable group of late nineteenth-century army officers, all of whom had been associated with the Raj, mainly as the mess officers of their respective regiments, and who fell in love with Indian cuisine and subsequently developed it for the English palate. The most interesting of these was a cavalry officer, Colonel Kenny-Herbert, who not only wrote four excellent cookery books but eventually retired from the army altogether to found the Commonsense Cookery Association which had a school on its London premises in Sloane Street. He devotes a whole chapter to curries in his *Culinary Jottings*.

Lamb kidneys (or for that matter any kidneys) are ideally suited to curries. They have little fat and what there is can be trimmed away. They also make delicious gravy.

This dish takes quite a long time to prepare. Allow yourself two hours at least and don't try to hurry it.

1 kg lamb kidneys
2 onions, finely chopped
150 g ghee
1 teaspoon turmeric
1 tablespoon sesame seed
¾ tablespoon cumin
½ teaspoon cayenne
4 chopped tomatoes
2 bay leaves, powdered
pinch of salt
½ teaspoon mace

Steep the kidneys in lightly vinegared water for 24 hours prior to cooking. Wash them in a colander under a tap and dry them. Skin them, halve them and trim away the fat and membranes. Grind and pound the aromatic ingredients to powder beforehand if necessary. In an iron pot fry the onions in the ghee (clarified butter) until they are deep brown then add the sesame, turmeric, cumin and cayenne. Fry together briefly. Add the kidneys and fry over medium heat for five minutes more, stirring continually, then add the tomatoes, powdered bay and salt. Pour over half a cup of water and sprinkle with mace.

Now comes time to exercise patience. Gently cook the mixture until it is dry. Add a further ¼ cup of water and cook it dry again, then fry it until it is deep red. Do not try and hurry this by turning up the heat, or you will burn it. Stir it throughout. Add enough water to cover the meat by at least an inch, bring it to the boil and then cover it and simmer it until the kidneys are tender and the sauce thick. It can then be kept simmering gently until it is ready to serve.

A curry like this is best served with plain boiled rice, some hot and sweet chutneys and poppadoms. Until a couple of years ago I used to laboriously prepare my own ghee until a friend in the dairy industry told me that you could obtain the stuff tinned and that we have a major export trade in it with the Middle East. Ghee is excellent for frying. Because the impurities in the butter have been removed it can be heated to quite high temperatures without burning and for that reason you should keep some on hand if you should ever be seized with an uncontrollable urge to fry yourself a steak. Which brings us to beef.

Beef

Objects of my withering scorn include those who, confronted with any restaurant menu, invariably order steak, medium rare. I put them in the same category as those tourists who return from Italy saying that the trouble with Florence is you can't get a decent cup of tea there. The steak that is served here in restaurants is usually abominably prepared and served, largely I suspect because the chef is infuriated that after all the thought that has been put into the menu someone has ordered a steak.

Now, lest it be imagined that I do not like steak, let me disabuse you of that notion straight away. I adore steak. The big question is: how should it be prepared? I once took a wager with myself that I could eat steak every Friday for a year and manage never to eat the same dish twice. This turned out to be ridiculously easy to accomplish. I suspect I could have gone on indefinitely, but I became bored.

That there is apparently an endless variety of ways to serve beef should not surprise us; the English have been eating cattle for at least four millenia;

and they have been renowned for this habit during the last four hundred years.

If you must have fried steak, proceed as follows. Buy the best you can afford and trim any fat off it. Put each steak between a piece of greaseproof paper, folded over, and beat it out to about twice its size with the flat of a steak hammer. Dribble a little olive oil and a little soy sauce on it, sprinkle it with a dozen or so *green* peppercorns and roll it up upon itself. Leave it for at least half an hour at room temperature before frying. Use a pan that is very hot and if you do not have any ghee use half butter and half oil, just covering the surface. The meat should be cooked very quickly so that the inside is still pink (but not raw), which should take about seven minutes at the most.

Brillat-Savarin dwells at some length on the theory of frying. 'The whole merit of frying,' he says, 'consists in the *surprise*; for such is the name given to the sudden action of the boiling liquid which carbonises or scorches the surface of the substance in question, at the very moment of its immersion. By means of this surprise a sort of ceiling is formed over the object, which prevents the fat from penetrating it and concentrates the juices inside, so that they undergo an internal cooking process which gives the dish all the flavour of which it is capable.' He concludes: 'It takes no longer to fry a four pound carp than it does to boil an egg.' All of which could hardly be more economically expressed.

Frying steak for a dinner party of six requires a certain confidence and adroitness in the kitchen. It is a good idea to have two or even three pans at work at the same time so that all the meats can be cooked concurrently. This takes some practice but one can in a short while become adept at it. It goes without saying that the other components in the main course will need to be either preparable in advance and served cold, such as salad, or something which requires neither split-second timing nor attention to minute detail in the moments before serving, such as ratatouille.

STEAK BERCY

Preheat your oven and have an ovenproof serving dish nearby. Heat 50 g of butter and a tablespoon of oil in each pan you are using and when it is very hot turn the heat to a point where it will keep it that way without burning. Sauté your steaks for about three minutes on each side. Transfer the meat to a serving dish and keep it hot in the oven. Pour the fat out and put another 50 g of butter in each pan. Add three tablespoons of chopped spring onions and cook gently for about a minute, then pour on 150 ml of dry white vermouth. Boil this down rapidly, scraping up all the bits in the pan until you have a thick liquid. Take it off the heat and beat in about 150 g of softened butter and salt and pepper to taste. Sprinkle with parsley, pour over the steaks and serve.

If you would like to take this dish a step further, then try it as a combination with oysters and grilled sausages. Put 200 g of chopped spring onions in an iron casserole and cover it with 250 ml of good wine vinegar. Let this boil rapidly until there is almost no liquid and then just keep sufficient heat under it to keep it hot. Meanwhile grill some bratwurst sausages (two for each guest) and when they are nearly done sauté the steak as described above. Serve steak, sausages and a little of the onion sauce to each guest together with half a dozen raw oysters. This, according to Elizabeth David in *French Country Cooking* is how they like their beef in the Bordelais and Basque country. It certainly leaves carpetbag steak a long way behind.

STEAK CASANOVA

I cannot speak for the aphrodisiac qualities of this dish but it certainly has its spectacular side. Season six steaks with salt and pepper, rub them very lightly with olive oil and leave them to absorb these flavours for at least two hours. Sauté them very quickly in the usual way for a minute on each side. Keep the steaks warm in the oven, pour off the oil and replace it with 50 g of fresh butter. In this melt 125 g of goose pâté or other strong pâté and add four tablespoons marsala. Cook this bubbling for a minute and then return the steaks to it. Meanwhile have a cupful of cognac warming in a small pan. Set it alight and pour it over the steaks, shaking it so that it keeps burning. By the time the brandy has finished flaming the meat will be cooked and can be served in its sauce. Do this for yourself a couple of times before trying it on guests. If you can do it within sight of the dining table then so much the better.

STEAK AU POIVRE

Pepper steak is possibly one of the most abused of all dishes. I have seen it on sale so smothered in pepper that eating it must be not so much a meal as a test of manhood. Try it this way instead.

Take a dessertspoon each of black and green peppercorns and crush them roughly in a pestle and mortar. Add a ¼ teaspoon each of white pepper and cayenne. Rub this mixture into the meat and then let the steaks stand for a couple of hours wrapped in greaseproof paper.

Sauté the steaks and keep them warm in the usual way. Pour away the fat in the pan, melt 50 g of fresh butter and fry 2 tablespoons of chopped spring onions until they are soft. Add 125 ml of beef stock and render it rapidly with the contents of the pan. Then add about 50 ml of cognac and boil it for about two minutes. Take it off the heat, melt 50 g of softened butter into it and serve poured over the steaks in their serving dish.

STEAKS IN BLACK COFFEE

Yes, that's right, coffee. I approached this sauce from Elizabeth Ayrton's *The Cookery of England* with some scepticism but I can thoroughly recommend it. You will need 300 ml of cold, strong, strained black coffee (not instant!). Into this stir a teaspoon of salt, some pepper and the juice of half a lemon and marinate your steaks for about two hours. Take the steaks out and put the marinade to simmer, leaving aside just a little to baste the steaks with. Sauté the steaks, basting them twice as you do so. Thicken the heated marinade with a tablespoon of cornflour mixed to a smooth paste with a little cold water. Put the steaks to warm and pour the thickened marinade into the pan to cook for a minute. Pour a little over the steaks and serve the rest as a gravy in a sauceboat. This is an unusual but effective flavouring for meat. Chocolate, as shall be seen, may be used in a similar manner.

If you find this rather decadent and French you are in good company. Parson James Woodforde, the eighteenth-century epicure, after attending an elaborate dinner complained that 'most of the things were spoiled by being so Frenchified in the dressing', that is, in their method of preparation. He was not usually so peevish. His diary, eventually published in five volumes between 1926 and 1931, and now alas almost unobtainable, is a treasure trove of what was eaten in the eighteenth century. He was so interested in food that he daily described what he had for dinner. Although he was by no means against steak, he had even heartier fare on his mind most of the time. I am with him in his view that the truly English thing to do with your beef is to make a steak and kidney pudding out of it.

STEAK AND KIDNEY PUDDING

This archetypal English dish puts in an appearance rather late in the recipe books. It actually makes its début in Mrs Beeton's famous *Household Management* of 1859 although there is a similar dish in Eliza Acton's *Modern Cookery* (1845). Perhaps it was so familiar that like the hippopotamus it was thought so unique no one found it necessary to describe it. It is almost certainly much older than the nineteenth century. Two clues lead to this conclusion: the combination of fish and meat, and the method of cooking (which suggests it would originally have been boiled in a leather or linen bag in a cauldron). Whatever its origin, it is one of the great dishes of English cuisine and is particularly suited to winter eating.

You will get a better pudding if you make the filling in advance and let it rest for a day in the refrigerator. Certainly you should never put it hot into the crust or you will steam the interior and make the pastry soggy. For the filling:

1 kg blade steak
500 g ox kidney
2 tablespoons seasoned flour
1 large chopped onion
50 g butter
300 ml beef stock
300 ml red wine
250 g mushrooms
2 dozen raw oysters in their liquor
bouquet garni

Don't buy ready-chopped steak and kidney. It is almost always nasty gristly stuff and full of fat besides.

Trim the meat and chop the steak and kidney into neat pieces. Lightly flour it. This is a bit of a messy job if you do it in an open plate. I prefer to put the flour and meat together in a plastic bag and to shake it vigorously for a few minutes, which does the job admirably. Lightly brown the onion in most of the butter, remove and put to one side and increase the heat. Brown the meat rapidly in batches and add it to the onions in a casserole. Pour the stock and wine into the frying pan and boil it vigorously so it gathers in all the bits on the bottom of the pan and boils off the alcohol. Add this to the casserole. Fry the chopped mushrooms in the remaining butter and add them to the casserole with the bouquet garni. Cook covered in the oven at 150°C for a little more than an hour. Remove and store.

For the crust:

300 g self-raising flour
1 teaspoon baking powder
½ teaspoon salt
a little white pepper
½ teaspoon thyme
150 g chopped suet

The combination of one part suet to two parts flour is the classic suet pudding preparation. Mix the dry ingredients in a bowl with your hands and slowly dribble in the water until you have a stiff dough. Be sparing with the water, or the flour will become sticky and unmanageable. Put a quarter of it to one side and roll out the larger part into a circle. Butter a large pudding basin and press the circle of dough into it, leaving a little overhang. Add the filling.

If the filling seems a little watery you may need to heat it on top of the stove until it has reduced, although this will be a nuisance because you will then need to cool it again. Add the oysters at this point and remove the bouquet garni. Don't forget to include the oyster liquor. Test the seasoning

147

and add more if necessary. Roll out and fit the pastry lid by folding over the overhang and pressing it firmly into place. Fit the lid of the pudding basin, set it in a few inches of water in a saucepan and simmer. It will take about two hours to cook this pudding but once it is cooked it can be left simmering for up to a further hour without spoiling, thus allowing you flexibility to deal with other items for your meal.

To serve, it is best not to turn the pudding out. This can lead to a tragic disaster with the pudding bursting its banks all over the kitchen bench and the cook having a nervous breakdown. Instead, pat the pudding basin dry, remove the lid and tie a white starched napkin around it for serving. This looks frightfully traditional. If you like, rather than boiling down the filling when you first make it, you can ladle the excess off and bring it to the table boiling hot in a jug with the pudding. Then, after you have served a couple of helpings, pour this into the pudding, and it will amalgamate with the gravy. You can do the same thing with beef stock if you have any to hand.

You will not need any potatoes or other starch with this of course, but a dish of plain steamed vegetables complements it very well. I prefer brussel sprouts but the vegetable of the season is always best.

The inclusion of thyme as a savoury in the suet crust is particularly appropriate to a beef dish. The Greeks, who burned thyme as an incense, named it *thumus* as the giver of courage, fitting attribute of the bull. It was also reputed to inspire eloquence. Pliny remarks that it could drive away all things venomous, which suggests a use for it in politics. During the French revolution, it was the symbol of thorough-going republicanism. In country lore they say that if you look at a fairy ring through thyme oil in a phial washed first with rosewater you will see the fairies dancing. On balance my preference is to eat it. It also goes superbly with poultry.

I think there is nothing finer than steak and kidney pudding, but some people find it rather homely. If you are on the lookout for a rather more grand traditional English dinner dish, then the next one is for you. It is in the same line as the lamb royale already described.

BOMBARD OF VEAL

When you see this dish in its final form you will understand why it is so named. It has the sort of ornamental form and colour that medieval cooks liked very much, although this is an adaption of an eighteenth-century recipe. There is quite a lot of work involved in it and you should be prepared to devote most of an afternoon to its preparation, with breaks for reviving cups of tea. In fact if you don't have any stock to hand you will need to start the day before. The result, when it is borne in in triumph, is worth the effort.

1 leg fillet of veal cut into thick slices (one for each guest plus two extra)
1 litre of strong beef stock, well seasoned and with all fat removed
a large tin of tongue
4 rashers of lean bacon
180 g breadcrumbs
120 g lean cooked ham
240 g mushrooms
3 large artichoke bottoms
2 tablespoons of fresh parsley
1 teaspoon each of thyme, marjoram and mace
2 lemons
120 g suet
200 g cooked, chopped spinach
3 egg yolks
1 medium onion, chopped
seasoning to taste

Open the tin of tongue and cut the meat into six pieces. Put the jelly separately into a bowl and combine with half the breadcrumbs. Mince two slices of the veal with the bacon and the ham and mix this with the breadcrumb mixture, half the suet, the mace and the pepper and salt. Bind it with two of the egg yolks. Make this into a ball.

In another bowl combine the remaining suet and crumbs, the spinach, chopped onion and the parsley, thyme and marjoram. Bind this with the remaining egg yolk. Now, here is the tricky part. You must work this around the other ball so that you have two round shapes one inside the other, the outside one being green. This is called the bombard, because of is resemblance to a cannonball. Sit down now and have a cup of tea. The bombard is baked in a well buttered, covered casserole in an oven preheated to about 180°C. It takes about an hour or maybe a little more.

The artichoke bottoms should be cooked in advance (in salted water for about 30 minutes) and as the bombard begins to cook (say twenty minutes in the oven) warm the artichoke bottoms in butter. Sauté the mushrooms in butter also and keep them warm. You should also have your stock simmering gently on the top of the stove, and your remaining veal steaks dusted in seasoned flour. When the bombard has been in the oven for about thirty-five minutes, begin to poach the veal in the stock. When the bombard is cooked take it out and cut it in half. Turn the oven down to 100°C. Lay both halves flat side up on a *large* ovenproof serving plate. Lay the fillets of veal around it, interspersed with the sliced tongue. Ladle a little of the stock over the veal and tongue and intersperse the mushrooms and artichokes. Cover the whole thing with foil.

By now the oven should be at a reduced heat. Return the whole dish to the oven where it will keep hot but not overcooked for a little more than half an hour. Round up your guests and serve them the first course which should be something prepared in advance. You will then be able to slip out to the kitchen and with a negligent 'I just knocked this up' air, bear in the uncovered bombard. As with the steak and kidney pudding a very simple dish of steamed vegetables is all you need with this.

For a while after preparing such a dish you will want to rest on your laurels a bit. There is nothing better for that purpose than beef stew, cooked in a casserole by the slow method. Here are two recipes which can both be prepared the night before and put into an oven at 100° C on the morning of the dinner to cook all day. This is very useful if you have an elaborate or complicated dessert or other course to prepare because it allows you complete flexibility. It is almost impossible to overcook these dishes if you use the slow method and they are there whenever you want them. I also find a stew useful if I am entertaining during the week. I just slip the dish into the oven before I go to work and when I come home it is done and waiting while I prepare the vegetables. If you plan properly you can raise the oven temperature once you have taken out the meat dish, and while you are eating the main course, cook a dessert you have also prepared in advance.

STIPHATHO

I'm not much in the habit of repeating dishes. If they are good they might get a return once or twice a year. *Ars longa, vita brevis* as Sir Francis Bacon was wont to remark. But this one I come back to again and again. The recipe is Greek and I first ate it on the island of Crete, but in every European cuisine there is an equivalent. In English we would simply call it a stew; it can be made with almost any meat but it is best with beef in my view.

> *1200 g beef, after removal of fat*
> *4 tablespoons olive oil*
> *600 g onions, chopped*
> *3 cloves garlic, chopped*
> *6 tablespoons tomato purée*
> *250 ml red wine*
> *salt and pepper, flour, bouquet garni*

You can use cheap cuts of meat for this dish. In fact if you buy too expensive a cut you will not get such a good dish. Once as a joke I served this at a dinner party made with the meat I usually feed my cat as the principal ingredient. Nobody knew that they were not getting the best steak and they were astonished when told afterwards. It's partly the combination of ingredients and partly the slow cooking which accounts for this. The intention is to produce a very rich sauce.

Heat the oil in a pan and brown the onions and garlic. Remove. Trim the meat, cut into neat cubes, then flour, season and brown. Transfer to a casserole with the onions and the other ingredients. If you like you can add a bay leaf. Then just put it in the oven for ten hours minimum at 100°C. It is really one of the simplest dishes I know. In the mountainous northern region of Spain, the Asturias, they make the same dish with wild pig and using a mixture of white wine and vinegar instead of the red. There it is called *jabali estofado*.

STEAK CASSEROLE WITH WALNUTS

When I was a child we had a very large and ancient walnut tree from which was slung a canvas hammock. Walnut trees are marvellous to climb and I remember mounting high into the branches or swinging lazily in the hammock on summer Saturday afternoons. I expect some self-righteous ass has now chopped the tree down. Each autumn we collected the ripe nuts and put them to dry out in an outhouse. We never thought to preserve or pickle the soft green unripe fruit, which always fascinated me.

The tree was well-known to the Romans. Pliny says it was introduced from Persia. Walnut trees grew in Italy as early as 100 BC and have always been common in France but were not introduced into England until Tudor times. Nicholas Culpepper, the seventeenth-century herbalist, says that walnuts are very good infused with onions, salt and honey for treating the bite of a mad dog. I am not inclined to test this theory.

Walnuts have a delicious spicy taste when pickled. If you are lucky enough to have a walnut tree and want to pickle your own you will find an excellent recipe in *Jams, Pickles and Chutneys* by David and Rose Mabey. Eliza Acton has a rather interesting one too. Otherwise they can be bought fairly readily.

1200 g steak
12 pickled walnuts
3 bay leaves (from a tree if you have one)
3 tablespoons plain flour
250 ml red wine (or half wine/half beef stock)
3 chopped onions
300 g chopped tomatoes
teaspoon sugar
salt and pepper to taste

Cut the fat off the meat, cube it neatly and roll it in the flour. Put it in layers in a casserole with the other ingredients. Sugar, used sparingly, brings out the flavour of tomatoes. Sprinkle in the left-over flour and pour over the wine. Cook slowly in the way described above. The walnuts impart a smooth texture and superb dark brown colour to the dish.

Culpepper also had views on the subject of bay leaves: 'Neither witch nor devil, thunder nor lightning, will hurt a man where a bay tree is.' So if you have never been bothered by these afflictions you now know the reason why.

Pork

Pork occupies a more exalted place in New Zealand cooking than it does in England, where it is one of the cheaper meats (insofar as any meat in England can be said to be cheap). When a friend of mine is searching for a description of the ultimate in costly celebration he always ends by exclaiming 'and pork chops ran in the gutters'. This is probably because the English colonists who came here, being mostly rural labourers, had always kept a pig as an asset, 'the gentleman who paid the rent', and had a feast of pork only when the beast was slaughtered. The folk memory survives, although it is growing dimmer as factory farming gets into its stride (and flavour goes out the window).

There have been domestic pigs in Britain since pre-Roman times and porkers were introduced here as a domestic animal very early in our colonisation. They should not be confused with the animals released by Cook and subsequent early European navigators. These pigs ran wild and are still rooting up the hills. They are game rather than meat and we will get to them in due course.

We all have a vision in our minds of the sucking pig with the apple in its mouth borne in to the medieval feast. Although I have several recipes for a roast suckling pig I have never got around to cooking one. Frankly I am not too sure how my butcher would react if I asked him to get me one.

December was the ritual hog-slaughtering month in medieval Europe when stock could not be kept during the winter. During preceding weeks they were driven out to feast on the acorns in the woods. 'Masterage', that is, the right to graze hogs in the woods in November, was a jealously guarded medieval privilege. Such foraging must have imparted a marvellous flavour to the meat, although there were apparently certain attendant risks. 'At Michelmas safely go sty up thy boar/Lest straying abroad ye do see him no more,' warned Thomas Tusser. Medieval manuscripts abound with pictures of pigs as food. The *Da Costa Hours* produced in Bruges in 1520 has an extraordinary illustration of a pig being bled prior to butchery. And in the recent Italian cinema production *The Tree of Wooden Clogs* there is a fascinating pig slaughtering sequence — although it is not for the squeamish.

If you can bring yourself to eat pork again after that you might care to try the following:

MITOON OF PORK

I don't know the origin of this name except to say that 'oon' apparently means great or large when used as a suffix. This dish, which comes from the north of England, is almost a terrine of pork, but not quite because the pork is used in strips rather than minced. It requires some preparation in advance but can then be cooked very quickly and easily. I suspect it is a variation on a similar dish now out of favour called a 'pulpatoon', of which more hereafter.

8 rashers of lean bacon
1 kg of pork strips
1 teaspoon mace
50 g butter
300 ml strong jellied stock
500 g forcemeat

Bake the pork strips in the oven for about an hour, covered, at 180° C. Allow to cool.

Make a forcemeat as follows: mix together 250 g of breadcrumbs, 125 g of suet, 125 g chopped smoked ham, 2 teaspoons chopped parsley, 2 teaspoons mixed herbs, salt and pepper. Bind the whole with two well beaten eggs. Thoroughly butter a casserole and line it with the bacon. Press a layer of forcemeat about a centimetre thick into the bottom. Slice the pork strips finely and layer them on top. Season with mace, salt and pepper. Pour in the stock and cover with the remaining forcemeat, which should be dotted with pieces of butter. Cook in an oven at 180° C for forty or fifty minutes and turn out onto a serving dish for the table if you feel confident it will not go everywhere as you are doing so. I usually serve it from the casserole.

This is a similar dish to the tongue and mushroom crumble described earlier. It is a rather unconventional use of pork just as the following is an unconventional use of bacon.

QUORN BACON ROLL

The Quorn is one of the oldest hunts in England and one of the few which still survives in all its glory. Whatever you may think about blood sports (abattoirs are not very pleasant places either), the sight of a hunt in full cry is an astonishing and exciting spectacle. I suspect a good deal of the opposition to foxhunting or harecoursing is as much a matter of dislike of the upper class yahoos who do it as of cruelty to animals. I know that bulks large in my consideration; I never used to like them in restaurants in England either.

This dish was served to the servants who followed the hunt, while their betters were tucking into their post-hunt galantines or whatever upstairs. My mother would have called it a roly-poly.

153

240 g plain flour
180 g shredded suet
800 g rolled bacon in a single piece
1 teaspoon sage
1 onion, finely chopped
salt and pepper
1 tablespoon chopped fresh parsley

Mix the flour, suet and a little salt, and add enough cold water to make a stiff dough. Roll this out thin enough to wrap right around the bacon. If you have trained your butcher well enough he won't stare when you ask for bacon in the piece rather than sliced rashers. Do ask him however how salty it is and if necessary soak it overnight if you suspect it of being too salty. If you do not it will be uneatable. Cut the strings and fold it out. Put the sage, onion, a little salt and rather more freshly ground pepper in the centre and roll it up again. If it won't stay rolled, skewer it. Now enfold it in the suet dough and seal the joins by moistening and pressing. Wrap it up tightly in a well floured cloth (a teatowel, say) and tie it. Pop it in a pot of boiling water for two hours, at the end of which time it should be cooked, but if you are a little unsure give it a little longer. Unwrap it and serve it with a hot apple sauce.

APPLE SAUCE

Where would pork be without apple sauce? Everybody has their own recipe. Here is mine.

250 g tart cooking apples
1 small quince if you can get one
150 ml water
heaped tablespoon sugar
1 strip orange zest
50 g butter
freshly ground black pepper

Cut the apples coarsely without peeling or coring. Peel, core and grate the quince. Simmer with the water, sugar and orange zest until it is soft. Sieve it and return it to the pan. The pips and skin should remain in the sieve. Cook the purée briskly until it is drier, say three minutes. Remove from the heat, beat in the butter and grind pepper over it. With the above bacon roll and sauce, steamed green peas or beans are the best accompaniment.

BAKED PORK WITH ORANGE

If you are unalterably wedded to the notion of a joint of pork then here is a summer recipe for a joint to be served cold.

> *a joint of pork, about 2 kg*
> *150 ml clear chicken stock*
> *dried parsley, marjoram and rosemary*
> *4 tablespoons dry white vermouth*
> *3 oranges*
> *olive oil*
> *3 cloves garlic*
> *salt and pepper to taste*

Bone and skin the pork joint and skewer it into a roll, more or less. Chop the garlic and rub it and the dried herbs well into the meat. Alternatively you could secrete them in the bone cavity before skewering, in which case about a teaspoon of each herb will do. Barely cover the bottom of a baking dish with water, put in the meat and add the skin and bones. Cook at 200° C for about 15 minutes to sear it. Reduce the heat to 155° C. While that is happening remove the dish and pour in the stock. Return to the oven and cook uncovered for 3 hours or perhaps a little less. Baste it from time to time with the stock.

About half an hour before the end of the cooking, remove the bones and skin and discard. Squeeze the juice of half an orange over the joint and add the vermouth. Slice the remaining oranges into very thin slices and blanch them for three minutes in boiling water. Remove the meat from the dish and put on a serving plate to cool. Strain the sauce into a pan and cook it for a further 30 minutes or so. Poach the drained orange slices in it for five minutes and drain them again. Arrange them around the joint. Strain the juice into a serving boat and leave to cool. When it is cold, skim the fat and serve this with the joint the next day. This is a superb dish on a summer evening with a fresh salad dressed with orange segments accompanied by fresh bread. In my experience indeed there is only one better way to eat cold pork, and that is to brawn it.

PIG'S HEAD CHEESE

Why 'cheese'? I have often asked but I have never been able to find out. My guess is that in earlier times the same technology was used as in the dairy for the making of cheese — the mould, the press and so forth. We would more usually today call this a brawn but the old name is quite evocative and should be kept. Making a brawn from the head of a pig is an old tradition.

Until the fifteenth century at least, wild boars were common in England and were hunted in winter not with hounds but with the much larger mastiffs. Anyone who has hunted wild pig in this country will know why; they are extremely fierce. In medieval times the brawn made from the head and forepart was a delicacy served on Christmas Day, but by Tudor times it might be eaten at any time over the twelve days of Christmas. Its place in the feast had also changed. In menus of the thirteenth century it appeared last with the game birds, along with a rich pottage called peverade (still served with venison as poivrade, i.e. pepper sauce — originally a bread sauce but now made with vinegar, stock, tomato and pepper). Or it was served as a sweet in a spiced syrup of wine and honey. Meat in a sweet syrup seems odd to us but is very common in medieval recipe collections.

A couple of hundred years later it had become a traditional first service. At the feast for the enthronement of Archbishop Nevill in 1467 we find 'first' brawn and mustard out of course served with malmsey', i.e. sweet wine from Monemvasia in Greece. Note the appearance of mustard, still the traditional accompaniment to cold pork or ham. The first published recipe for pigshead brawn is by William Harrison in the reign of Elizabeth I. 'A great piece of pork to be served at the table', he describes it, 'from November until February be ended, but chiefly in the Christmas time. With the same also we begin our dinners each day after each other.'

Obtaining the head of a pig is not too difficult if you warn your butcher a few days in advance. Sometimes they are on display and you can simply buy them then and there. They are relatively cheap although there is a lot of waste bone and other bits and pieces. Get the butcher to split the head into two or three parts and be sure that you have got the tongue, which is a principal ingredient. You may on the other hand discard the brain unless you like to eat it, in which case there is a famous and much celebrated dish *bouchées à la Reine*. The Queen in question was Marie Leszczinska, daughter of the King of Poland and gourmet wife of Louis XV. It involves brains, mushrooms, cream and *béchamel* sauce served in a vol-au-vent. Personally I do not care for brains and so my cat dines well when I make this dish.

You may find it best to put your pig's head in a brine for a couple of days. This not only improves the flavour but gives the meat a good pink colour. A recipe for brine is:

3 litres of water
325 g sea salt
325 g brown sugar
60 g saltpetre

You may have a little trouble with the saltpetre, as it is one of the principal constituents of gunpowder. You will get a suspicious look at the pharmacy and be asked to sign for it. My chemist is now used to me and asks cheerily, 'Pork brawn again is it?'

Clean a large pan very carefully and rinse it with equal care. Bring the ingredients to the boil, take it from the heat and add the following tied up tightly in a muslin cloth:

1 teaspoon of juniper berries
small piece of whole nutmeg
1 bay leaf
1 teaspoon thyme
1 teaspoon peppercorns
4 whole cloves

When it is cool, put in the pig's head and a pig's trotter. If you don't have a container big enough for this you can strip some of the meat off the bones first, particularly around the jawbone, which should be discarded. Leave this to soak for two or three days in the refrigerator, well covered. At the end of that time discard the brine and bring the head to the boil in clean water to draw off the salt. Discard the water and replace it so that the head and trotters are covered. Now add the following ingredients:

2 onions
2 carrots
2 leeks
2 cloves of garlic
2 bay leaves
2 sprigs of parsley
1 teaspoon thyme
8 peppercorns
2 tablespoons wine vinegar

Cover the pan tightly and bring this slowly to the boil. Simmer it gently for at least four hours until the meat is dropping from the bone. Strain and keep the liquid. Pick the meat off the bones and throw the bones and vegetables away. Chop the meat into small pieces, except the tongue which should stay whole. *Don't* mince it. Season it with a mixture of allspice, cloves and nutmeg ground very fine.

For the jelly, take 400 ml of the strained liquid, add half a bottle of dry white wine and boil it down to 400ml again. Add two teaspoons of salt and a tablespoon of lemon juice. Simmer the meat in it for 20 minutes and let it cool. Put the meat in a mould. Pour the liquid over the top. Refrigerate overnight and turn out the following day, by which time it should have set.

I serve this dish at Easter. Not only is it good for a long weekend but it is a melancholy farewell to summer and autumn before winter sets in in earnest. Being a valedictory it naturally needs a mustard sauce.

Frightful things are done to mustard in the interests of sauce. You should not buy it made up, but make up your own fresh whenever you need it. Complaints against made mustard are nothing new. After giving a recipe in *Delights for Ladies* in 1600 (not the sort of book it sounds like), Sir Hugh Plat goes on to say: 'I thought it verie necessarie to publish this manner of making your sauce, because our mustard which we buy from the Chandlers at this day is many times made up with vile and filthy vinegar, such as our stomack woulde abhorre if we should see it before the mixing thereof with the seeds.' Nothing has changed, it seems, in four centuries. It is best to get mustard and soak it overnight in vinegar. The usual is a white seed *Brassica alba* although there is apparently a *Brassica nigra* also which I have never seen. Then the next day strain it and grind it to a smooth paste with wine vinegar, wine and a little honey and a pinch of cayenne. This at any rate is the method of Robert May who published *The Accomplisht Cook* in 1660, and was endorsed by Alexandre Dumas in 1873. Who am I to argue in such exalted company? Boulestin, a famous chef of the thirties, once dismissed a waiter on the spot because the mustard was wrong. That's probably taking things too far.

When you get your pig's head, you will find that the ears are missing. I don't know what they do with all those ears. Perhaps they are made into silk purses. There is however another use for them and that is to eat them. The French have been doing it for years and it has never done them the slightest harm; if you want to surprise your friends then here is how to do it:

PIG'S EARS WITH LENTILS

If your friends are of a retiring disposition tell them that the dish they are about to sample is made from *oreilles de porc*. With your butcher you will need to confront the matter head on (if you'll pardon the expression) and earn yourself some odd looks. You may also be interested to know that until the nineteenth century the English ate pigs' ears as a matter of course. Parson James Woodforde dined upon them with his patron Charles Townsend, MP for Yarmouth, in 1791. It doesn't seem to have done them any harm either.

2 pig's ears for each person
12 garlic sausages or bratwurst
small piece (say 300 g) smoked bacon
500 g brown lentils
1 large onion
2 leeks
2 carrots
3 cloves garlic
bouquet garni
butter, salt, pepper, parsley, lemon juice

Wash the ears thoroughly and singe off the bristles. If you brine at the time, pickle them for two or three days. Simmer them gently in a *court-bouillon* for about an hour and a half but keep an eye on them to make sure they do not disintegrate. Drain and put to one side. Put the lentils, the chopped onion and garlic, the whole white part of the leeks and the carrots, the smoked bacon and the bouquet garni in a pot, burying the ingredients in the lentils. Cover with water and simmer in the oven for an hour. Don't add the salt at the beginning, it will make the lentils go hard. Remove the pot and add the pigs' ears by just laying them gently on the top of the dish. Return to the oven and continue to simmer covered for about another half hour. You will have to use your own judgement as to the amount of water. Not too sloppy and not too dry. When the dish is cooked you should then remove the bouquet garni, add the salt, pepper, lemon juice and enough butter to taste without overdoing it. Chop the parsley and sprinkle it over. In the meantime grill the sausages separately. Bring the whole thing to the table in the cooking pot with the sausages. Again, this dish is good with a mustard. Your friends will either leave at once or enjoy it immensely. Either way they will dine out on the experience for a long time.

Lentils have been around for centuries. They ate them in ancient Egypt and still do today. The Lady of Han, wife of the Marquis of Tai, an important gentleman in China in the second century BC, was so fond of them she was buried with a bag of them, presumably to sustain her in the afterlife. We do not eat them much, which is a pity; they are really rather good and very nutritious. Brown or green lentils are to be preferred; the red or orange ones not only disintegrate (and are thus suitable for *dhal* in Indian cookery) but they can bring on frightful attacks of flatulence. Unlike most pulses they do not need to be soaked. But watch out for grit. I shall have a little more to say about them when we get to the vegetables.

Main Course: Poultry & Game

My heart's in the Highlands, my heart is not here;
My heart's in the Highlands a-chasing the deer;
Chasing the wild deer, and following the roe;
My heart's in the Highlands wherever I go.

— Robert Burns

WHEN I WAS a child our Christmas treat was a 'chook'. About a week before the great day my mother could be espied marching grimly in the direction of the hen run with a tomahawk in her hand. My father could never be induced to play any part in this activity and the rest of us offered up a silent prayer that the scene of the crime would be hidden by fruit trees and bushes. There would come a frightful squawking and eventually mother emerged bearing the headless corpse of this year's hapless victim to be bled, plucked and gutted in the wash-house. On Christmas morning the result would be stuffed with bread sauce and roasted.

My mother was acting out a scene which was archetypal until this generation and the invention of the battery hen. Marcel Proust in *Swann's Way* recalls the cook, Françoise, performing the same rite in his childhood.

> I saw her in the scullery, which opened onto the back yard, killing a chicken which, by its desperate and natural resistance, accompanied by Francoise beside herself with rage as she attempted to slit its throat beneath the ear, with shrill cries of 'Filthy creature! Filthy creature!', made the saintly meekness and unction of our servant rather less prominent than it would do, next day at dinner, when it made its appearance in a skin gold-embroidered like a chasuble and its precious

160

juice was poured out drop by drop as from a pyx. When it was dead Françoise collected its steaming blood which did not however drown her rancour for she gave vent to another burst of rage and gazing down at the carcass of her enemy uttered a final 'Filthy creature!'

Mother would have been surprised to know that what she was doing had been thus celebrated in literature; she was merely preparing her annual festival offering.

For the rest of the year we ate mutton or mince. Certainly, until I was an adult, I never tasted turkey, although on a couple of notable occasions wild duck came our way. The thought of eating a goose, pheasant or pigeon would never have occurred to me. Game, strangely enough, was different. Wild pig or venison we had from time to time although I forget how it was cooked. Some of the cheaper eating houses in Christchurch actually had deer meat on the menu but it was regarded as pretty poor fare. Rabbits I knew had been eaten in the past because my father and his friends talked about it but these were no longer available because of 'disease'. Of the wealth of food varieties and recipes available for poultry or game I had no inkling. Chickens are now of course commonplace, although the means of their raising makes them tasteless in comparison with the birds of my childhood. And rabbits more recently have also put in a mass-produced appearance. Pheasants, hare and wild pig can be got if you know where to look. Regrettably the farmed venison we now obtain has not the lean and gamy quality of its wild relations. If you want that, you must cultivate the hunting fraternity.

Recollect as you do so that both poultry and game have been eaten since the dawn of recorded history. The domestic hen, however, at least as we know it, is descended from a Northern Indian bird, and did not arrive in Europe, via Persia, until classical times. It was in Britain before the Romans, according to Julius Caesar, although he himself observed a taboo against eating both chickens and geese, probably totem birds of the *gens* Julian to which he belonged by adoption.

No such inhibitions have since that time prevented generations of Europeans from eating both land and sea fowl. The medieval English enjoyed a wide range of birdlife at which we would today turn up our noses. Cranes, peacocks and other exotic creatures found their way to the pot. Among now virtually extinct methods of hunting them were falconry and a curious sport in the area from Yorkshire to Dorset which involved chasing and running down bustards with greyhounds.

Medieval markets always had an area given over to poultry and most manors boasted a dovecote. Birds were roasted or stewed in a pottage. Even the poor could enjoy this type of food although they largely ate rooks, thrushes or even wrens which they had snared for themselves. Roast birds were usually stuffed with onions and fruit; it is from this that cockie-leekie is descended. Large birds such as peacocks were reserved for the nobility. They often formed the highly decorated centrepiece at a formal banquet. 'Take a peacock,' begins a medieval description of a bird, 'in his hackle (i.e. in his feathers), break his neck and cut his throat and flay him the skin and feathers together and the head still to the skin of the neck . . . ' and it ends: '. . . and then wind the skin with the feathers and the tail about the body, and serve him forth as if he were alive.'

Swans seem to have been treated in a similarly undignified manner on special occasions. Dame Alice de Brynn gave a great feast for a hundred people on New Year's Day 1413 and two swans figured prominently on the menu (along with twelve geese, twenty-four capons, seventeen rabbits and two pigs). The great Northumberland Percys by their account books ate five swans every Christmas, four for Twelfth Night and two on St Stephens Day. Some curious customs concerning rights to swans still survive in England.

Until the eighteenth century or later even the poorest ate a goose at Christmas or harvest home if they could get one. Turkeys of course came from the Americas, with the returned explorers. Most traditional methods of cooking poultry and game birds, as galantines, for example, survived into the early nineteenth century but they have now all but died out. I feel this is a great pity and have included a recipe for a very simple galantine in this chapter. The habit of eating a large bird at Christmas came to this country with the first settlers from Europe. I suppose my mother's annual descent upon the hen run in the guise of the grim reaper is a survival of that tradition. Buying a turkey at the supermarket isn't the same somehow. You need not of course always get one drawn and plucked.

Drawing, Plucking and Boning Poultry and Feathered Game

The ability to bone a bird prior to stuffing and roasting is one of those skills which every competent cook needs to master. Plucking and drawing is an ability needed more rarely but is something useful to know, because certain types of game birds in particular, if they come your way, will almost certainly be in their undressed state. You will need to know what to do with them.

You should take particular care to ensure that the blood has been properly drained, particularly if the birds are to be hung. Blood goes off rapidly and can taint the whole carcass. In medieval times it would have been kept for making a sauce; this is considered a bit grisly these days (although quite proper in the case of furred game). Game birds should usually be hung, otherwise their flavour will not be noticeably different from chicken and you might just as well not have bothered. Hang them up by the neck in an airy, cool place, feathers, insides and all, for about four days to let the meat mature if they are freshly killed when you get them. This will startle your friends if they come into your kitchen and find themselves unexpectedly confronting a row of dead pigeons or whatever, but that cannot be helped.

When you come to pluck the bird(s) do it somewhere where you will not be bothered by feathers flying about. Some people like to pluck over a bucket of water which certainly keeps the feathers down but you then have the problem of what to do with a bucket of water and feathers afterwards. I pluck into a plastic bag. Pluck from the tail towards the head, taking care not to damage the skin. You will find that the feathers will come out quite readily if you pull firmly, although you will be astonished by the number of feathers on even the smallest bird. You may need a pair of tweezers to get the last of the small feathers out. After you have finished plucking, pass the carcass over a flame, e.g. of a gas ring, to singe off the down and fine hairs, and wipe it over.

Drawing is not much fun and is best done onto several thicknesses of newspaper. I wear rubber gloves, a refinement my mother would have scorned. Cut the head off the bird so as to leave a certain amount of neck and then split the skin and remove the crop. In a larger bird you might like to keep the neck for making stock or gravy. If you do, rinse it well. Insert your fingers through the hole at the neck and carefully break the threads attaching the organs to the interior of the carcass. At the other end cut off any soiled part of the vent and slit it to widen it. Again, insert your fingers and loosen the inside, then carefully draw out the entrails. Above all try not to break the gall bladder which is attached to the liver. This will taint the meat with a bitter taste if it is broken. Keep the heart, the liver and the fat, and wash out the interior of the bird thoroughly. Pat it dry with a paper towel. Finally you will need to remove the feet and leg sinews. Cut off the feet at the first leg joint. If the sinews do not come away with them, make a lengthways slit in the leg to expose them, hook a skewer under them and pull them out. In both this and in boning, practice makes perfect, although it is not for the squeamish.

BONING

Most people confronted by this task for the first time are terror-stricken and do not believe they can do it. In fact it is quite easy and speed and skill come with experience. The trick is to use a very sharp small knife and to take it slowly. If you hurry you will pierce the skin and end up with something that is literally a dog's breakfast. What you are doing is creating a container to subsequently stuff. Begin by cutting a deep slit down the back of the bird to expose the backbone and then, cutting as close to the bone as you can, cut and scrape the meat away from the carcass down one side. When you come to the joints of the leg and the wing, very carefully insert the knife in the joint and cut through. Keep going until you reach the ridge of the breast and then stop, turn the bird over and do the same on the other side. By this time the whole thing will look like an unholy mess. You should not however be discouraged. Cut along the breast to complete the task and lift out the carcass bones complete. Use this for stock. Some think you should also bone the upper leg and wing bones but I think this is in the 'stuffed mushroom'

163

category; too much trouble in relation to the result. If you now take the bird and lay it down on what was its breast on a flat surface and spread it wide, your boned carcass will be ready to stuff. As with the caucus race, so with boning a bird; the only real way to explain it is to do it. It is really a good deal easier than it sounds and once you have done it a couple of times you will wonder how you ever got by without this skill.

Once you have got the bird stuffed you might like to sew it and truss it. This makes it easier to handle but there is the problem of getting the thread out afterwards. I prefer to skewer it and then to lace thread through the skewers. At the end of cooking I then remove the skewers and the lacing simply lifts off. If you do sew it, it is best to use fine string and a small sailmaker's needle. You can finish by making two or three loops around the whole thing as if you were tying a roll of meat or an old-fashioned parcel, by tying the wings into the body and finishing with a loop over the legs to tie them in tight too. This will give you a neat finished item and the bird will not lose its shape during the cooking. It is particularly important to do this if you are going to cook the bird in a pastry case. Armed as you now are with these skills no bird will hold any terror for you.

Chicken

Almost anything which can be done with chicken can be also done with a rabbit. Chickens stuffed with a range of ingredients have been favourites since at least Roman times. These ingredients have varied. One recipe from Apicius incorporates pepper, lovage, ginger, chopped meat, breadcrumbs, a brain, eggs, peanuts, garum and oil. Every age to its flavours I dare say. By the time of Geoffrey Chaucer most manors kept chickens and geese in a courtyard; their care usually fell to the dairymaid. In a large town such as London, chickens could be obtained from specialised and licensed poulterers. Medieval market laws were strict and punishments severe for those who infringed them. The markets are commemorated now only by place names but they make a fascinating study. In medieval English they were designated 'cheaps' and their doings were strictly regulated by the ringing of bells. Poulterers from outside London for example were confined to Leadenhall, while the freemen poulterers used Cornhill along the west wall of the church of St Michael. Wholesale chickens could only be sold prior to 6 am, which was the hour of 'prime' and none after the vespers bell. If you sold anything at all after the hour of 'nones' you could have your goods seized. The purpose of this was to prevent 'eve chepynges' which often ended in a riot because of the numbers of thieves, pickpockets and prostitutes who congregated at markets in the evening. If you were able to obtain your chicken in the midst of all these rules you would have cooked it something like this:

FARSED STUFFED CHICKEN

1 large roasting chicken (2-3 kg)
200 g lentils
400 ml beer or stout
300 ml chicken stock
350 g cherries
300 g ricotta cheese
300 g oats
2 tablespoons butter
½ teaspoon dried basil
teaspoon salt
200 ml white wine
3 or 4 slices of bread, crumbed

Soak the lentils in the beer overnight. Next day cook them in the liquid for about 15 minutes. Drain them, and reserve the liquid. Mix the drained lentils with the pitted cherries, ricotta, oats, salt, butter and basil. Bone the chicken, stuff it with this mixture and skewer it. It should then be roasted at 180°C for about 2 hours. Whenever you are roasting a chicken (or any bird) lay some strips of fat bacon over its breast and rub the flesh with butter. Put a very little butter in the roasting dish. This will stop the flesh from drying up. This chicken should be served with a sauce made by simmering together the wine, breadcrumbs, 300 ml of the lentil liquid and salt and pepper, for about ten minutes.

As with other dishes fruit was widely used in cooking poultry in medieval times and it survives in one or two well-known dishes today. One of these is that famous Scots delicacy cockie-leekie.

COCKIE LEEKIE

There are always arguments about whether this is a poultry dish or a soup. In my view it is the former and is one of the few remaining examples of a method of cooking, i.e. in a cauldron, which was the widest known from the time of the invention of the iron cooking pot until almost the present. Why this particular way of cooking chicken has been long regarded as typically Scottish I do not know; perhaps pottages simply survived there longer than in England or elsewhere. It had become specific to Scotland as early as 1598. Fynes Moryson who was there then and didn't think much of the food remarked nevertheless that in a knight's house 'the upper mess instead of porridge had a pullet with some prunes in the broth.' The prunes were particularly important. In 1743 Lady Grisell Baillie wrote a special note to her housekeeper requiring her to put them in the dish. It has even been known to move the Scots, a people legendary for their dour solemnity, to verse:

I've supped gude bree i'mony a howff
    Wi'in Auld Reekie
But non wi' seccan a gusty gowff
    As cock-a-leekie.

That is to say, that while many of the taverns of Edinburgh serve tasty savoury soups, there's none so good as cockie-leekie. Quite right and an opinion endorsed by the chef Alexis Soyer.

1 chicken leg for each person, or a boiling fowl
500 g prunes
1 kg stewing beef in a piece
1500 g trimmed leeks
salt and pepper to taste

Soak the prunes overnight. Four hours before the meal put the beef trimmed of fat in a pot (which will also later hold the chicken). Cover it with water, bring it to the boil, skim it and let it simmer for an hour. Add the chicken, salt and pepper and half the leeks, whole and tied together. Twenty minutes before the end of the cooking take out the bundle of leeks and put in the prunes. Slice the remaining leeks and add them to the dish 5 minutes before serving so they stay crisp. Give each person a slice or two of beef and a leg of chicken (or a piece), some prunes and leeks and pour the liquid over it. It needs nothing else with it.

This dish has shared exalted company. According to that almost legendary Scots tavern keeper, Margaret Dods, who kept the inn at Howgate and who wrote *The Cook and Housewife's Manual* (Edinburgh 1826), the diplomat and gourmet Talleyrand, dining with Lord Holland, praised the dish and made some enquiries concerning it. Regrettably Sidney Smith was not present that day so we have no record of a learned and witty disquisition on the matter. The only Scot present, Lord Justice Jeffrey, was unable to help. Margaret Dods was of course immortalised by Sir Walter Scott in *St Ronan's Well* as Meg Dods who presided over the Cleikum Club at the Cross Keys Inn in Peebles. The inn still stands although I have not eaten there.

There is a much more elaborate version of the same basic dish called Hindle Wakes in English cookery. It is obviously a medieval festival dish and involves stuffing a hen with a suet and prune forcemeat, steaming it for some hours and then roasting it wrapped in bacon. It is then eaten hot or cold with a lemon sauce. There have been a number of fanciful attempts to explain the 'Hindle' in the title of the dish, none of them satisfactory. 'Wakes' were periods of overnight vigil kept prior to the patronal day of parish churches, which were holidays. Feasting would have been a part of this holiday and the dish served came to share the name.

A pottage of chicken is common to most cuisines. The Spanish have a version which is particularly tasty.

POLLO EN CHAMFAINA

This dish comes from Catalonia where George Orwell served with the anarchist militia during the Spanish Civil War. The food at the front, he wrote afterwards, was 'good enough' but he wasn't any more specific than to say it was composed of bread, and stew cooked in a cauldron. He does mention a café in Barcelona but not because of the food — he was in fact throwing bombs at it because it was full of Civil Guards. I am sure that if he had eaten chicken in chamfaina sauce he would have mentioned it; it is a most memorable dish.

1 chicken (or 1 leg for each person)
1 tablespoon lard and the same quantity of oil
1 onion
2 aubergines
2 courgettes
100 g of smoked ham
1 green and 1 red pepper
6 tomatoes
200 ml chicken stock
a bay leaf, thyme, nutmeg, salt and pepper

Cut up the chicken if you are using a whole one. Brown the pieces of chicken in an iron pot in the olive oil and lard, which should be very hot. Chop and add the onions, unpeeled courgettes and aubergines, and the ham. Sauté this for ten minutes then add the chopped tomatoes, a teaspoon each of the nutmeg and thyme, the bay leaf and salt and pepper to taste, pour in the stock and cover the pot. Simmer gently for three-quarters of an hour. Serve with sippets of toast.

Olive oils can differ vastly. Spanish olive oil is a beautiful pale yellow and has a particularly sweet taste. Other olive oils can be strong and the quality of some from other countries is questionable; Spanish oil is always of consistent quality in my experience. It is of course much cheaper to buy it in quantities of four litres or more.

CHICKEN GUMBO

European pottages crossed the Atlantic to the Americas with the early explorers and traders and there they survive in regional cuisines. A particularly good example is gumbo from the southern part of the United States, coastal Louisiana.

For many years I thought that *file gumbo* was a gumbo made of steak. Only recently I have discovered that *file* is actually powdered leaves of sassafras, a large tree growing along the eastern seaboard of North America. Its leaves are widely used as a flavouring and thickening agent in the Cajun sub-culture of the region. I have never seen it on sale in this country so I have no idea what it does to the taste of this dish. Just to confuse the matter, Cajun music is also called gumbo, or so my musicologically inclined acquaintances tell me.

250 g cubed ham
6 chicken legs
125 g chopped onion
3 cloves chopped garlic
1 red pepper, seeded and chopped
375 g okra
lard
1 tablespoon flour
250 g chopped tomato
1 tablespoon tomato concentrate
bouquet garni
1 or 2 dozen mussels
salt, pepper, cayenne, parsley

Heat the lard in a pan and in turn brown the ham, chicken, onion, garlic, pepper and okra. Transfer them as you go to a large iron pot. When you have done them all, stir the flour into the pan, cook for a minute then add the tomato, the concentrate and enough water to make a thin sauce. Pour this over the browned materials in the pot and add the bouquet and seasonings. Simmer for about an hour and about ten minutes before the end add the mussels. Remove the bouquet and sprinkle on the parsley before serving with plain boiled rice. Chicken and mussels is a traditional combination.

Okra (sometimes known as ladies' fingers) is a most unusual and elegant vegetable. It is actually a native of tropical Africa; its name derives from Wi language *nkurama* and the word gumbo from an Angolan Umbundu word *ochignnombo*. It crossed the Atlantic with the slavers and the word became part of black slave patois in New Orleans. This patois is called gumbo as well. Okra gives a magnificent jelly-like smoothness to a stew and is particularly good in combination with tomatoes. It can usually be obtained tinned, and very rarely fresh.

CHICKEN PIE

Another European import which acclimatised itself to the eastern seaboard of the United States and settled down to become a native American was the chicken pie. Thomas Jefferson, who was not only third president of the Republic but a noted gourmet who employed two French chefs at his mansion Monticello in Virginia, was particularly partial to it.

One of the pleasantest meals I have ever eaten was at Old Sturbridge Village, a 'living museum' of the late eighteenth and early nineteenth centuries, in Massachusetts where, among other attractions, there is an inn serving food which is contemporary to the Federalist period in New England. A favourite dish there is chicken pie. What characterises it in particular is that the chicken filling is cooked in a sauce, prior to its encasement in pastry.

1 large chicken
flour and butter
salt and pepper
120 g lard
300 ml milk
½ teaspoon salt

Cut up and boil the chicken in water until it is tender. Let it cool, and strip the meat from the bones. Reserve the broth. While this is cooking make a pastry by melting the lard and blending it with the milk. This should then be poured into sufficient plain flour to make a stiff dough. Roll this out to about a quarter of an inch thickness. Cut off about a quarter of this and put it to one side. Line a deep pie dish with the rest.

Make a roux from 3 tablespoons of butter melted in a small pan and a tablespoon of flour seasoned lightly with salt and pepper. Cook this for 3 minutes, stirring constantly, and then blend in 400 ml of the chicken broth. Cook for a further five minutes.

Cut the chicken into chunks and strips and lay in the pastry case. Pour enough sauce over to cover it. Cut the left-over dough into strips and arrange in a lattice over the chicken in sauce. Bake at 200°C for 20 minutes in a preheated oven then lower to 180°C and cook for a half-hour or until the pastry is cooked. This dish is best hot, and traditionally is eaten with glazed beets.

The day I ate lunch at the inn at Old Sturbridge, the waitress was inclined to chat and told me that the recipe for the pie I was having came from Vermont. Sometimes this pie is prepared and cooked in the kitchen of the Pliny Freeman Farmhouse at Old Sturbridge in conditions mirroring those which would have obtained in the early years of the nineteenth century.

Traces in the cooking of that period in New England allow the links with the earlier European tradition to be seen. A part of that tradition which does not seem however to have translated across the Atlantic was the use of garlic. As I have remarked in an earlier chapter, this herb also fills many New Zealanders with horror and many prejudices abound concerning it. As recently as 1969 a cookery writer, in a book still in print, could describe garlic as 'an evil-smelling plant' and go on in all seriousness to say: 'Its use has come into Australia and New Zealand since the war with Continental (*sic*) people who have been used only to poor meat. While we eat hogget, they have been used to horseflesh. (That is one reason why French sauces are so good — they have to disguise very often what is underneath.) We have no real need to follow imported fashions that are unsuitable to our own food, but there's no accounting for taste.'

So much for five hundred years of French culinary tradition. Of course quite apart from the question of what a lot of people in other countries think of our fat lamb (uneatable rubbish), the writer of the passage quoted seems entirely unaware that 'garlic' is an Anglo-Saxon word and that it has been a constituent of English cooking for centuries. It was well-known in ancient times (it gets a mention in Homer) but not everyone is enraptured by its aroma. Horace remarks upon its unpleasant smell and Shakespeare has Bottom say in *A Midsummer Night's Dream* 'eat no onions nor garlic for we are to utter sweet breath'. Since medieval times there has been an annual garlic fair at Tours on St Anne's Day (July 26th) which is still very much an event. More recently it has been celebrated in film. If you ever get the opportunity you should see Les Blank's *Garlic Is As Good As Ten Mothers* which is a very witty and uncritical paean of praise to *Allium sativum*. Which is not only my way of saying that I am an equal fan of garlic but also my preamble to the following recipe, which is one of those culinary improbabilities that turn out to be a delight. And just incidentally, like most good cooking it is the height of simplicity.

GARLIC CHICKEN

2In his very interesting book on Provence, Ford Madox Ford tells the tale of an elegant model in London who loved garlic but found it combined badly with her profession until she realised that *uncut* garlic eaten as a vegetable left no taint. That, as it happens, is to my certain knowledge untrue, but it does not detract one whit from the pleasure of this recipe; if my friends cannot tolerate garlic then they are no friends of mine. Season a large chicken both inside and out and peel at least 500 g of garlic. No that isn't a misprint. Leave the peeled garlic whole and put about half of it inside the chicken. Use a roasting dish or better still a chicken brick. Make a layer of the remaining garlic on the bottom of the dish interspersed if you like with fresh chopped green beans. Seal the dish and roast the bird for approximately an hour and a half at 190°C. For the last ten minutes or so you can take off the top and allow it to brown. Serve the garlic (and beans) as a vegetable garnish with a crisp green salad. Although the peeling of all that garlic will take some time it is well worth the effort, the smell of the dish cooking is indescribable, and it will exude juices which the vegetables will absorb. It is excellent in late autumn.

More suited to summer is the next and final chicken recipe which is a simple galantine.

CHICKEN GALANTINE

A galantine broadly speaking is a dish made from meat, poultry or fish and served in its own jelly. Such dishes were very common in the medieval and Tudor periods. The jellies were often very highly spiced; last survivor of this is the cranberry jelly we still traditionally eat with poultry and game, or Cumberland sauce for venison. Nobody much eats galantines these days except as a part of a terrine, which is a pity because they are excellent summer fare.

2 kg chicken
2 pig's trotters
2 or 3 onions
4 cloves garlic
1 leek
1 carrot
2 bay leaves
350 ml dry white wine
salt, pepper, and lemon

Blanch the trotters in boiling water for ten minutes and skim off the grey foam. While that is doing rub the chicken with the cut lemon and season it to taste inside and out. Put it in a large pot with the vegetables, the bay leaves, a few peppercorns and the blanched trotters. Cover it with about a litre of water and simmer it for two hours. After the first hour add the wine. Very carefully remove it from the pan (boiled chicken has a tendency to fall apart) and set it to cool. Cook the liquid for another hour and then strain it into a bowl retaining the carrot. The next day it should have jellied, but if it has not then after removing the fat you should reduce it. In either event the chicken should be put in its serving dish, surrounded by the pieces of cooked carrot, and the warm liquid strained over it. It should set in a refrigerator. The chicken is carved in the usual way and the jelly served with it. Again, a crisp salad is the best accompaniment.

The tradition of cold food served in its own jelly is at least as old as Apicius; the pig's head cheese recipe given in an earlier chapter is a galantine. The recipe above is simpler than some others. For instance a duck may be boned, stuffed and encased in pastry. After its cooking the pastry may be lifted and a jelly poured in.

Game

Chickens have come to be rather in a category of their own. Other birds are really feathered game, although the domestic breeding of duck and turkey particularly on a factory scale puts them somewhat between the two. Wild duck are more flavoursome and harder to obtain than the domestic variety;

171

there are no wild turkeys in this country. Pigeons and pheasants are game properly speaking and are now coming available. Just a few years ago pheasants were unprocurable, whereby hangs a tale . . . but in due course. Other birds such as goose or quail I have never seen on sale although the latter are fairly readily available in Sydney and Melbourne. Perhaps in time we will have the advantage of seeing them here.

DUCK

My first attempt with duck was rather disappointing. That was my own fault because ducks need special care in their handling. They have two drawbacks. They can be very fatty, so that they need to be carefully cooked to make sure a fair bit of that fat goes in the process (although not all or they would then be too dry); and there is not nearly as much meat on them as you would find on many other birds. This is resolved by boning and stuffing them. In particular ducks respond to being cooked with fruit and preferably a fruit which is a little tart. The classic dish in that regard is the famous *canard à l'orange*.

Sometimes when you get a duck or other gamebird it will be moot as to whether it died of gunshot wounds or old age. Old birds are tough and should be steamed for twenty minutes or so preliminary to all else. The younger the bird, the more tender. For the following recipe use duckling.

DUCKLING WITH ORANGE

The credit for this classic must go to the nineteenth-century chef Denis Vuillemot, who collaborated with Alexandre Dumas on his famous *Dictionnaire*. It was a particular favourite of Dumas. Contrary to my rule ducklings are not boned because they are quite small. Beware incidentally of the descriptions on the exterior packaging of ducks. For some unfathomable reason they are sometimes denominated 'duckling' when they are mature adults. If you want real duckling you will have to cultivate your poulterer. Make sure you get the livers and giblets.

2 ducklings with livers and giblets
2 carrots
2 onions
large stalk of celery, chopped
3 spring onions
butter
350 ml of dry white wine or vermouth
250 ml beef stock
3 oranges
2 egg whites
pepper, salt, lemon juice

172

Melt some butter in an iron casserole and brown the chopped vegetables, then add the ducklings and some salt and let them heat and begin to render their juices for about ten minutes. Then add the wine, stock, giblets and livers. Cover and simmer until cooked, perhaps 2 hours.

While that is going on prepare two of the oranges. Peel off the zest and blanch it. Cut the zestless oranges into segments and towards the end of the cooking of the duck simmer these gently in water for about ten minutes. Put the ducklings on their serving tray surrounded by the orange segments and keep them hot. Pour away the fat from the cooking liquid and strain the remaining juices into a shallow pan. Boil them down and drop the egg whites into them. These will draw out the impurities in the sauce and coagulate on the surface. When you have the right concentration strain off the now clear liquid and add pepper, the zest and the juice of the third orange. Pour a little of this around the duck, put the rest in a sauce boat and . . voilà, *caneton à l'orange* just like Alexandre Dumas used to make.

Duck is traditionally served with unminted green peas. I recommend it particularly in combination with plain boiled rice to absorb the juices and any fat which may have slipped through the skimming. The next recipe is also with fruit but in this case dried apricots. If you can get a wild duck so much the better. Most duck in this country is shot over fresh water. If your duck has been near the sea it may taste obtrusively fishy but this can be reduced by cutting an onion in half and leaving it inside the duck for a couple of hours. It will absorb most of the fishiness and can be discarded.

DUCK WITH APRICOTS

1 large duck
½ an onion, sliced
3 stalks from the heart of celery
1 teaspoon thyme
50 g butter
1 tablespoon flour
1 tablespoon bitter marmalade

Stuffing:
150 g dried apricots
60 g breadcrumbs
100 g butter
½ chopped onion
2 large tablespoons chopped celery
salt and pepper

Soak the apricots overnight and drain them. Chop them roughly and mix with the breadcrumbs and the onion. Cook the celery gently in the butter for ten minutes then add both to the apricot mixture with salt and pepper and mix thoroughly. This is your stuffing.

Bone the duck and keep the carcass to make stock or soup. Salt the boned duck (remembering that there is already salt in the stuffing) and stuff and skewer the duck. Lay it on a bed of celery and onion in a deep roasting dish and pour in water until it is about half an inch up the side of the duck. Put it covered into a slow oven at 160° C for about an hour and a half. Remove it to a serving dish and keep it hot. Strain the liquid into a pan and boil it down to about half. Knead the butter and flour thoroughly together and beat it into the liquid which should be kept just below boiling point. As it begins to thicken, stir in the marmalade. Serve this sauce separately in a sauceboat.

In her book *French Country Cooking* Elizabeth David has a variation on this recipe, using figs instead of apricots. The fruit is soaked overnight in sauternes and the strained sauternes provides the cooking liquid. This would be too sweet a dish for me so I have not tried it, but it sounds interesting. A method of cooking duck with a sweet glaze that I *have* tried was certainly worthwhile.

ROAST DUCK HYMETTOS

The appearance of 'hymettos' in a recipe title is a trigger word. If 'florentine' indicates spinach and 'crécy' indicates carrot then 'hymettos' tells us the dish contains honey. Honey has of course been used as a sweetening agent in cooking since time immemorial. In medieval times the important occupation of wild honey gatherer had a special name — *mellitarus*. From the late Middle Ages honey was increasingly replaced by sugar although it was still common until the eighteenth century. Lately it has been making something of a comeback. Traditionally the best honey in Europe has come from Mt Hymettos near Athens where it was doubtless flavoured by the wild thyme which abounds in the Greek uplands. For this recipe you should use the clear dark honey sold as 'bush' honey in health food shops.

> *1 large duck, about 2-3 kg, with giblets*
> *1 unpeeled onion*
> *2 tablespoons honey*
> *lemon juice, salt, pepper, oil, butter*
> *1 tablespoon arrowroot or cornflour mixed with two teaspoons water*

Stuffing:
> *60 g butter*
> *1 onion, chopped*
> *125 g walnuts*
> *150 g breadcrumbs*
> *grated lemon zest*

1 teaspoon each parsley, sage, thyme, marjoram, cinnamon
salt and pepper
beaten egg
lemon juice

Brown the giblets in a little oil, add the onion, salt and 500 ml of water to make a stock. Strain and set aside. For the stuffing, melt some of the butter and brown the onion until it is soft, add a little more butter and fry the walnuts until they are golden. Turn these into a bowl and mix thoroughly with the rest of the stuffing ingredients. Bone, stuff and truss the duck. Rub the exterior of the duck with butter and then spread with the honey. Pour the stock around and roast in a hot oven 190°C for an hour and a half. Remove the duck to a serving dish and keep it hot. Skim the fat from the juice, strain the remainder, add the lemon juice and arrowroot or cornflour mixture and heat until it thickens. The honey should have formed a sweet glaze on the outside of the duck. All these recipes for duck are much of a piece. Here is one on the other hand which bears little resemblance to them and is indeed something of a curiosity.

CASSOULET OF DUCK

Traditionally a cassoulet is made with a goose potted in its own fat. I have never seen such a bird on sale in this country. This one is made of duck. The traditional version, the *cassoulet de Castelnaudery,* includes haricot beans, goose, onions and smoked sausages, cooked in an earthenware pot or *cassol,* thus the name. This dish is I suspect an older forebear of the same dish. It must be subsequent to the sixteenth century because haricot beans are a New World contribution to European cookery. But its sweet and sour flavour is typical of pre-eighteenth-century European cooking. It is said to derive from French Canada and to have entered American cooking by way of New England. It is similar to Boston baked beans in its use of molasses and that simpler dish may have derived from it. Certainly, such a survival isn't uncommon in colonial societies which are conservative about the traditions they have brought from 'the old country', long after the original has developed into something else entirely.

½ kg dried haricot beans
1½ litres of beer
½ litre beef stock
2 bay leaves
2 chopped onions
a piece of chopped fresh ginger
1 lemon, chopped

1 teaspoon raw sugar
125 ml treacle
2 tablespoons Worcestershire sauce
1 tablespoon English mustard
½ teaspoon cumin
1 teaspoon dried savory or mint
125 g belly pork
1 large duck

Soak the beans in the beer overnight. Without draining them put everything except the duck in a large iron pot and bring it to the boil covered. Then bake it for three hours at 180° C making sure from time to time that the liquid is still covering the beans. If it is not, add hot water. While this is going on bone the duck and cut it into six pieces (or however many are eating the dish). Brown these pieces lightly in lard and when the beans are done take the pot from the oven and remove half. Place the duck on top of the remainder and then cover by returning the other beans. Give the dish a further three hours as before. By the end almost all the liquid should have been absorbed by the beans. They should be served in that form with a plain green vegetable.

This dish is very rich and its combination of strong flavours is not to everyone's taste. If your friends are not adventurous in their eating you would be unwise to serve it to them. But for me it is an ideal dish to introduce those embarking on a voyage of culinary exploration to the notion of other times, other food.

TURKEY

The turkey ranks with a few other products — tomatoes, chocolate, white beans — which have had a profound effect upon European cuisine since their introduction from the Americas three or four hundred years ago. Turkeys seem to have come into European cuisine about 1520 although they had been domesticated in Mexico long before. It is well known that the settlers at Plimouth Plantation ate turkeys for their first thanksgiving dinner, though theirs were the wild variety. Turkeys quickly replaced cranes and peacocks as a suitable great fowl for feasts in Europe, to the extent that they were prohibited in 1541 in an ordinance of Archbishop Cranmer's against extravagance among the clergy. By the seventeenth century they were traditional Christmas fare and were driven on foot to London in great herds from East Anglia. These drives took three months and must have been an extraordinary sight to behold.

In France where the bird was known as the *coq d'inde* they appear first as a children's pet in 1528, but by 1549 Catherine de Medici was serving

sixty-six of them at a banquet. By 1767 the *Dictionnaire portatif de Cuisine* enumerated more than forty ways to prepare them for the table. The paramount luxury then, apparently, was to stuff them with truffles; given the price of these latter it still is. Sir Kenelm Digby liked to stuff his with garlic; Brillat-Savarin stuffed his with garlic sausages. There is a description of a New England wild turkey hunt in *The Philosopher in the Kitchen* in which the turkey got away (a variation on the fish) but in which the sportsmen bagged some fat partridges. The painter, Claude Monet, who like many of his fellows was a considerable gourmet, did a superb painting of white turkeys feeding on a green slope. No doubt he enjoyed them cooked and stuffed as well as he liked the birds as painter's models. In Normandy they stuff turkey with apple and chestnuts, a recipe I have never tried. In fact I have only one recipe for turkey, which I have been using every Christmas for as long as I can recall. Every year I tell myself that I must try something new but always I return to this recipe because it is so delicious.

turkey
350 g each of pork and veal
the giblets of the turkey
250 g smoked bacon

3 onions, chopped
3 cloves garlic, chopped
1 green pepper, chopped
parsley, spring onions and the leaves from a bunch of celery
50 g butter
200 g chopped mushrooms
200 ml sherry
salt, pepper, bay leaf, ½ teaspoon each of nutmeg, thyme and sage
3 beaten eggs

Put the meat, onions, garlic, green pepper, parsley and celery through a mincer. Mix it thoroughly with the seasonings, the sherry, eggs and the mushrooms cooked in the butter. Cook the whole mixture in a pot for about 20 minutes, stirring so it does not burn.

Bone the turkey. This is just the same as boning a chicken only bigger and thus a longer job. Stuff it loosely, skewer and truss it. Put it in a roasting pan on a rack and brush it all over with melted butter. Cover the breast with a piece of larding fat, which your butcher will probably have available. (Ernie knew immediately what I was talking about. If your butcher looks at you non-plussed he doesn't know his business; change your butcher.) Roast the bird in a very hot preheated oven (230°C) for twenty minutes. This will sear it. Reduce the oven heat to 160°C. While it is cooking add to the pan 200 ml of port, plenty of black pepper, salt and a bouquet garni. Roast the bird for about three hours, basting from time to time.

Shortly before serving, remove it and keep it hot. Drain the fat from the pan juices, remove the bouquet and thicken the juices with flour to make a gravy.

The bird is just as good cold, in which case the accompaniment should be not gravy but a tart fruit sauce. Cranberry is the most traditional but this can only be obtained tinned and is not terribly flavoursome. If you can get some red or white currants (increasingly rare these days) they can be boiled with 500 ml of water to each 500 g of fruit and the strained result in its turn boiled with 500 g of sugar to each 500 ml of juice. This should set into an excellent jelly.

There is an entertaining description of jelly making and the difficulties associated with it in this sanforised, deodorised fast-food age, in the novel *Birds of America* by Mary McCarthy.

I prefer to serve this turkey as part of a cold collation. It seems to me the height of foolishness to turn on a massive hot roast meal in the middle of summer (although who has not at some time?). Tempers fray, cooks become hysterical, and the season of goodwill goes out to sea on the resultant flood of tears. Much better to have the cold turkey, game pie, a selection of salads and custards, etc. The following dish can also be served cold and is better for it, in my view. It will surprise and delight you, if only you are able to obtain the appropriate principal ingredient.

PIGEON PIE

I once became friends with a lady who worked in the delicatessen where I buy many of my more unusual ingredients. Until she left to open a pâtisserie of her own (out of my reach, which was lucky for my waistline) we would exchange recipes. One day she startled me by asking me if I would like a couple of pigeons. Her husband, it transpired, kept racers and from time to time weeded out his flock. Of course I said that I would, and before very long there they were hanging in my kitchen, feathers and all, to the disgust of my son and the shock of casual visitors who wandered in.

We ought to eat pigeons as often as we eat chicken. Until a couple of hundred years ago or less, they were a staple in English cuisine. During the Middle Ages almost every manor had a dovecote. Some still stand, curious circular towers without roofs and the walls honeycombed with nesting holes. The local peasantry never cared much for the keeping of pigeons as they lost too much of their grain crop as a result. To the gentry, however, pigeons were an everyday food item. They appear almost as often as chicken in Alice de Brynne's daybook for 1413. They made a most welcome addition in particular to the winter dietary when fresh meat was unprocurable. The Ingatestone Hall account books for 1552 record 1080 pigeons killed and eaten that year. Early settlers to New Zealand ate the native wood pigeon but these are now of course protected.

However you obtain your pigeons you will have to pluck and draw them for yourself. They need to be washed out thoroughly; pigeons have a great deal of blood in them.

2 pigeons
30 g butter
700 g shin of beef, cubed
1 litre chicken stock
salt and pepper
aspic jelly
200 g button mushrooms
puff pastry
beaten egg

Brown the pigeons and beef in the butter in an iron casserole, season, add the stock and simmer for about two hours. Allow to cool and separate the meat from the carcass, discarding the bones. Put the meats and the washed mushrooms in a pie dish with a funnel. Dissolve the aspic in the cooking liquid and cover the solid ingredients with it in the dish. Roll out the pastry, leaving a good overhang, and trim away the excess. Use this to make decorations. Dampen the rim pastry and press the cover onto it, making a hole in the centre. Press the edges with a fork to seal them and then gild the pastry and decoration with the egg. A pinch of salt dissolved in the egg will darken the glaze. Bake for about 30 minutes in an oven preheated to 180°C. Serve cold. You will be surprised at how delicious this pie is. It cannot however compare to a pheasant.

PHEASANT

'I am a great partisan,' remarks Brillat-Savarin, 'of secondary causes, and devoutly believe that the whole race of fowls was soley created to fill our larders and enrich our banquets. Over all these birds the pheasant takes precedence.' I wouldn't disagree with him, although I cannot go along with his suggestion that it should not be eaten unless it has been hung until it is high. Four days is enough for me. Pheasant is also unique in having never been domesticated, although it is hand reared. Thus, even although raised in partial captivity, it never loses the flavour of the wild.

My first introduction to pheasant was a little unusual. As part of a book I was writing, I went one day to see a man who had fought with the commando rearguard in Crete, in the same unit as Evelyn Waugh, who describes the experience in his novel *Officers and Gentlemen*. This man was head gardener on one of the great English landed estates, which I entered through the home farm. It was a beautiful late autumn morning. The wheat was ripe and golden and as I drove along I thought that the weather could hardly have been more perfect. Suddenly a pheasant darted out of the field and before I could brake it had glanced off the bumper and expired by the side of the road. What was I to do? I could hardly arrive bearing a dead prize pheasant, but neither could I leave it there. I flung it in the back, covered it guiltily with a blanket, and proceeded to my interview. Later it graced my table. Luckily I am no longer forced to such desperate expedients to eat pheasant.

PHEASANT WITH GRAPES

Among the things which January means to me is the appearance of cheap white grapes in the fruiterer, and then I know that the time has come to cook one of my favourite pheasant dishes. It is the simplest of meals but a rich luxury nevertheless.

a brace of pheasants
1 kg of white seedless grapes
120 g butter
2 glasses of white wine
salt and pepper
250 ml chicken stock

Season the birds inside and out and fill the cavity with as many grapes as the birds will take. Sew up the vent. Brush the pheasants with the melted butter and place them side by side on a rack in a roasting dish. Put a strip of larding fat on the breasts. Pour in the stock and the remaining grapes. Sometimes I add a little grape juice as well. Roast uncovered at 180°C for about 45 minutes. You must baste the birds often with the pan liquid or they will dry out and be spoiled.

When they are cooked, keep them warm with the grapes while you heat up the pan juices with the wine. Serve this separately in a sauce boat. There is only one accompaniment to this dish, and that is plain boiled brussel sprouts and lots of crusty baguette bread.

My other favourite dish of pheasant is a classic of French cooking.

FAISAN NORMANDE

This pheasant stuffed with apples is one of the glories of the European cuisine. For the stuffing:

50 g butter
2 onions, finely chopped
2 pheasant livers, chopped
200 g breadcrumbs
2 tart apples, peeled, cored and diced
parsley, salt and pepper

Fry the onions and livers in the butter for three or four minutes. In a bowl mix with the other ingredients to make the stuffing. Fill the interiors of a brace of pheasants and skewer them up. Truss and season the birds and brush their outsides with melted butter. Drape fat bacon or lard over their breasts and roast them side by side in a pan for 30 minutes in an oven preheated to 180°C. Remove them from the oven, pour 6 tablespoons of calvados over them and return them to the oven for ten minutes to brown. Keep them hot and add to the pan juices six tablespoons of chicken stock and four of cream. Heat this through and serve as a sauce.

There is a recipe for stuffing a pheasant which I have not tried; it comes from Georgia (the Russian one) and involves grapes, oranges, walnuts, Frontignac and an infusion of green tea. It all sounds rather too much for me but the chef Escoffier used to swear by it. He in his turn had it from *La gastronomie en Russie* published in 1860 so presumably it came back from the Crimean War by courtesy of a French officer. Pheasants can also be braised successfully in gin.

I remarked earlier that there was a tale to be told concerning pheasants. On one occasion I served Faisan Normande to, among others, a member of parliament. It transpired that about a decade previously he had been approached by a constituent who operated a poultry farm on the banks of the Waimakariri river. To his already formidable range of products this farmer wished to add pheasant, but had discovered that in our over-regulated society the law forbade it, pheasant not being contained in the appropriate schedule to the Poultry Act. My friend took the problem to Wellington, fount of all solutions, and there the deed was done — pheasant could then be sold in accordance with the Act. And now, a decade later, he was sitting down to enjoy the fruits of his political endeavours. Would that all such endeavours led to such gratifying results. In the light of the history of the English game laws it was deeply ironic that the author of this enlightened legislative move should have been from the Labour benches.

The game laws of England are one of those historical pecularities which, when come upon for the first time, beggar belief. It seems incredible now, but just over a hundred years ago it was absolutely forbidden to kill game except on landed estates beyond a certain quite substantial value. Even then the shooting had to be done by the eldest sons of esquires or persons of higher rank. No one else was allowed to kill game, to buy it or sell it, or even to *eat* it unless it came as a gift from a landowner. Penalties for the breach of this privilege were quite extraordinarily savage. In earlier centuries a man could be hanged for helping himself to a rabbit which, by law, belonged to someone else, and even as late as the early nineteenth century transportation was usual for those convicted of poaching.

Some squires took cynical advantage of this. In 1814 the Oxford Assizes record the case of Sir William Clayton who was sued for compensation. Sir William, it transpired, was in the habit of having his keepers drive his game into neighbouring farmland to the intense irritation of the farmers who were prevented by law from killing the offending animals. One of them, exasperated beyond endurance, had set his dog on them but the dog had run upon a trap at the outskirts of Sir William's estate and been speared by a javelin. The case, which was successful, sought recompense for the death of the dog.

Reformers, including the redoubtable Reverend Sydney Smith, mounted an eventually successful campaign against these laws and their associated paraphernalia of spring guns and mantraps. But while the law was in force there was little sympathy for landowners who relied upon its provisions. Juries were strangely reluctant to convict men who poached a rabbit in order to relieve the sufferings of their starving families. It was a circumstance indeed which led Mark Twain, after a visit to New Zealand where rabbits were considered vermin, to make a capital suggestion in *Following the Equator*:

> In England any person below the Heir who is caught with a rabbit in his possession must satisfactorily explain how it got there, or he will suffer fine and imprisonment, with extinction of peerage; in Bluff the cat found with a rabbit does not have to explain — everybody looks the other way; the person caught noticing would suffer fine and imprisonment with extinction of peerage. This is a sure way to undermine the moral fabric of a cat. Thirty years from now there will not be a moral cat in New Zealand. Some think there is none there now. . . . In England they fine a poacher, whereas he ought to be banished to New Zealand. New Zealand would pay his fine and give him wages.

This, as it transpired, was not necessary. Introduced disease all but wiped out the rabbit. This was fine for the farmers but had the unfortunate consequence that rabbit and hare disappeared from the market as food items. Now that they have come available again we have rather got out of the habit of eating them, which is a great pity because they are delicious. This is particularly so of hares which are still supplied from the wild (and are hard to come by) whereas most of the rabbit on the market is farmed and correspondingly blander for it. I suspect that the same thing will happen to venison.

Not, I hasten to add, that there is anything wrong with the farming of game. We have no foolish game laws here — with one exception. Trout alas cannot be legally cultivated readily and is reserved for those who can afford the privilege of fishing for it, an increasingly élitist pursuit. The sooner the farming of trout is introduced the better, I say, on behalf of all those whose idea of a good time is eating, not standing up to the waist in chilly water for hours on end.

RABBIT STEW

I had this recipe from my friend Ray Braine, a ruddy-faced forester from Bude. It was my culinary introduction to rabbit and so I have a soft spot for it. It is, I have since discovered, a very traditional recipe. In its original version it calls for a whole rabbit but rabbit legs are now obtainable and I prefer to use those.

6 rabbit legs (or one for each person)
200 g bacon cut into strips
120 g sultanas
12 prunes
3 large onions, chopped

500 ml dry cider
butter, sugar, flour, vinegar
salt, pepper, thyme

Melt about 50 g of butter in an iron casserole and brown the bacon and then the rabbit. When they are nicely browned, sprinkle a tablespoon of flour over them and pour on the cider. Add the onions, salt, pepper and a teaspoon of thyme. Simmer for about an hour, add the sultanas and prunes and simmer for an hour more. Just before serving, melt together three tablespoons of sugar and a tablespoon of vinegar. When it begins to darken, stir it into the rabbit stew. Serve on plain boiled rice.

PULPATOON OF RABBIT

This dish is variously named. I have seen it as Dorset rabbit but I prefer it as above. Pulpatoon is one of those peculiar English words like Cholmondely or Marjoribanks which is not said as it is spelled. This word is pronounced 'pupton'. A pulpatoon is a pie with a forcemeat crust. As a dish these were quite popular until the early years of the nineteenth century and then they inexplicably vanished from the cuisine. This is a shame because they are quite outstanding. This same use of a crust of crumbs is found in the cassoulet of Castelnaudery; the tongue and mushrooms crumble described earlier (and surviving fruit crumbles) are also pulpatoons.

6 rabbit legs
200 g bacon
2 tablespoons fresh sage
½ cup milk
salt and pepper

For the forcemeat:
4 large chopped onions
50 g butter
250 g breadcrumbs
zest of a lemon, chopped
3 tablespoons chopped parsley
1 egg
a little milk

Soak the rabbit pieces overnight in plenty of cold salted water. This will remove all the blood. Drain, rinse and pat dry. Roll them in seasoned flour and pack in a deep casserole with the bacon and the milk. Season them well and sprinkle with the sage. Make the crust by cooking the onions in a little butter until it colours and then mixing it with the crumbs, zest and parsley.

184

Bind it with the egg and the milk but be careful not to get it too wet, otherwise the dish will not work properly and the crust will be soggy.

Spread the forcemeat over the rabbit and cook in a preheated oven at 180°C for two hours, by which time the crust should be nicely browned. If it looks as though it is going to burn, cover with foil. The rabbit meat under the crust will be succulent and faintly pink. I am thinking of starting a movement to bring back the pulpatoon.

ROAST STUFFED RABBIT

This recipe is from the Canary Islands and is in Spanish *conejo guisado*. It's rather grand in my estimation, and just right as main course for a dinner. In the original recipe there's an ingredient *tocino* which is a form of salted pork fat and quite unprocurable here; I've substituted the Central European 'speck'.

> *2 medium rabbits*
> *100 g speck, diced*
> *1 cup of breadcrumbs*
> *100 g suet*
> *500 ml milk*
> *6 rashers of bacon*
> *1 glass white wine*
> *4 large onions, chopped*
> *2 cloves*
> *salt, pepper, parsley*

Soak the breadcrumbs in the milk for a couple of hours. Mix in the suet, speck, parsley, pepper and salt. Stuff the rabbits loosely with the resulting paste. Skewer. Put two of the rashers of bacon on the bottom of a roasting dish, put the rabbit on top and cover with the remaining rashers. Pour the wine over and roast at 190°C for about an hour and a half, basting from time to time. When it is just about ready make a purée from the onions in a little water with the cloves. Remove these latter when the onion is cooked, mash up the purée and serve with the rabbits which should be borne in on a platter and carved at the table.

The painter Toulouse-Lautrec in his collection of recipes published posthumously by his friend the chef Maurice Joyant also has a recipe for stuffed rabbit *lapin de garenne au gîte et aux olives* 'rabbit at rest with olives' which is as Provençal as the recipe above is Spanish. The stuffing includes mustard, beef, pork, liver, kidneys and stoned black olives, and the whole is swaddled in lard and roasted at a high temperature.

As far as we can tell, rabbits were originally natives of the Iberian peninsula, which makes the dish above particularly apposite. They were

185

introduced by the Romans everywhere they went and in some areas where rabbits had no predators they became at once a nuisance; the people of the Balearic Islands had to ask the Emperor Augustus for military aid to get rid of them. They were introduced into Britain as elsewhere and were bred in special enclosures called *leporaria* but they seem to have disappeared with the withdrawal of the legions. They were reintroduced by the Normans and again kept in artificial burrows known as conygers. There was a medieval specialist to look after these — the warrener. The rabbits, as rabbits will, quickly escaped and became feral.

The poor have always eaten them, despite the game laws of a later time. Special breeds of dogs were developed for coursing both rabbits and hares — greyhounds in particular. They were also netted and ferreted. Between 1529 and 1551 there was a closed season on both because they had been hunted almost to extinction. Unlike rabbits hares seem never to have been bred in captivity but to have always been game. They are native to all Europe and most of Asia. If you value your teeth, watch for shot in a present-day hare.

HARE IN CHOCOLATE SAUCE

I know that sounds odd as a flavour but I urge you to attempt it. Chocolate was introduced from the New World in the sixteenth century and is still an important ingredient in both the Mexican and Iberian cuisines. I first ate it at a Mexican restaurant in London as a constituent of a sauce for turkey. I took a lot of encouraging to try it but eventually was persuaded and found it quite delicious. We are so used to eating chocolate combined with sugar that we forget that it has a bitter flavour in its natural state. Even so-called 'cooking' chocolate has sugar in it. You should try and obtain some bakers' chocolate. Combined with that other American import, the tomato, it makes a sauce of strong flavour ideal for serving with game. It is too sharp for other meats.

1 hare, jointed
3 rashers bacon, chopped
lard
2 large onions, chopped
2 large carrots, chopped
400 g tomatoes, chopped
2 cloves garlic
beef stock
2 cloves
1 tablespoon wine vinegar
3 teaspoons bakers' chocolate
1 glass sherry
salt, pepper, nutmeg, parsley

Brown the hare and bacon in the lard. Put the meat in a casserole, add the vegetables and cover it with stock. Stir in the parsley and other seasonings to taste with the exception of the chocolate and sherry. Simmer until the meat is cooked. Keep it hot while you put the liquid and vegetables through a blender, transfer it to a saucepan and stir in the chocolate and sherry. Cook for about five minutes and pour it over the hare to serve. This needs something very plain as an accompaniment. Buttered tossed noodles are ideal. At Bilbao they cook a dish of partridges this way *perdices à la bilbaina*. Whenever I serve this dish I challenge my guests to tell me what is the main flavouring in the sauce. Nobody has got it right so far.

HARE PIE

From the exotic to the traditional. This recipe can be used to make one of those magnificent free-standing cold game pies which are a triumph at any table. You will need a pie mould to get the proper effect. Prepare the filling in advance.

For the filling:
  1 small hare
  1 sliced carrot
  2 sliced onions
  bay leaf
  2 glasses port
  aspic
  salt and pepper
  200 ml beef stock

187

Strip the meat from the carcass and cut into chunks. Keep the carcass for game stock. Cook these chunks very gently in a casserole with the vegetables, stock and seasonings for about three hours at 150°C well covered and let it cool. Keep the port and aspic separate and to one side for a moment.

For the pastry:
  500 g plain flour
  125 g butter
  125 g lard
  5 tablespoons water
  salt, pepper and a teaspoon of thyme

Put the flour in a bowl and make a well in the centre. Fill this with the chopped butter and lard. Bring the water to the boil and pour it over the fats, which will soften and dissolve. Mix in the flour and the seasonings. It should form a fairly stiff dough. Cut off a piece for the lid, roll out the rest and use it to line the bottom and sides of the pie mould. Put in the cold hare filling. Dissolve the aspic in the port and pour this in too. Roll out your cover and put over the top. A pie funnel is useful. Make a small hole in the top to allow the pie to steam, and gild and decorate the lid. When you are putting on the lid raise the rim up about half an inch. It will improve the look of the final product. Now (and this is most important) leave the whole thing uncooked in the refrigerator overnight for the pastry to stiffen.

Bake it in a hot preheated oven, 200°C, for about thirty minutes. When it has cooled, carefully remove the mould. Of course it can be eaten hot if you prefer but this is to miss the effect of the aspic. Try a hot chestnut purée with this. In some parts of Europe they serve both hare and rabbit in a walnut sauce; I know of at least one restaurant in Wellington where this is a standing item on the menu. Nuts and small game make a very interesting combination. For larger game however it is fruit which, in my estimation, makes the most delicious dish.

VENISON WITH CHERRIES

With a growing export market, the introduction of lucrative domestic farming enterprises and a decline in numbers because of more efficient culling methods, good wild venison is getting harder to obtain. In most countries *de facto* game laws apply; hunting venison is an occupation for the very rich. When I was living in Britain some years ago I was told by an acquaintance who was a senior forester with the Forestry Commission that a week's shooting cost at least the equivalent of ten thousand dollars without any guarantee of even seeing a deer. Doubtless the cost has not gone down in the meantime but there was no shortage of takers. We are not yet at that stage, the saints be praised. It is still possible for anyone who can afford the gun to indulge. If you have neither the time nor the inclination, find a hunter and cultivate him or her.

Most of the deer in New Zealand are red deer, liberated in Nelson's Matai Valley in 1851. There are however a number of other species — fallow, wapiti, sika, sambar and even moose. Good quality venison is dark red and has very little fat. The best cuts are the haunch and the loin. Almost all deer needs marinating unless it is very young, and even then it needs a good deal of basting during cooking to ensure that it does not dry out. The enthusiast can try larding; personally I find it too much bother.

1 loin or haunch, at least 2 kg
150 g butter
3 sliced onions
1 tablespoon flour
150 ml kirschwasser
2 cups pitted black cherries
zest of lemon
salt and pepper

Marinade:
juice of three lemons
2 tablespoons olive oil
1 teaspoon crushed coriander
2 teaspoons thyme
2 cloves garlic
bay leaf
350 ml red wine

Marinate the meat for at least eight hours, turning it from time to time. Drain and pat dry. Brown the meat in the butter in a large iron casserole with the onions. Flame it with the kirsch, sprinkle on the flour and strain the marinade over it. Simmer it covered on top of the stove for 2½ hours. About half an hour before serving, add the cherries and sprinkle the chopped zest on top. Serve on a hot dish surrounded by the cherries and the sauce poured over the top or served in a sauce boat. Venison needs plain potatoes and a strong tasting vegetable such as sprouts or broccoli. I have sometimes used a slow cooking technique but this is risky because venison shrinks and can become very dry and fibrous unless carefully watched and basted. One of the best ways to avoid this is to bake a joint in a pastry case, preferably made with suet.

VENISON EN CROÛTE

I have never been able to fathom why a joint of meat cooked in a pastry shell has become associated with the Duke of Wellington. There is no record that he was a noted gourmet or even that he was particularly fond of this or any other dish. On the contrary he was such a boor over food that his chef left him. Personally I think he was a frightful man who bitterly opposed the extension of the franchise in the Reform Act of 1842, thought soldiers should on no account be allowed to have opinions on anything at all and when asked why he had joined a particular London club replied that it was so that when it rained he could stand in the window 'and watch the damned people get wet.' Naming a boot after such a man is very fitting, but a dish as lordly as venison — never! Besides, the habit of wrapping meat in pastry preceded him by many centuries.

Parson James Woodforde, at the same dinner in 1791 at which he had the grilled pig's ears, also records that he had 'beef-stake tarts in turrets of paste'. The practice actually goes back to medieval times when pastries enclosing meats and moulded in fantastical shapes were common at banquets and feasts. Gervase Markham gives a recipe for a leg of mutton in a pastry case. It was a good way of keeping in the juices when there were no plates but only bread trenchers, and it gave you something to hold on to while you were eating it. You will need quite a lot of pastry.

1 haunch of venison
1.2 kg plain flour
600 g chopped suet
water
salt and pepper
125 g butter
150 g strong game pâté
cooking foil

For once you will not need to marinate this joint, although you can if you like using the marinade from the previous recipe. Make a stiff pastry from the flour, water and suet seasoned to taste. Smear the joint with softened butter and the pâté and season it well. Wrap it in the rolled out pastry so that it is well sealed and then wrap it again in cooking foil. Some people find this easier to handle if the joint is boned and trussed, in which case fill the cavity with pâté. Cook for three or four hours in an oven at 180° C. This may seem a long time but the foil will prevent it burning.

Remove the foil shortly before the end so that the pastry can brown properly. Alternatively you can use the suet pastry from the steak and kidney pie. The Reverend Sydney Smith (who said that some people's idea of heaven was eating pâté de foie gras to the sound of trumpets) and who was a deep-dyed political enemy of Wellington, was also extremely fond of venison. Lord Lansdowne, who was one of his political cronies, once sent him a present of a haunch but the label was lost and it was some time before

Sydney found out who had sent it. In his belated letter of thanks he remarked: 'It struck me at the time that to send venison to the clergy without saying from whence it came was an act of high-principled and profound charity.' I thought of calling this dish Venison Sydney Smith. He was at least a noted gourmet and has more right to the honour than that man Wellesley. He would also have known that there is only one fitting accompaniment to large game — the following.

CUMBERLAND SAUCE

This sauce is named not after a place but a person, Ernest, Duke of Cumberland, brother of the Prince Regent, last independent ruler of Hanover, and a contemporary of Sydney Smith. Why it was named after him nobody seems to know, although the sauce itself is very German. Take the zest of two oranges and two lemons and blanch it. Heat together 250 g redcurrant jelly, a teaspoon of mustard, the juice of the oranges and lemons, the drained zest, 5 tablespoons of port and a teaspoon each of ginger, salt and pepper. Simmer this mixture for five minutes and strain; serve hot or cold. This sauce will keep for up to a week. It goes as well with a leg of wild pig as for the marinated venison above. To my astonishment I was once given a leg of wild pig in a street in Auckland by a man I hardly knew. I shared this astonishment around by taking the pig leg back to my hotel and inviting the receptionist to put it in the freezer until I was ready to go.

Although she was a little non-plussed by this strange request she complied. You meet all sorts working in a hotel no doubt. Its subsequent journey by air to my table did it no harm; it was delicious. Wild pig in Queen Street is rare; for yourself you will probably have to go to more rural parts to get it.

Although any venison recipe can be adapted to wild pig I promised earlier some recipes specific to itself. Here European cookery books will do you little good. They speak of wild boar as if it were as rare as unicorn. Most give a single recipe as much for its curiosity value as for practical purposes. The latest that Elizabeth David could find to quote in *French Provincial Cooking* had last been published in 1913. Lilli Gore, in a book devoted to game, actually includes it in a chapter given to such curiosities as bear paws and buffalo steaks. As she appositely remarks, if you find a wild boar in Britain it must have escaped from a zoo. On the other hand they still have it running around loose in Sicily where this recipe comes from.

BOAR IN SWEET AND SOUR SAUCE

Sweet-and-sour we associate too readily with the Chinese. As this book has shown already, there are a number of traditional European combinations of these flavours.

Marinade:
    600 ml dry white wine
    300 ml wine vinegar
    1 onion, 1 stick of celery and 2 carrots, chopped
    bouquet garni
    3 cloves
    10 crushed juniper berries
    2 tablespoons olive oil
    salt, pepper and thyme to taste

Boil these ingredients together, let them cool and marinate the wild boar in them for forty-eight hours. Remove it, dry it, bone it if necessary and roll and tie it. Keep the marinade.

    lard
    salt and pepper
    6 rashers bacon, diced
    bouquet garni
    1 carrot and 1 onion, chopped
    200 ml strained marinade
    30 g baker's chocolate

100 g sultanas
10 prunes
a little wine vinegar with a tablespoon of raw sugar dissolved in it
candied peel and pine nuts
water to cover

The chocolate and pine nuts betray the origin of this dish.

Brown the meat in lard. Add the bacon, carrot and onion and brown these also. Put in the seasonings, bouquet and marinade and simmer this to dryness. Cover with water and simmer again until tender. Remove the meat and keep warm. Skin and sieve the liquid. Add the remaining ingredients and simmer to thicken. Slice the meat and pour this sauce over it to serve.

Sweet and sour meat dishes are very common in medieval collections. Richard II of England (who came to an unbelievably sticky end which I won't dwell upon) had his own recipe book, the *Forme of Cury,* which contains a recipe for rabbit done in sweet and sour syrup.

Unlike such exotic curiosities, local cookery books abound in quite straightforward recipes for wild boar. Not only roasts but steaks and casseroles. The following is one of these.

WILD PORK AND PEAR CASSEROLE

800 g diced wild pork
lard
1 chopped onion
350 ml of stock mixed with three tablespoons tomato purée
4 pears peeled, cored and chopped
teaspoon each of ginger and rosemary
salt and pepper to taste

Brown the meat and the onion in the lard. Add the other ingredients to these in a casserole and cook tightly covered for two hours at 180°C. This dish, which is a variation on the common stew of European cooking, goes very well with brown rice. Addicts of this grain will know of its unique nutty flavour although it takes about twice as long to cook as polished rice.

Vegetables

If he's content with a vegetable love
which would certainly not suit me,
why what a most perfectly pure young man
this pure young man must be.

— W.S. Gilbert

I HAVE ALREADY REMARKED several times that we don't eat sufficient vegetables, and this truth deserves to be emphasised. Given their cheapness and their profusion and variety in summer I'm surprised that from November to February we eat anything else.

There are two reasons for a lack of appreciation of vegetables. The first is straight out snobbery as the following anecdote illustrates.

In M.F.K. Fisher's *Serve It Forth* she recounts how she and some friends are out walking in Switzerland. As the day draws to an end they find themselves in a tiny village restaurant. The waitress brings in a dish of vegetables, dark green and purple. One of those present, a Mrs Davidson, asks what it is and Fisher answers:

> 'That's a ring of spinach around chopped red cabbage, probably cooked with ham juice.' At the word spinach her face clouded, but when I mentioned cabbage a look of complete and horrified disgust settled like a cloud. 'Cabbage,' her tone was incredulous. 'Why not?' James asked mildly. 'Cabbage is the staff of life in many countries. You ought to know Mrs Davidson, weren't you raised on a farm?' Her mouth settled grimly. 'As you know,' she remarked in an icy voice, and her face gradually looked very old and discontented again, 'there are many kinds of farms. My home

194

was not a collection of peasants. Nor did we eat such — such peasant things as this.'

Alas, we are cursed with a surfeit of Mrs Davidsons, whose hungry ancestors ate vegetables to keep alive. They rarely saw meat and they regarded it as a great luxury — meat was what the gentry had. So when they came to a country where, to their astonishment, they found they could eat meat every day, they did, and came to think it natural. Vegetables they despised as fit only for the lower orders — for people such as they had been themselves scant years before, although they were doing their level best to forget it. In so doing they were depriving themselves of a great deal.

The second reason for disaffection with vegetables is to do with the abominable manner in which they are cooked and presented here. My mother's generation knew only one cooking technique for vegetables and that was boiling. So they boiled — and boiled and boiled. The results were unfit for human consumption — floury potatoes, soggy pumpkin, peas and beans unrecognisable and cabbage indescribable. There was an exception in my childhood, a nearby family of vegetarians, from whom I might have learned better, but sadly they were not a great encouragement.

There are some people, George Orwell remarks, who are attracted to progress in the same way that bluebottles are attracted to a dead cat. Among those he instanced were sandal wearers, fruit-juice drinkers, ninety-mile hikers — and vegetarians. He was being unfair but I know what he means. There is a class of person who will fight the abuses of privilege with all their heart but who will also put up with unacceptable and uncomfortable circumstances in the interest of 'progress'. They will do the two things side by side without irony. Puritanism takes many guises, and my neighbourhood vegetarians took up one of them. They ate vegetables because they were good for you and heaven forfend that anything which was good for you should be pleasurable. In fact vegetables were good for you *because* they tasted awful. This put me off vegetarian cooking for many years, although I know better now.

In fact in my whole childhood the only vegetables which I can remember enjoying were those we not only grew ourselves (which was most of them), but which we ate raw, such as tomatoes and radish, and sometimes carrot or even cabbage stalk (which is delicious, by the way). I make an exception for the green peas and new potatoes we had for Christmas dinner; I think this was because they were cooked by my grandmother who had too much respect for vegetables to mistreat them. Nor had she any snobbish qualms about eating with relish and delight those foods which her family had enjoyed for generations past. It has taken me many years to arrive at the same conclusion.

Basic vegetables have actually changed very little over the centuries, although selective breeding has improved some. Not all of course, particularly those which have been 'improved' to suit the convenience of the grower and distributor. The Celts of Iron Age Britain and their Roman successors ate garlic, onions, radish, cabbage, lettuce, cucumber, marrows and asparagus in forms very similar to those we eat today. To this repertoire have been added some other standards following European contact with the Americas — in particular the pulse-bean, tomato and above all the potato. Many new varieties of green vegetables were cultivated in England largely thanks to the pioneering work of the seventeenth-century diarist John Evelyn whose book on vegetables and their culinary uses, *Acetaria*, still makes fascinating reading. And we now take for granted those delicious items which were unheard of in my youth: the capsicum, aubergine, courgette and a range of other sometime exotica.

How are they to be brought to the table at their best? The more I read and practise on the subject the more I incline to the French approach. If vegetables must be cooked as an accompaniment to something else, then they should be cooked as little as possible. That rule does not necessarily apply equally to dishes of vegetables which are a principal item in themselves, but even they need less cooking by far than their meaty counterparts.

The key to the French approach is blanching and rinsing. That is to say, all green vegetables prior to their cooking are dropped briefly into a large pan of boiling salted water. They are then immediately refreshed by being plunged into or rinsed with cold water. This process, although it is a nuisance until you are used to it, ensures that the colour, texture and flavour of the vegetables is preserved. Any further cooking should then, in my view, proceed by steaming. This takes a little longer than boiling but is to be commended because it ensures that as little as possible of the flavour and juices are lost. It's possible to buy quite elaborate steaming utensils but they aren't necessary. I use a colander over a saucepan. This secret of steaming vegetables has been known to the Chinese since the dawn of time. You will no doubt be familiar with their bamboo utensils for the purpose. I own a set and use them sometimes for fun but they really are not as efficient as a colander with a lid.

For most vegetables to accompany a meal the rules are simple. Buy whatever is in season (or failing that, frozen). Get them as fresh and of the highest quality as you can and cook them as little as you can, i.e. until they are just tender. But having said that, let me now contradict it. Sometimes it is a good idea, just for the sake of variety or to surprise your guests, to add something to the vegetable you are cooking to go with a principal dish, as in some of the recipes which follow. We commence with the dreaded cabbage.

CABBAGE AND PAPRIKA

Poor old *Brassica oleracea*. It was recommended by Cato as an antidote to too much dining and as being good for the health (he liked it raw too). The

Greeks ate it with vinegar as a hangover cure. 'Wife, quick, some cabbage boil of virtues healing that I may rid me of this seedy feeling', Athanaeus quotes Eubulus as moaning. Pickled by the Germans. Introduced into England by Sir Anthony Ashley of Wimborn St Giles in the 1570s. Brought low by generations of boarding school cooks and the proprietors of 'family' hotels. Let us rehabilitate it.

Cook it short if you want to enjoy it long. There are exceptions of course to that as there are, sensibly, to every rule. Here is another of them.

According to Sir Harry Luke who wrote an entertaining cookery book, *The Tenth Muse*, cabbage used to be served this way at the Hotel am See, at Alt-Aussee, Styria, Austria, where Frau Frischmuth presided. The Germans always seem to have done best with cabbage.

1 cabbage
100 ml wine vinegar
1 onion
50 g lard
1 large green pepper
caraway seed, paprika, salt, pepper

Cut the cabbage into strips and marinate it in the vinegar, caraway, salt and pepper for most of the day. Slice and fry the onion in the lard, add the cabbage, sprinkle with paprika and put a lid on the kettle. Let it stew over a very low heat for about an hour then mix in the seeded and chopped pepper and serve. This is a step in the direction of that peculiarly German delicacy, sauerkraut, which descended to them from the Romans and has the great advantage of being antiscorbutic. In essence it is cabbage preserved in salt (with no vinegar thank you). The cabbage ferments in the brine so formed, and this is decanted off and the sauerkraut washed thoroughly before use. It makes a delicious salad mixed with some cubed pineapple and olive oil, and goes particularly well with duck or with salami. There is an excellent game and sauerkraut dish in Poland called Hunter's Bigos.

DOLMADES LAHANA

If memories of boarding school make you rebel even at Sir Harry's method then you might like to try these stuffed cabbage leaves. We usually think of them as Greek but they are common all over Europe.

16 large cabbage leaves
170 g rice
2 chopped onions
2 cloves garlic

1 tablespoon pine nuts
1 tablespoon sultanas
nutmeg, salt and pepper
3 chopped tomatoes
lemon juice

Make the stuffing first, frying the rice for two or three minutes in a little oil. Then add the onions, garlic, pine nuts and sultanas and keep frying until this mixture begins to turn golden. Add the tomatoes, nutmeg and seasoning and simmer for five minutes.

Meanwhile blanch the cabbage leaves and trim the central stem out of each one, otherwise they will not roll. Put a spoonful of the stuffing on each and roll it up, tucking in the ends as you go. Pack these neatly on a plate in a saucepan, cover with salted water and add lemon juice. Cover with another plate or they will disintegrate and simmer very slowly for about half an hour.

Dolmades can be served hot or cold depending on the time of year, and your own taste in such things.

SPROUTS

Cabbage has a number of relatives which, if treated with equal culinary respect, will reward you by tasting good. Brussel sprouts are a species of cabbage (*gemmifera* for the botanically minded) but why Brussels? Because that's where they come from, of course. As early as 1215, about the time the Sheriff of Nottingham and Robin Hood were playing peekaboo in Sherwood Forest, they rated a mention in medieval records. But they remained a local delicacy until the early nineteenth century when Thomas Jefferson introduced them to America. An attempt by Jean Baptiste Van Mons, Professor of Rural Economy at Louvain, to do the same for England in 1818 failed and it is not until the 1850s that they begin to appear in cookery books. They are now of course a winter staple and also very good with game. They mix well, curiously, with grapes. Cook about 700 g of sprouts and when they are done toss them for a couple of minutes in 30 g melted butter. Then mix in about 300 g of seedless white grapes and serve as an accompaniment to pheasant. The combination will surprise you.

BROCCOLI

Equally unlikely is a combination of broccoli with chilli and sweet pepper. Steam a kilo of broccoli until it's just cooked. Heat a little olive oil in an iron kettle and gently fry a couple of red chillis in it for a few minutes. Put in the broccoli and a chopped red capsicum (removing the seeds of course). Put on a lid and let it stew until it is reheated through, then serve. This is a Roman dish *broccoli al peperonciono*. The name of the vegetable is itself Italian meaning 'little sprouts'. It is mentioned in Evelyn's *Acetaria* of 1699 but was first introduced widely into English cooking by the eighteenth-century nurseryman Stephen Switzer. The same recipe can also be used, but less successfully I think, for cauliflower.

CAULIFLOWER WITH WINE

Cauliflowers were first developed by the Arabs and began to appear in European herbals in the Middle Ages. Again, it was Thomas Jefferson who introduced them to America after the United States consul sent him some seed from Naples in 1824. This recipe, appropriately, comes from Sicily.

Separate a large cauliflower into small flowerets. Pour a little olive oil into an iron pot and put in some anchovies. Add the cauliflower pieces, some sliced cheddar cheese and about 200 ml of red wine. Cover and stew gently until the cauliflower is cooked. The wine should have been absorbed but if it has not been so entirely that doesn't matter. Serve directly from the pot at table.

CAULIFLOWER CHEESE

No mention of cauliflower would be complete without a recipe for this dish. It is of course a principal course on its own. I find this version very tasty. Cauliflower cheese, incidentally, was a great favourite in the eighteenth century. A hundred years earlier caulis were eaten pickled instead.

1 cauliflower, separated into flowerets
30 g butter
30 g flour
350 ml milk
200 g grated mozzarella
teaspoon salt
pepper, tabasco, Worcestershire sauce
30 g breadcrumbs
30 g grated Parmesan

Cook the cauliflower. Preheat oven to 160° C. Butter a casserole in readiness. Make a roux of the flour and butter and cook for a minute or so. Heat the milk to boiling and whisk it in. Stir in the mozzarella and seasonings and combine into a smooth sauce. Distribute the cauliflower in the casserole and pour the sauce over. Combine the breadcrumbs and Parmesan and sprinkle on the top. Bake for about 45 minutes. Cauliflower cheese is one of those things you love or hate. If the former then vegetarian guests will thank you for making it a principal dish for a dinner. If you don't like cheese sauces an equally good one can be made of prawns.

CAULIFLOWER IN PRAWN SAUCE
This recipe is similar to one given by Jane Grigson in her *Vegetable Book.*

600 g prawns in their shells
400 g fish trimmings
1 onion stuck with 3 cloves
1 carrot, quartered
bouquet garni
600 ml water
3 tablespoons dry white Vermouth
30 g butter
30 g flour
150 ml cream
1 tablespoon Parmesan
salt, pepper, parsley
1 large cauliflower

Break up the cauliflower into six pieces and cook. Keep warm. Shell the prawns and reserve the meat. Combine shells, fish, onion, carrot, bouquet, water and Vermouth and simmer covered for about half an hour. Strain off the liquid and boil it down to about 400 ml. Make a roux and cook for a few minutes. Add the cream and fish stock and keep cooking to form a creamy sauce. Add the Parmesan and prawns and heat through thoroughly. Season. Pour over the cooked cauliflower and scatter with parsley to serve.

SPINACH

This vegetable was the bane of my childhood. Many a time I was made to sit at the table and eat it all up. Understandably I developed an aversion to it. One of the joys of growing up was being able to determine that I would never eat spinach again. Then, one night, some friends took me to a Greek restaurant. They recommended the spanokapita, which was quite outstanding. I was astonished to discover that its principal ingredient was spinach.

Pies of spinach and other greenstuffs have a long culinary history, going back at least to medieval times.

In the chapter on desserts you will find a sweet version.

10 sheets filo pastry
2 kg spinach
aniseed
2 chopped onions
olive oil
salt and pepper

In addition to the aniseed the Greeks would add thyme, rosemary and chopped dandelion leaves. These last have an intriguing flavour, which more people should try.

Cook the spinach in a little salted water with the herbs if you are using them. Fry the onions until soft in the oil and mix them into the cooked spinach. Chop it all together with the aniseed and more salt and pepper to taste. Line a pie dish with five sheets of the pastry, each one brushed in turn with melted butter. Put in the filling and then the remaining pastry sheets in the same way. Bake at 190°C for about forty minutes. If the pastry browns too rapidly cover with foil.

If you want to serve plain spinach then it should be cooked with a little butter. Alexandre Dumas gives a recipe which involves cooking it on five consecutive days, adding more butter each day. That I'm afraid would be too rich for my palate. In southern Italy a few anchovies and a little lemon juice are added to pique the flavour — which they certainly do. Spinach has not always been a lowly dish. The T'ang emperor T'ai Tsung, who was sent some by the ruler of Nepal, regarded it as a great delicacy. It came to Europe from Persia through Arabia, hence its name, from *aspanakh*, and has been in English herbals since at least 1568.

Interestingly there is a unique New Zealand variety, *Tetragonia expansa*, which was taken back to England in 1770 by Sir Joseph Banks and developed at Kew Gardens in the 1820s. It's quite popular in France but is not usually on sale here. Most New Zealanders are unaware of its existence.

HARVARD BEETS

Cognate with spinach in my chamber of horrors as a child were beets. Served cold and dripping with malt vinegar they stained red everything with which they came into contact. In New England they are traditionally served hot instead, in a sweet and sour sauce.

This recipe is so called because red is the football colour of Harvard College, in case you didn't know.

400 g cooked beetroots, sliced
150 ml of the reserved cooking liquid
2 teaspoons cornflour
1 tablespoon butter
salt, pepper
2 tablespoons sugar
60 ml vinegar

Mix all the ingredients except the butter and beets. Boil this gently for five minutes, stirring to avoid catching. Add the beets and the butter and heat through to serve. This is the traditional accompaniment to the recipe for chicken pie given in an earlier chapter.

For me this recipe redeems beetroot somewhat. Some of the best northern European recipes for beetroot are to be found in *Home Cookery* by Jessie Conrad, wife of the novelist Joseph, who remarks somewhere that of all books only cookery books are above suspicion being devoted as they are solely to human happiness.

CUCUMBERS IN ORANGE SAUCE

The other vegetable we usually eat cold, but which is just as good hot, is the cucumber. Most people blanch at the thought of a cooked cucumber but this is only because of the unfamiliarity. In Puerto Rico they stew them in orange sauce and call them *pepinos en salsa de naranja*, a curious eighteenth-century survival, far from its place of origin.

3 peeled cucumbers
45 g butter
1 tablespoon flour
300 ml orange juice
1 teaspoon orange zest
salt and pepper

Cut the cucumbers lengthwise and scrape out the seeds, then chop them into thin slices. Cook them in boiling salted water for five minutes, drain and keep warm. Make a roux in a small saucepan and cook it for a couple of minutes, then add the other ingredients. Keep cooking until smooth and pour over the cucumbers.

Courgettes can be cooked in the same way and both can be done in a sweet and sour sauce as for the beets, but I prefer my courgettes done in a different way.

COURGETTES AND TOMATOES

These are simply small marrows eaten throughout most of Europe for centuries. The English, with innate conservatism, did not, it appears, use them in their cooking until 1931. That at least is what the Oxford English Dictionary says in allowing that 'courgette' is now an English word. Many people in New Zealand still turn their noses up at courgettes (or zucchini), which is extremely silly of them. This recipe is from Catalonia.

Wash a kilo of courgettes and slice them thinly, unpeeled. Sprinkle them with salt and leave them to drain in a colander for about half an hour. This will draw out their slight bitterness. Chop 500 g of tomatoes and two cloves of garlic and fry the latter gently in a little olive oil for a few minutes. Then add the courgettes and cover the pan. Stew for 15 minutes and add the tomatoes. Stew for a further ten minutes and serve. This begins to approach a very famous southern European vegetable stew which we will get to in due course. But first more on courgettes which can also be combined with pasta in an excellent salad.

COURGETTES AND RIGATONI

Rigatoni are large tubes of pasta, a bit like overgrown *macaroni curvi*, and each about 5 cm long.

1 kg courgettes
500 g rigatoni
30 g butter
2 tablespoons olive oil
2 cloves chopped garlic
1 teaspoon dried thyme
pepper and salt
Parmesan cheese

Wash, dice and salt the courgettes. Cook the rigatoni *al dente* and drain well. Heat the butter and oil and sauté the courgettes for about two minutes, then add the garlic and thyme and sauté for another minute or two. Add pepper and a little more salt to taste, toss with the rigatoni and sprinkle with grated Parmesan.

Courgettes appear in abundance and very cheaply in late December and keep on doing so until early February. Consequently I eat them in quantity throughout January because I can never easily go past the vegetables of the season. One year in early November the same abundance happened with asparagus. I don't know why this was so and didn't ask in case it went away as mysteriously as it had come. I merely thanked the good Lord and gorged on asparagus. Incidentally, when fresh asparagus is in abundance grocers tend to reduce the price of the tinned. Then is the time to stock up for the winter.

ASPARAGUS MOULD

Mostly we eat the green and violet variety of asparagus, but Europeans also eat a kind which is white and yellow. I have never seen it on sale here. The vegetable is ancient enough to have been mentioned by Pliny. Venice was famous for it in centuries past; it was sold in the market on the Rialto. Louis XIV loved it and Samuel Pepys records buying it in Fenchurch Street in 1667, a hundred spears for sixpence (lucky him). For summer he could have made an excellent mould, like the following, from his purchase.

600 g cooked asparagus
salt and pepper
breadcrumbs
1 onion, finely chopped
25 g butter
300 ml boiling milk
5 eggs
60 g grated Gruyère cheese
nutmeg

Preheat your oven to 160° C. Grease a soufflé dish and sprinkle breadcrumbs over its surface. Cook the onion in butter until soft and then combine this with the cheese, seasoning, nutmeg and 60 g of breadcrumbs. Beat in the eggs and the hot milk. Cut up the asparagus and fold into the mixture. Turn this into the soufflé dish and bake in a bain marie for about 40 minutes. Remove from the heat and allow to cool before turning out to serve. A sauce Mornay, i.e. a bechamel with cheese, goes well with this.

This sort of warm mould, known as a *timbale*, was particularly popular at the time of Marcel Proust. And Proust in his famous description of the kitchen at Combray dwells lovingly on the beautiful colours of the asparagus in its season. If you want to discover the source of his more than sensual delight you must go to the Louvre and there admire Manet's painting of a bundle of asparagus which he painted once when visiting Monet at Argenteuil, famous for its asparagus. To me asparagus is best steamed with a little butter, or in a sauce Hollandaise (hot) or vinaigrette (cold). At Combray, however, they sometimes ate it with peas, as Proust goes on to record. They also do this in Spain, where asparagus is plentiful.

ASPARAGUS WITH PEAS — ESPARRAGOS CON GUISANTES

This is a good way to use tinned asparagus.

450 g tinned asparagus
50 g butter
pepper, salt, sugar
750 g peas
1 tablespoon flour
fresh chopped mint
water and a little milk

Drain the asparagus. Make a roux and cook it for a few minutes and then stir in about 250 ml water to make a thin sauce. Add the other ingredients and simmer gently for about ten minutes. This will produce a thick asparagus sauce containing the cooked peas. You may need to stir this from time to time to prevent it catching. Bring it to the table piping hot.

PEAS

Thanks to a large food-processing company these are the most convenient and ubiquitous of all vegetables eaten in this country. We forget of course that this is a recent development. A mere twenty years ago my then aged godparents told me in some excitement how only a few days previously they had for the first time ever eaten tinned peas. They didn't like them.

Christmas morning for me is always not only in recollection redolent with the smell of fowl cooking but conjures a very vivid picture of my grandmother sitting on the back step shelling peas.

Tinned peas are rather nasty but frozen peas are excellent if lightly steamed. And of course they are a godsend in the winter. But one grows weary of peas on their own and therefore the occasional variation does not go amiss. Peas, incidentally, are one of those vegetables the flavour of which is heightened by the addition of a teaspoon of sugar.

PEAS IN CREAM

Peas with nutmeg or mace may sound a bit odd but they're not.

450 g peas
60 g butter
150 ml water
sugar, salt and pepper
½ teaspoon each nutmeg and mace
chopped parsley
2 teaspoons flour
180 ml cream
lemon juice

Simmer the peas with the butter, spice and seasonings in the water until tender. Mix the flour to a smooth paste with some of the cooking water, stir in the cream and return this to the pot. Cook until it thickens and then add a little lemon juice. This goes particularly well with lamb dishes, although peas are more traditionally the accompaniment to duck.

PEAS WITH EGGS

In southern Europe peas and eggs are cooked together in a dish which is proverbially a stew for the poorest of the poor. I'm glad they still have at least one traditional pleasure that the rich haven't yet taken from them. In fact this recipe is quite old. There's a version of it in Hannah Glasse's *Art of Cookery* which also relies upon nutmeg and mace.

750 g of peas
50 ml water
50 ml olive oil
½ teaspoon each nutmeg and mace
salt, sugar, black pepper
6 eggs
3 tablespoons cream

Cook the peas with the spices and a little salt, in the water and oil in a pot with the lid on. When they are half done add some sugar and pepper to taste. The liquid should not be covering the peas. With the back of a spoon make four depressions in the surface of the peas and slip an egg to poach into each one. This should take about ten minutes with the lid back in place. Beat the remaining two eggs with the cream and pour over the top to scramble and set before serving. If you should ever dine at Pedro's in Christchurch try a variation on this, *huevos a la flamenco,* which is done very well there.

Peas combine well with many other vegetables such as baby carrots. In Spain also they do them with the tiny onions we used for pickling. The onions are fried whole in butter with a little chopped ham and then peas, water, seasoning and herbs added and the whole thing simmered covered for about twenty minutes, strained and served.

Ultimately however the popularity of peas as a vegetable down the centuries has been based upon their amenability to drying and their place as a winter pulse. They were introduced into Britain by the Romans and have been used continuously since. The great advantage of the dried pea of course is that when recombined with water and cooked with other ingredients it makes an absorbant pottage which is as good hot as cold (although not in the pot nine days old). Ham and pea soup is in its present form one of the commonest of the medieval pottages, although not everyone could afford the meat bone to go in it. Its medieval name when combined with herbs and other greenstuffs was *joutes*. Some recipes for this in medieval manuscripts include the leaves of fruit trees. By the eighteenth century, pease pottage or pudding had become a dish of the poor and of the industrial north in particular. Just because frozen peas are available all year we should not forget the dried variety, which make a tasty dish in their own right.

DRIED PEAS AND PEPPERCORNS

The peppercorns used in this are the green, i.e. unripe, variety preserved in vinegar.

500 g dried green peas
1 chopped onion
1 sliced carrot
bouquet garni
60 g butter
1 tablespoon green peppercorns
salt and sugar

Soak the peas overnight. Cook them in fresh water with the onion, carrot and bouquet but don't salt until later otherwise you will harden the peas. When they are cooked strain them, remove the bouquet, and purée with the butter in a food processor. Add salt, sugar and a little of the juice along with peppercorns. Some people find this too peppery a vegetable but for me it is ideal with pork. You can make the same dish with lentils. In the end however just peas steamed with butter will do me. But definitely not with honey; I don't care if they *do* roll off the knife. If it bothers you use a spoon.

IMAM BAYILDI

I don't think I ever saw aubergines until I was an adult, but when I did I fell in love with them at once. Those glorious shining purple bulbs were to me the essence of the word 'vegetable'. When I first cut into one I was disappointed by the slightly floury texture but that lasted only until my first mouthful of Greek moussaka. Aubergines have an ancient pedigree with a name ultimately derived from Sanskrit *vatin-ganah* by way of Arabic *albadinjan*. They come in many colours besides purple, including a creamy white, but only the dark variety seems to be available here. They can be grilled on their own but they are at their best either stuffed or in a stew. Some say they should be peeled but I am not one of those. Like courgettes, however, they need half an hour's salting before use, otherwise they will be bitter.

Stuffed aubergines are to be found in the cuisines all around the eastern Mediterranean. Imam Biyaldi is a Turkish speciality and means 'the holy man fainted'. No one knows however who he was or why he did. The suggestion has been made that he fainted when he saw how much olive oil the recipe contained. The Greeks, who also claim this dish, call it *yalangi dolma*.

6 long aubergines
150 ml olive oil
sugar, salt
juice of a lemon
300 g onion, chopped
3 tablespoons olive oil
3 cloves garlic, chopped
parsley, finely chopped
300 g tomatoes, chopped

Cut the aubergines in half lengthways and scoop out the centre. Salt the hollow and leave for half an hour. Rinse. Soften the onion in the 3 tablespoons of oil. Add the garlic and stir for a minute. Remove from the heat and add the tomato, parsley and a little salt. Stuff the aubergines with this. Put them all side by side in a pan, pour in the 150 ml of oil and an equal quantity of water. Add sugar, salt and lemon juice. Simmer gently for one hour and remove when cool to a serving dish. Serve cold. The cooking liquid is of course thrown away.

MOUSSAKA

In revenge for the Turks claiming *imam biyaldi* the Greeks have claimed moussaka — and with about as much justification because the name is Arabic and the dish is general in the eastern Mediterranean. There are many variations.

3 aubergines
salt, pepper
oil
2 chopped onions
600 g minced lamb
1 teaspoon ground cinnamon
2 tomatoes, chopped
2 tablespoons tomato concentrate
chopped parsley
60 g butter
60 g flour
300 ml hot milk
grated nutmeg
1 egg yolk

Slice the aubergines thinly and salt them. Wash and pat dry. Fry lightly in oil and drain on absorbent paper. Fry the onions until soft and then add the lamb and fry until brown. Mix in the seasonings, spice, tomato concentrate and parsley. Add a little water and simmer for fifteen minutes. In a deep baking dish layer alternately aubergines and mince mixture, beginning and ending with the former. Make a roux and cook a few minutes. Add the milk, stirring until it boils, and season with salt, pepper and nutmeg. Beat the egg yolk and mix with a little of the sauce, then stir it slowly in off the heat or it will curdle. Pour the sauce over the layered mixture and bake for forty-five minutes at 190°C. Some recipes add layers of cheese also or a topping of mashed potato.

With this dish we have come to vegetables which are not so much accompaniments to other dishes, as main dishes themselves. These take many forms. The most interesting of these (and quite suitable for a dinner party) are the vegetable stews and their near relatives of one sort or another.

Vegetable Stews and Casseroles

While at the eastern end of southern Europe aubergines are used in the manner just described, in France, Italy and Spain they form the basis of a variety of vegetable stews, the most famous of which is ratatouille.

RATATOUILLE

For a few brief weeks in 1977 this was the most famous dish in England. It even pushed the Silver Jubilee off the front page. It all began when the sous-chef at Claridges was dismissed, allegedly for failing to put salt in the ratatouille, and sued the management for unfair dismissal. The public was agog as revelation after revelation emerged concerning the downstairs goings on in the kitchens of the rich. And the question was on all lips: 'What is a ratawhateveritis?' Eventually a chef appeared on prime time news on the BBC to demonstrate. The controversy came to its inevitable end with a cartoon in *The Guardian*. Man sits at restaurant table. 'Waiter', he says, 'there's an allegation of unfair dismissal in my ratatouille.'

As with moussaka there are many variations of ratatouille. This is how it is made in Nice, at least according to Jacques Medecin, and he's the mayor so he ought to know.

400 g aubergines
400 g courgettes
10 g flour
400 g green peppers
400 g onions peeled and sliced
600 g tomatoes, sliced

9 tablespoons-approx olive oil
6 cloves garlic
teaspoon thyme and of basil
3 sprigs chopped parsley
salt and pepper

Cut the aubergines and courgettes into slices and sprinkle with flour. Seed and slice the peppers, onions and tomatoes. Heat olive oil in two separate pans. In one, gently fry the aubergines, then the courgettes. In the other, fry the onions and peppers. In an iron kettle put the remaining oil and cook the garlic, herbs and tomatoes until they form a sauce. Add to this the other vegetables, salt and pepper and cook *very* gently until they are tender. Over-cooking is fatal to the success of this dish, which is served hot or cold with equal success.

In Provence there is a variation with tomatoes and aubergines only, but in a sauce of milk and anchovies. This is called *boumiano*. In Sicily, not to be outdone, they replace the peppers with celery and add vinegar, olives, capers, anchovies and pine nuts. This is *caponata*. This last, according to Elizabeth David in *Italian Food*, can be served with a garnish of lobster or of salted smoked roes. Ratatouille is also one of the few dishes to have travelled, to Guadeloupe and Martinique where the *ratatouille créole* contains in addition a couple of large cucumbers, the *gros concombre*, a speciality of the region.

Few of these dishes would exist were it not for one of the great contributions of the Americas to European cuisine, the pepper. In combination with another such contribution, the pulse bean, they make a stew in Bulgaria.

LENTIL, BEAN AND PEPPER STEW

Beans and related pulses are one of our most neglected food sources. Next to cereals they are the most important of human foods: they are higher in protein content than any other vegetable and to many people who never see meat they are the only source of such protein. Like other pulses their great culinary advantage is that they can be dried and when they are reconstituted they absorb the flavour of whatever it is in which they are cooked. It is a pity that our usual introduction to them is in a commercial baked bean preparation full of sugar. This creates a mindblock for most people which is entirely unjustified.

European folklore is full of beans and is not alone in that; the Hopi Indians have a major annual festival in their honour.

200 g brown lentils
200 g haricot beans

2 chopped onions
4 large red sweet peppers
40 g butter
300 ml stock (any variety)
4 tablespoons tomato concentrate
salt
sugar

Soak the beans and lentils in cold water overnight. Drain and rinse them. Fry the onions in the butter until they soften and then add the peppers seeded and cut into strips. Give them another five minutes and then add the pulses and the stock. Bring to a simmer and add the tomato, salt and sugar. Simmer for five more minutes. Put on a lid and transfer to the oven. This can then be cooked either at 180°C for about an hour and a half, or preferably all day at 100°C.

Beans improve with slow cooking and will take up more liquid. They improve even more with reheating (one of the fundamental precepts of Mexican cooking). The particularly attractive thing about this dish is its red rich colour. If you can get red kidney beans so much the better.

GHIVECHI
This vegetable stew from Romania is not red but multi-coloured. It traditionally makes use of everything available and goes superbly with some sour cream and baked jacket potatoes.

2 tablespoons oil
2 large onions, sliced
2 chopped celery stalks

250 g carrots, sliced
250 g parsnips, sliced
250 g marrow or courgette, chopped
400 g leeks, sliced
3 large tomatoes, chopped
4 potatoes, diced
20 g flour
600 ml stock
125 ml tomato purée
2 garlic cloves, chopped
salt, pepper, bay leaf

Heat the oil and fry the onion until soft. Add the other vegetables and stew with the lid on for five minutes, then sprinkle on the flour and add the stock and remaining ingredients. Bring to the boil and then simmer for about an hour. Vegetables alone, it need hardly be remarked, cook more quickly than meat and should be watched carefully so as not to turn mushy.

MENESTRA A LA PALENTINA

At the other end of the Mediterranean in Old Castille they also make a vegetable stew, but this one uses rather different ingredients. The contrast is interesting. This is very much a dish for spring.

2 tablespoons oil and a little lard
200 g smoked bacon, cubed
1 onion and 2 garlic cloves chopped
parsley
200 g green beans
1 lettuce
2 artichokes
2 courgettes
300 g new potatoes (small)
250 g green peas
250 g broad beans
200 ml white wine
salt, pepper, nutmeg
150 ml tomato purée

Heat the oil and lard in an iron pot and fry the bacon until crisp. Add the onion, garlic and parsley. Chop the lettuce, beans, artichokes and courgettes and wash the potatoes. Add these to the pot with the peas and broad beans. Add the wine and a little water. Season and stir in the nutmeg and purée. Simmer gently for an hour and serve.

And just to round it out, vegetable stews take on a life of their own if they become a curry.

VEGETABLE CURRY

It has already been remarked that the Raj has left an indelible imprint on English cuisine. The curries which have been one of the results are neither entirely Indian nor European but in some curious British way combine both. They are unique and one of the few desirable inheritances of empire. No other European cuisine can quite comprehend them.

250 g leeks
small cauliflower
3 potatoes
2 onions, chopped
1 tart apple, cored but unpeeled
350 g tomatoes, chopped
350 g okra
1 tablespoon flour
1 tablespoon turmeric
60 g lard
1 tablespoon curry powder
1 teaspoon coriander
3 tablespoons mango chutney
300 ml water
salt and pepper

Wash the vegetables. Chop the leeks, divide the cauliflower into flowerets and slice the potatoes. Toss these vegetables in the flour and turmeric mixed, and then fry them lightly in the melted lard. Add the apple, tomatoes, spices, chutney and water. Season and cook for half an hour, then add the okra and heat through. Curries, like beans, respond extremely well to reheating.

Take care with curry powders however. In Wellington a local grocer markets his own under the brand name Arbee and if you can get it it is very good. When I was a child the one to look out for was Vencat which was imported from India in a rather unusual packet not unlike the packaging of angostura bitters, a label badly printed, almost unreadable, tiny print, mostly testimonials from satisfied customers now long dead. This packaging is now alas no more, although the powder is still available. Some people prefer to make their own and in some dishes so do I but with some good ones ready-made it isn't generally necessary. This curry goes very well with brown rice.

BEANS

Let me return to beans, outside the context of vegetable stews, and deal with dishes which are beans but supplementary to a meat dish. The painter Monet loved the next dish. In fact he was very fond of food in general as his famous *Le Déjeuner sur l'Herbe* indicates, as do many of his other paintings which show fruit or domestic interiors at mealtimes. His life at Giverny revolved around eating and the entertaining he did there. He even designed his own blue, yellow and white dinner service. Art was a forbidden topic at his table; there one talked of food and if one could not join the conversation then in Monet's view you were a barbarian. I am with him there.

250 g dried haricots
150 g bacon in a piece
200 ml red wine
70 g butter
salt, pepper, parsley

Soak the beans overnight and drain them. Put them in a pot with half the bacon and pour in half the wine and enough water to cover. Simmer for about 45 minutes. Then add salt and leave them for a few minutes. Pour off the liquid, add the remaining wine and boil it down to about 150 ml. Cut the remaining bacon into cubes and fry it in half the butter. Add the beans to this but discard the first half of the bacon. Heat through stirring. Add the remaining butter to the concentrated wine. When it has been absorbed pour it over the beans and serve.

POROTOS GRANADOS

This is another bean dish, which hails from Chile and which will do equally as an accompaniment or as a main dish. It is particularly effective given to those who spurn vegetarian food, because of its interesting combination of flavours and of colours.

There is some argument over the origin of this dish. Some say it is a native of the Americas but there are similar dishes in Aquitaine and Euskedi.

250 g dried beans
2 tablespoons paprika
4 tablespoons corn oil
2 chopped onions
2 green hot chillies
250 g sweet corn
500 g pumpkin, cubed
500 g tomatoes, chopped
teaspoon oregano
salt and pepper

Soak the beans, haricot for preference, overnight. Boil them in unsalted water until they are tender. Drain them, keeping the liquid. Fry the onions in the oil with the paprika; a neutral vegetable oil like corn oil is best. Olive oil for instance is too strong for my taste in this dish although it adds an interesting flavour. When the onions are soft add the remaining ingredients. Let this stew for about five minutes with the lid on the pot, then add the beans and a little of the bean liquid. Simmer until the pumpkin disintegrates and thickens the dish. This takes about 30 minutes.

Pumpkin is usually served as a watery mush in this country. There is no need to treat it in this way however and it can be cooked with a variety of other ingredients. The Germans have a dish *Kurbishrei mit Apfeln* which involves not only apples but smoked bacon and lemon. And in his *Dictionnaire* Alexandre Dumas gives a recipe for baking pumpkin with nutmeg and Parmesan cheese. But the nicest and simplest recipe comes from the book of Toulouse-Lautrec's favourite recipes published posthumously by his friend Maurice Joyant. There is a famous painting of the artist at his oven by Vuillard, in which he seems to be preparing this dish.

GRATIN OF PUMPKIN

900 g pumpkin
flour
oil
500 g onions, sliced
450 g tomatoes, chopped
salt, pepper, breadcrumbs, butter

Peel the pumpkin and cut it into smallish pieces about an inch square at most. Roll these in seasoned flour and fry them in oil until they are brown. Remove from the pan and drain. Cook the onions, adding more oil if necessary until they are soft. Add the tomatoes and seasonings and cook a little longer. Return the pumpkin to the dish, scatter with breadcrumbs, dot with knobs of butter and bake for about three-quarters of an hour at 180° C. This dish makes a very good substitute for potatoes if you are one of those people who can't abide them.

POTATOES AND PEARS

I don't much care for potatoes, although I'm not entirely against them. This is probably because through my paternal grandmother I have an Irish inheritance and the potato famine, 'the great hunger', has got into my genetic make-up. Nevertheless I sometimes make myself a dish of potatoes and I am always agreeably surprised by the result. Of course just new and boiled with mint they are delicious but unless you grow your own you are unlikely to enjoy that pleasure. It isn't economic for commercial growers to lift their crop at the right time so proper new potatoes don't appear in the shops. The potatoes which are nowadays usually described as 'new' mostly aren't. When I was a child everyone seemed to grow potatoes but no more. Consequently I have no one to whom I can hand on all that esoteric oral lore about moulding and trenching my father taught me.

Potatoes have an interesting history. The ethnocentric English usually credit Sir Walter Raleigh with their introduction to Europe. It's perfectly true that he brought some back from his travels and cultivated them on his Irish estates. But a Spanish monk, Hieronymous Cardan, had already introduced them to Europe from Peru some fifty years earlier. They never caught on much in the south but the northern Europeans have made them peculiarly their own. It took a while, however. In 1774 the inhabitants of Kolberg had to be forced to eat them at gunpoint. At about the same time they were becoming popular in England where they eventually replaced pottages as a source of bulk. We now take them for granted as a staple. Potatoes can even be used to make a form of bread (likewise turnips and pumpkins), as John Evelyn remarks.

Alas the very success of the potato has been its downfall. The need to supply a mass market has led to the development of varieties notable only for their bulk and the abundance of the production of each plant. This has accelerated since the introduction of mechanical diggers. The result has been a decline in taste and in the tuber itself into a bland uninteresting lump of starch. I still like to make a shepherd's pie from time to time however, particularly in winter.

An unusual way for us to prepare potatoes is to serve them with pears. Less traditional for us, perhaps, but not for the Swiss, who have been doing it since at least 1580 when Montaigne remarked upon it while on a journey to Italy.

450 g small new potatoes
1 sliced onion
200 g dried pears
butter
pepper, salt, honey

Soak the pears until they reconstitute, and cut them up. Keep the water. Fry the onion in butter until soft, then add the pears and the scrubbed potatoes, the liquid, salt, pepper and a teaspoon of honey. The potatoes should be barely covered. Add more water if necessary and simmer them very gently until the potatoes are tender. Drain and serve.

This is particularly good with pork. Potatoes combine very well with a range of unusual other ingredients. Cheese most people know about but they also go with blanched almonds. In southern India they are mashed with chillies, coconut milk and green ginger. They also mould very well. If you wash and scrape them and slice them very thin they can be layered with butter in a soufflé dish, seasoned with pepper and salt and baked at 215°C for about an hour. If you then turn them out they can come to the table in a 'shape' which is a diverting way to serve them rather more formally for guests.

KUMARA WITH ORANGE

We would be better advised however to serve the relative of the potato, the kumara. Sweet potatoes are natives of both South and North America, noted by Columbus and introduced to Europe in 1526. They enjoyed great popularity there, much more than the potato, although the manner of their consumption seems odd to twentieth-century ears. They were glazed and crystallised as chestnuts still are; when Falstaff declares: 'Let it rain potatoes . . . hail kissing-comfits,' he is referring to crystallised sweet potatoes.

There is something of a debate over whether they were originally native to Asia or from the Americas. The former probably, as they seem to have come to New Zealand long before Europeans set foot in the New World. Unless you are a follower of the rather odd theories of Thor Heyrdahl, this means they arrived here via Indonesia. Certainly there were kumara fields, protected by a curious system of stone walls, in the South Wairarapa area as early as 1300 AD; or so my archeological friends tell me.

The sweetish floury consistency of kumara is complemented by the sharpness of orange in this dish. The bitter oranges of Seville would be even better but they are unprocurable here.

about 1500 g kumara
60 g brown sugar
juice of two oranges and zest of one
juice of a lemon and zest of half
60 g butter
salt and pepper

Peel, slice and cook the kumaras in salted water until just tender. Transfer them to a buttered oven dish. Sprinkle on the sugar and pour the combined juices, zest and seasonings over. Dot with lumps of butter and bake at 150°C for about half an hour. This dish can also be made with yams but less successfully.

POTATO GNOCCHI

In those parts of the world where potatoes have never been popular, such as Italy, they have had either to develop substitutes or to disguise them. This led the Italians to invent *gnocchi* for which I am prepared to forgive them a great deal — not that I know of anything for which they might need to be forgiven in any event.

> 900 g potatoes
> 250 g flour
> 2 eggs
> 30 g butter
> salt and pepper

Peel, cook and mash the potatoes. Mix in the other ingredients. The result is a soft, doughlike material. This should be rolled out into a long, sausage-like shape, but rather thinner, and cut into pieces about an inch long. Have ready a large pan of boiling salted water and drop the gnocchi in one by one. When they rise to the top they are done. This should take about three minutes. They can be done in batches, kept warm in the oven and sprinkled with cheese and a little pepper before serving. In Genoa they are served with the famous basil sauce *pesto*. They go well with any dish and particularly with game.

If they seem a little bland to you in this form you can make the well-known *gnocchi verdi*, which have nothing to do with music and everything to do with spinach.

> 700 g chopped cooked spinach
> 120 g butter
> 350 g cottage cheese
> salt, pepper, nutmeg
> 2 eggs
> 3 tablespoons flour
> 80 g Parmesan cheese

Thoroughly mix the spinach, the cottage cheese and about half the butter. Heat this in a pan for a few minutes stirring so as not to burn. Remove from the heat and add the flour, the eggs and about half the Parmesan. Cook spoonfuls in simmering salted water. Then in a baking dish sprinkle them with the remaining butter and Parmesan and bake them in a hot oven for a few minutes. They may be served as an accompaniment to many dishes.

There is another Italian dish that goes very well with game, especially when there is a rich sauce. The staple of northern Italy is not traditionally pasta, as you might expect, although they eat it there in all its glorious variety. Instead, it is *polenta*, particularly in Lombardy and the Veneto. This is a form of cornmeal porridge also known as *mamaliga* and can be made very simply. Use a largish double boiler because in this way you will not burn it. Bring about a litre of lightly salted water to the boil and stir in 500 g of fine maize flour. As it cooks and thickens stir in lumps of butter. Keep it cooking for about twenty minutes to half an hour. It will absorb almost as much butter as you like to stir in but I use about 200 g and a fair grinding of pepper. Turn it out into a dish or loaf tin to set. It is not meant to be eaten alone in which form it is bland and, some think, rather unpleasant. It can be stored for long periods in the refrigerator or a freezer. When you need it, cut thin slices and fry them brown in oil. Keep them warm and serve as an accompaniment to strong meat dishes. In the Trentino and further east in Romania it is served smothered in a rich sauce of walnuts, garlic and olive oil (or sometimes yoghurt).

In some parts however they dispense with flour or starch entirely and use one of the most under-rated pulses, lentils. In an earlier chapter I remarked upon their particular popularity in Early Han China. In England in the Middle Ages they were used as a pottage base. They go superbly with game.

BASIC LENTILS

30 g butter
2 chopped onions
500 ml stock, beef or game
600 g lentils, washed
1 bay leaf
salt and pepper
parsley and spring onions

Do not soak the lentils. The whole point about this dish is to absorb the stock and if you soak them you will spoil this effect. Also remember that pulses should not be seasoned until after they are cooked. Melt the butter in an iron pot and fry the onion until it is soft. Pour in the stock, add the lentils and the bay leaf and simmer until all the stock is absorbed. This should take about forty minutes. You can add the salt and pepper after about half an hour. Stir in the chopped onions and parsley and a knob of butter if the lentils seem a little dry, and serve.

This is delicious but as an accompaniment can be taken a step further if your guests can handle strong flavours in combination. In many parts of southern Europe dishes are piqued with the taste of anchovy. This habit used to also be a feature of English cooking but survives now only in bloater pastes and in some Victorian savoury recipes. In Catalonia it is still widely popular.

LENTEJAS Y ANCHOAS

500 g brown lentils
2 chopped onions
2 small tins anchovies
4 tablespoons olive oil

3 cloves garlic
100 g butter
salt and pepper

Wash the lentils and cover them with water in a pan. Bring this to the boil and then take it off the heat and let it stand for an hour. Cook the onions and garlic in the olive oil for a few minutes and then add them to the lentils. Chop up the anchovies and add them to the mixture with their oil. Return the lentils to the heat and put in just a little salt (anchovies are quite salty) and plenty of pepper. If the lentils have absorbed all the water add just a tiny amount more so that they do not catch and simmer for about twenty minutes, slowly adding the butter a knob at a time. If you think this is rich I must tell you that the Catalans use more than twice as much butter and think nothing of it but my heart goes pit-a-pat at the very thought. This also does very well as a main dish for summer with a green salad. I would thoroughly recommend it to accompany plainly braised game birds if you can get them — a brace of pheasant, some quail or some partridges.

KHICHRI

Rice as a source of carbohydrate has never been much regarded in England although it was used sometimes in the Middle Ages as a base for sweet pottages such as 'frumenty'. When the English conquered India they discovered it in another form, spelt as above and, as they did with curry, they transformed it into something quite unIndian called kedgeree, a breakfast dish of fish and rice. The something they transformed had no fish in it but comprised rice and lentils.

60 g ghee
300 g long grain rice
300 g lentils
1 chopped onion
salt
tablespoon tarmarind pulp
¼ teaspoon each ground ginger, white pepper, allspice and cardamom

Soften the onion in the ghee, then stir in the spices and salt and let them fry for a couple of minutes. Add the rice and the tamarind and just cover with water. Simmer for about ten minutes and then add the lentils and some more water if necessary. Lentils cook slightly more quickly than rice. If you put them on together the lentils will go mushy while the rice is still hard. Simmer uncovered until both are cooked. This is good with chicken.

How the English got from here to kedgeree is one of the great unexplained mysteries of international cuisine. Perhaps they added Bombay duck, that is saltfish, as a piquant flavour and went on from there to make smoked fish the main ingredient. We shall never know. They should perhaps have stuck to suet pudding.

LEEK AND ONION PUDDING .

In the winter this dish is an excellent accompaniment to meat, particularly beefsteaks.

300 g flour
teaspoon baking powder
150 g suet
salt, pepper, thyme, sage
1 chopped onion
3 or 4 chopped leeks
butter

Make a suet crust by mixing the flour, baking powder, suet, salt, pepper and thyme to a firm dough with a little water. Line a pudding steamer with two-thirds of it and fill this with the leeks and onion. Add sage and some knobs of butter, and a little more salt and pepper. Put on the pastry lid and cover and steam or boil for about 3 hours in the usual way.

Leeks are one of the most delicious but under-rated of all vegetables. At one time they had their own festival in Northumbria. But the English eventually came to associate them with the Welsh, the poor, and worst of all with a cure for leprosy. In William Langland's famous passage in which Piers Ploughman describes his diet, leeks figure prominently. They therefore turned their noses up at them and those who still eat them hastened their decline by serving them with white sauce. I should like to see leeks make a comeback.

We have in the past decade grown used to eating the unusual and the frowned upon. While we are at it we might very well learn to eat stuffed peppers.

SICILIAN STUFFED PEPPERS

There are many recipes for stuffed peppers. Almost any savoury stuffing can be used but this one is my favourite. It can also be served as an entrée. You will need to choose large green peppers (which are crisper than red) and ones with relatively flat bottoms so they will sit up to be cooked. It is essentially a dish for summer in much the same way as the preceding is for winter. Both can be eaten at any time but all things have their appropriate season.

12 large green peppers
150 g chopped onion
3 cloves chopped garlic
olive oil
200 g pine nuts
300 g breadcrumbs
150 g sultanas
2 tins anchovies
juice of two oranges
lemon juice, salt, pepper, sugar
parsley

Cut the stalk end off the pepper and retain it, as a cap. Clean out the seeds and membrane. Fry the onion and garlic in a little oil and then stir in the crumbs and pine nuts and heat through. Remove from the heat and mix in the other ingredients including the oil from the anchovies. Divide this stuffing evenly between the peppers and replace their caps. Set them upright and sprinkle with olive oil. Bake at 190° C for about an hour. Some say the peppers should be blanched, or even grilled, beforehand and their skins removed but that seems unnecessary to me.

If you are using this as an entrée then halve the numbers. And if it is summer you will almost certainly be serving that other great summer delight, a salad.

SALADS

In second place in my mother's bestiary of vegetables there came lettuce. When she grew tired of torturing cabbage she would seize a lettuce and savagely chop it up with a knife. Its shredded remains would be mixed with tomato and cucumber and a mess of condensed milk, mustard and vinegar poured over it. Sometimes it was stained red with beetroot as well, doubtless to simulate its life's blood. The result, which should have been given a decent burial, was presented as salad and eaten with pressed ham on summer Sunday evenings. It was not for some years that I learned never to cut a lettuce, as the resultant bruising ruins it. It should be shredded.

Salads are one of the oldest of all dishes. The Romans ate them with relish and so has everyone since, but the ingredients have changed considerably over the years. The Romans for instance put flowers, both leaves and petals, in theirs. You still can of course. Nasturtium flowers are excellent, they have a refreshing sharp flavour and they add an interesting touch of colour. Borage flowers do the same. Borage is included in a salad recipe of 1393 along with parsley, sage, mint, fennel, cress, onions, leeks, rosemary and purslain.

In medieval times they were into colours in rather a big way. A most interesting medival salad can be made by combining shredded raw cabbage with cooked and quartered beets, turnips and parsnips, and with dried fruits and nuts, e.g. almonds, prunes, dates, figs, raisins and apple. Sprinkle over the top a little salt, brown sugar, mustard and carob powder. This last, known at St John's bread, was particularly popular as a medieval ingredient. It is now used as a substitute for chocolate by some 'health food' buffs although not very successfully I think.

Salads have never gone out of fashion. Gervase Markham speaks of them at length, although his archaic use of language makes his recipes hard to follow. 'Bean-cods' for example in his recipes are fresh young beans and 'chibols' are spring onions. Joan Cromwell, wife of the Protector, and noted in her time for her frugal housekeeping skills, once served a salad including not only vegetables but shrimps and pickles.

But the greatest of all works on salads is John Evelyn's *Acetaria* of 1699 which lists not only seventy-two different salad herbs and vegetables but contains a salad calendar. This allows for a different salad in almost every week of the year. In his day of course there were no tomatoes. He also gives a number of recipes for dressings.

Thomas Jefferson, Jane Austen and Alexandre Dumas all speak approvingly of salads. Sydney Smith, never one to be outdone, actually composed a poem which is a recipe for a salad dressing. It begins:

To make this condiment your poet begs
The pounded yellow of two hardboiled eggs . . .

and ends:

Serenely full the epicure would say,
Fate cannot harm me, I have dined today.

Who are we to argue with all of these people? And who wants to?

The key to successful salads is always to compose them just before serving, to use the freshest vegetables available and to always put the dressing on at the very last. We all have our favourite dressings. John Evelyn was very

223

down on vinegar. The English, he said, used far too much of it and I agree. Try mixing equal parts of olive oil and lemon juice and you may be surprised at the result. My standard comes from a most interesting book *Leaves From Our Tuscan Kitchen* published first in 1899. It was compiled by Janet Ross who lived just outside Florence with her husband, Henry, a Mesopotamian archeologist. Together for thirty years they carefully compiled a collection of the recipes of Giuseppe Volpi, their cook. They suggest mixing equal quantities of olive oil and wine vinegar, a pinch of salt, a teaspoon of majoram and a teaspoon of honey. Blend thoroughly.

There are quite literally hundreds of dressing recipes. Two things to be avoided like the plague however are ready-mades and condensed milk. Beyond that the sky is the limit.

One begins almost invariably with lettuce. The lettuce, says Evelyn, 'ever was and still continues the principal foundation of the universal Tribe of Salads.' They have been around since at least the ancient Egyptians who made them sacred to the god Min and painted them in detail on the walls of tombs and temples. They found their way from Egypt to the Greek Islands, to Italy and then to Avignon during the Renaissance. When making salads however, don't forget that lettuce is not the only possibility. Celery and fennel are both very good. Cabbage is too, although it has been rendered disreputable by mass caterers who have introduced onto the market something they describe as coleslaw. It bears little resemblance to the real dish of that name which should be served with sour cream and vinegar and was originally brought to the Americas by Dutch settlers on Manhattan. Its name seems to derive from *cal* and *sla*, two words meaning respectively cabbage and salad, which became run together and their pronunciation smoothed by time. Some salads, particularly those based on potatoes, are equally good hot with a hollandaise sauce or one of its many variations. In the field of salads I cannot be your mentor. You must invent your own.

But here is one recipe for salad in aspic which adds a little something special to a summer dinner.

1 litre of aspic jelly
120 g cooked green peas
120 g cooked diced young carrots
60 g cooked corn kernels
120 g cooked prawns
2 hard-boiled eggs
lettuce
mayonnaise dressing

Make up the jelly with half water and half white wine. Remember to season it well. In a mould slowly layer and set the jelly, the vegetables, the prawns and the sliced eggs. Turn out onto a bed of lettuce and serve with the mayonnaise of your choice.

Desserts

Blessed be he that invented pudding,
for it is a Manna that hits the
palates of all sortes of people.

— M. Misson

THE FRENCHMAN MISSON travelled in England in the early eighteenth century. He was delighted with English food, possibly the last visitor from across the channel to voice this opinion although there is little justice in its contrary. My mother would echo Misson's view; in my childhood no main meal was complete without a pudding of some sort. Mind you the pudding to which Misson referred was not necessarily the sweet course as we now know it. The original purpose of pudding in the tradition of eighteenth-century country cooking we follow was twofold — sugar to give energy for heavy work and bulk to fill out what was an often frugal meat course.

Over the last several decades the tradition of the pudding with every meal has fallen on evil days. Desserts are rarely served. A surfeit of joggers and other puritanical punishers of their bodies under the guise of health have ensured that suet puddings and even tarts and fools have become a thing of the past. Fanatics are always with us; it is a pity they have now invaded the realm of food. Desserts are accompaniments now largely to dinners and festivals alone.

This is a shame, not least because it puts an end to an ancient and honourable tradition which commenced when sugar came to Europe with the returning Crusaders in the eleventh century. Originally sugar was an extremely costly substance and was used only as a spice. In 1289 Bishop

225

Swinfield was paying sixpence a pound to buy it in bulk in London. In the provinces it went for as much as eightpence, a great sum. Alice de Brynne's household accounts record the purchase of about a pound avoirdupois per annum. Royal households were more extravagant. Edward I used over three thousand pounds of it in a single year; it was given, among other uses, to his son Henry who was often ill as a child, to build him up. Perhaps too much sugar kept him that way; certainly his teeth must have suffered. A much later writer remarked upon the blackness of the teeth of Elizabeth Tudor and attributed this to a surfeit of sugar. By the sixteenth century it had quite driven out honey as a sweetener.

Medieval cooks span astonishing sugar confections for banquets or combined it with cream or eggs in custards and syllabubs. Sometimes it was combined with almonds to make marzipan and used to model figures, which were greatly admired as centrepieces at feasts. Such fancies no longer attract us. They survive only as the icing on cakes for special occasions.

By the eighteenth century puddings and desserts had evolved pretty much into dishes we eat today, and Misson would at once recognise many of our traditional dessert dishes. In his encomium to the English pudding he said: 'Ah, what an excellent thing is an English pudding! To come in pudding-time is as much as to say to come in the most lucky moment in the world. Give an English man a pudding, and he shall think it an able treat in any part of the world.' Even, I may say, in the far antipodes. Only recollect one thing; desserts are to finish the *meal* rather than the guests. A light dessert is usually to be preferred. Not everyone can handle a Sussex pond pudding after a roast; they would be much better off with a custard, a meringue, a sorbet or even simply fresh fruit and cheese. We should begin therefore with some of these lighter confections.

Creams and Jellies

The seventeenth century was the great age of such dishes. The works of Gervase Markham and Sir Kenelm Digby are full of blancmanges and whipped syllabubs. There were so many varieties that words such as suckets, lozenges and codinacs, which have now fallen entirely out of use or changed their meaning, had to be invented to differentiate them. Some few survive and one of these particularly brings back memories of my childhood.

SPANISH CREAM

When we went to Sunday lunch with my grandmother she always made this dessert. The curiosity of it was that she could never get it *quite* right, and the cream and the jelly used to separate. That left it perfectly edible but granny always muttered and grumbled about this peculiar 'Spanish cream effect'. She was a very fine traditional cook and it irritated her. I am ashamed to say that we children used to tease her about it, but now that I have made it myself a number of times and have also had grave difficulty with it more than once I am sorry we did so.

1 tablespoon gelatine
600 ml milk
2 eggs, separated
50 g sugar
3 drops vanilla essence

Soften the gelatine in a saucepan with a little of the milk and then add the rest of the milk and heat over a low burner until the gelatine is dissolved. Add the sugar and the lightly beaten yolks and continue to stir until this custard coats the back of a wooden spoon. Take care it doesn't curdle by keeping the heat low, even if this takes longer. Patience is an indispensable accompaniment to the cooking of any custard. Remove from the heat to cool. Beat the egg whites until they are stiff and fold them in with the vanilla. I suspect it is inadequate folding which causes the separation. Pour into a wet mould and leave to set in a cool place. This can be made the day before and unmoulded just before serving. It is delicious with stewed fruit. Of course it is really a simple version of the dish which follows.

ORANGE BAVARIAN CREAM

No one seems to know why this cream is said to be Bavarian any more than the one just described is naturally Spanish. It just is. It takes somewhat longer to make however and is consequently grander. Keep the two extra egg whites for sorbet.

2 large oranges
1 tablespoon sugar
15 g gelatine
7 egg yolks
5 egg whites
120 g caster sugar
2 teaspoons cornflour
450 ml boiling milk
150 ml cream
2 tablespoons orange liqueur

Peel the oranges, cut the zest into thin strips and chop finely. Blanch and strain. If you don't blanch the orange zest you will get a bitter tinge to the flavour. Add the tablespoon of sugar, the squeezed juice of the oranges and the gelatine. Set this aside.

To make the custard, beat the egg yolks, the caster sugar and the cornflour together until it is creamy. You will know this is happening when you see it 'form the ribbon'. That's to say when a whisk drawn through it leaves a path behind. Stir in the milk and then simmer the mixture in a double boiler until it thickens. The French call this a *crème anglaise.* Let it cool for a moment and then stir in the orange and gelatine mixture. Make sure that this is properly dispersed and dissolved in the custard or the cream will not set. Beat the egg whites until they are stiff. You can add a tablespoon of sugar and a pinch of salt to this if you like. Fold the stiff whites into the custard and put in a cool place. Folding it again several times as it cools will prevent separation. When it is cold but not set, whip the cream lightly and fold it in also together with the liqueur. Pour into a wetted mould.

A Bavarian cream needs nothing else. It should simply be turned out and served. Other flavours than orange may be used — almond, say, or chocolate. For the latter, proceed as above but use 150 ml of strong coffee, a little vanilla and some cooking chocolate dissolved together to melt the gelatine, and rum or a coffee liqueur rather than orange. Some recipes I have seen add a sauce made by heating together 150 ml cream, 70 g of caster sugar and 120 g cooking chocolate, a little rum and cinnamon and a handful of chopped almonds. This is chilled and then poured over the cream just before serving. It can all be made the day before. The famous dessert *Riz à l'Impératrice* is also a Bavarian cream and has not any resemblance or family relationship to the dreaded cold rice pudding of my childhood. That notwithstanding, the connection by name is enough and I have never made it.

Most jellies, by contrast, are much simpler than this. Unfortunately they have developed a bad reputation, created by mass food manufacturers with their over-sweet biliously coloured products. The original and traditional jelly desserts were rather more a variation on creams. Some of them are almost a soufflé. Possibly you cannot.believe that anything of such a hybrid nature could be worth the eating and I agree that they sound rather like something designed by a committee. But I do commend this next one to you. It involves a very sixteenth-century combination of flavours — cinnamon and chocolate. It became fashionable when Spain began exporting the products of its territories in the Americas to Europe.

CHOCOLATE PAVLOVA SOUFFLÉ

I don't know how pavlova got into the name. Perhaps it's the egg whites. Sometimes this dish is called a chinchilla.

5 egg whites
40 g unsweetened cocoa
80 g caster sugar
1 heaped teaspoon ground cinnamon

Mix together the dry ingredients. Beat the egg whites until stiff and then thoroughly fold in the dry mixture by beating further. Add a jigger of rum if you like. Scrape the mixture into a buttered mould, preferably a ring, and stand this in a water bath in an oven pre-heated to 160°C for an hour. The dessert will rise tremendously. At the end of that time turn off the oven and leave the door ajar until the whole thing has cooled. It will contract down again. When cold it can be turned out of the mould and kept in the refrigerator.

COFFEE CREAM JELLY

Still with the same sort of flavour, this is a true jelly and one that goes very well as a light end to a meal.

300 ml double strength coffee
3 tablespoons sugar
15 g gelatine
300 ml cream

Warm the coffee. Don't let it boil — it will become bitter if you do. Dissolve the sugar and gelatine in the warmed coffee. Cool until almost set. Beat the cream until thick and fold it into the coffee. Pour into a wetted mould and turn out to serve. Jelly from a mould always looks good on the table. There are some very nice ceramic moulds about but I prefer something in metal. No fear of breaking it when you give it a sharp tap on the bottom to loosen the contents. Of course you can also make the same jelly without the cream by doubling the other ingredients and brewing the coffee with cinnamon, nutmeg, cloves and cardamom (which should be strained off before moulding). This looks good served in individual glasses with a decoration of whipped cream on top. Jellies which are simply a flavour captured in a setting agent can be made with almost anything.

LEMON SOLID

This is the traditional name for this dish which is a sort of milk jelly.

750 ml milk
300 ml cream
25 g gelatine
2 lemons
150 g caster sugar

Grate the zest from the lemons and squeeze the juice. Set aside. Let the gelatine soak in 600 ml of the milk. Bring the balance of the milk and the cream to a good heat and dissolve the sugar in it. Add the zest and the remaining milk and gelatine then slowly stir in the lemon juice. Don't worry if it curdles slightly; it's supposed to. Pour into a mould to set. You can make most jellies using this or the preceding recipe. It's quite fun to experiment.

Tart fruits are best to my taste, particularly raspberries or currants. One thing you should not use a jelly for, however, is for a trifle.

Fools, Flummeries and Trifles

Long before I made them or ate them, fools and flummeries attracted me by the name alone. Trifle was something else. From my earliest memory it was the cold dessert for family state occasions — funerals, weddings and Christmas tea. At least that which passed for trifle — bought sponge soaked in commercial jelly and covered with packet custard. The fastidious will doubtless recoil in horror although to be frank I have clear memories of eating it with relish and coming back for more. In fact I could never understand why the grown-ups were eating ham and salad when all that trifle was going to waste. I still enjoy trifle but I've now discovered that there's an upmarket version, that is to say, the real thing, which leaves the confections of my childhood in the shade.

All of these dishes have an interesting history. In medieval times a flavouring for dessert and other sweet dishes was manufactured from almonds, ground and infused in milk. In the sixteenth century this was combined with calves-foot jelly and coloured red to produce a dish known as a lechemeat to be eaten with a wine sauce. Some time in the seventeenth century people began to leave out the almonds, use cream and sometimes add oatmeal as a thickener so that the dish would hold its shape when moulded. It was flavoured with fresh fruit. Fools and trifles are variations on this dish which became known in the eighteenth century as 'flummery'. Why the name changed it is hard to say. Flummery, in the colloquial English of the time means flattery, or polite nonsense. If you make this dish you'll see the connection — and of course its relationship to 'trifle' is clear enough.

About the middle of the eighteenth century people began to put their fruit and cream on a base of macaroons or ratafia biscuits soaked in fortified wine, a combination of the flummery with yet another dish, the floating island. It was from this that our present trifle developed.

BLACKCURRANT FLUMMERY

My parents always had currant bushes in their garden and made pies and tarts from them as well as jam. Topping and tailing them was a long and tedious task which always seemed to fall to my grandmother when she came to stay. I rather think she insisted on it because she couldn't bear to see fruit going to waste. Then for a long time currants couldn't be easily obtained. They are now coming back. I hope flummery and fool comes back with them.

450 g blackcurrants
250 ml milk
225 g sugar
1 teaspoon lemon juice
4 tablespoons semolina

Simmer the currants with the sugar and just enough water to prevent burning. When the fruit is soft and pulpy add the lemon juice and remove from the heat. Separately warm the milk and stir in the semolina. Bring it to a simmer and stir for three or four minutes. Blend in the fruit and put in a bowl to cool. Serve with whipped cream or even better a syllabub (of which more hereafter).

Contrariwise, if you are proposing to mould the flummery then stir 15 g of gelatine into the milk along with the semolina so that it will stand when turned out. You can make the same dish with gooseberries, another fruit which is coming available again, or blueberries which are a favourite in traditional New England cookery in which flummery was sometimes known as 'grunt' or 'slump'.

Semolina, which is wheat with the bran and germ removed leaving only the endosperm, or protein, and starch, as a thickener has been largely driven out by cornflour, although in my view it is much superior. In Italy of course it is used as the base for the famous *gnocchi alla romana*. Just to muddle you it is not the same as semola or semolino which is flour made from durum, a very hard wheat suitable for pasta. Both words of course derive from Latin *simila* meaning 'fine flow'.

GOOSEBERRY FOOL

Gooseberries usually appear in the shops for about two weeks in early December or thereabouts. They don't freeze at all well; being almost all liquid they burst in the freezing and turn watery when they thaw. So if you want to make this dish you'll really have to do it when they are fresh. Luckily that's early summer (even in Wellington where I live). I am sure you will be able to stand the strain of eating so many gooseberries at one time of year if you are also making some of the other gooseberry dishes in this book. Tinned gooseberries *can* be used but they aren't the same, mostly because of the heavy syrup in which they are usually preserved. If you don't like or can't get gooseberries you can use this recipe with almost any soft fruit.

500 g gooseberries
60 g butter
a little sugar
300 ml cream
3 egg yolks

Melt the butter in a pan and add the topped and tailed gooseberries. Cover and cook on low for a few minutes. Gooseberries, along with rhubarb, raspberries and some other soft fruit, contain enough liquid to literally stew in their own juice. When the fruit is soft mash it with a fork off the heat and stir in sugar to taste but not so much as to destroy the tart flavour. Make a custard of the cream and eggs by bringing the cream to the boil in a double boiler and then blending in the beaten egg yolks. Stir constantly until it thickens, remove from the heat and when almost cold mix in the fruit. Gooseberries go very well with Frontignac and you could stir in a tablespoon of that if you can get it, although that is not so easy. If you want to do a quicker and simpler version of this dish substitute whipped cream for a custard.

Gooseberries (botanically *Ribes grossularia*) grow all over northern and central Europe, as far east as Nepal, and as far south as Morocco. They have transplanted most successfully to both the Americas and the Antipodes. Only the English appear however to have developed them for the purposes of desserts.

In medieval times the leaves of the bush were eaten as a vegetable and the fruit was thought to ward off the plague. Ineffective I should think, but a pleasanter way to go. My herbal also remarks: 'An infusion of the leaves taken monthly will be found a useful tonic for growing girls.' The Germans and Italians use them as the base of a sauce for veal. Despite their name they have nothing to do with geese; the name derives from Old French *krusil* meaning a crisp berry.

TRIFLE

This is the acme of summer desserts. I once served it at a dinner party at which my youngest son then aged eight was present. This above all else I thought he would like (the other food being too strong in flavour for the taste of a child). Apparently not, however. When I quizzed him later he said he thought 'there was too much beer in it'. When you make it you will see what he meant. The sponge I use comes from the *Edmond's Cookery Book* which ought to be a standby in every kitchen. I also always make the trifle in a transparent bowl so that the layers and colours can be seen to best advantage.

sponge cake
Madeira wine
1 glass brandy
600 ml cream
2 egg yolks
2 eggs
1 tablespoon semolina

caster sugar
500 g fresh raspberries or blackberries
syllabub (see below)
candied orange and lemon peel

Cut the sponge to fit the bottom of your bowl. Pour about 150 mls of Madeira over it and the brandy. Seal with plastic film and leave overnight. Next day make the custard by bringing the cream to a gentle simmer and then mixing in the beaten eggs and the semolina and stirring in a double boiler until it is very thick, adding sugar to taste. Pour it over the sponge and leave it to set. When it is cold spread the fruit over the top and cover that in its turn with a layer of syllabub. Decorate with the peel. This is best made well in advance so that the flavours can percolate. It can then be refrigerated until serving.

SYLLABUB

When a friend of mine was in Edinburgh a few years ago he visited the Georgian House Kitchen, an *in situ* museum. He sent me a postcard which was a recipe for whipt (sic) syllabub which purported to be Scottish. Syllabub was actually almost a universal European dish in the sixteenth and seventeenth centuries. At its simplest a milkmaid directed a squirt of milk from the cow into a bowl of spiced cider or ale. After a little while this separated into a curd and a sweet whey. What Little Ms Muffet was doing on her tuffet was eating a syllabub. Charles II was so fond of this refreshment that he kept cows in St James's Park to enable him to indulge himself when out walking.

Wine and fruit juices were also used, and sometimes cream. There is a recipe for one such in Sir Kenelm Digby's *Closet Opened*. He suggested 'a tiny sprig of rosemary' in each glass. I should remark of course that this fashion coincided with the introduction of the cow as the universal provider of milk. Up to the sixteenth century sheep and goats were the milch animals and cows were mostly kept for meat.

Celia Fiennes, a traveller who published a book of her journeys in the 1680s, remarks upon the little wooden cake stalls at Bath and the syllabubs which could also be bought there. However, some people preferred a syllabub which did not separate, which was rather more substantial and which did not have to be consumed at once. This is one such.

8 tablespoons white wine
2 tablespoons brandy
zest and juice of a lemon
60 g sugar
300 ml cream
nutmeg or cinnamon

Put the wine, brandy and lemon in a covered bowl overnight. Next day strain them and dissolve in the sugar. Slowly pour in the cream and add a light grating or dusting of the spice. Beat the mixture until it is stiff. This of course can be eaten as a dessert on its own but I prefer it on the trifle. I have also tried it on a pavlova but it's less successful that way. Hannah Glasse in one of her recipe books (1760) gives a mixture which includes half a bottle of claret as well as sherry, cream and orange juice. Reading eighteenth-century cookery books it is difficult to escape the impression that people were slightly intoxicated most of the time.

The 'floating island' from which trifle derives involves a 'sea' of cream and fruit purée with fingers of sponge covered in jam resting on it and the whole covered over with whipped cream. This and another variation — the whim-wham — were very popular until the latter part of the nineteenth century but they seem to have fallen out of favour. They are still to be found in old-fashioned cookery books. Sometimes as a variation egg whites were combined with the whipped cream. This was known as 'snow'.

Meringues and Others

The combination of sugar with the beaten egg whites to be baked to a brittle surface and a chewy centre — the meringue — does not seem to have appeared in England until the beginning of the eighteenth century. Its first general appearance in a cookery book was in 1691 in the works of the Parisian Francois Massialot. Little did he know that he was spawning the pavlova.

PAVLOVA

You're not going to like what I'm about to tell you but you'll just have to be strong. The pavlova as we know it is not a native of New Zealand. The name seems to have been applied to an existing dessert in Australia in the nineteen-thirties to honour the dancer. But the dish itself is European. I discovered this some years ago when I was at an international gathering in Stockholm. One evening the Danish delegation gave a supper and there on the table were some pavlovas. When I expressed nationalistic delight the Danes professed puzzlement. They had never heard it referred to by our name and explained that it had been in their cuisine for several hundred years. Perhaps it travelled to this country with Scandavian settlers in the nineteenth century. The tradition of putting sliced Chinese gooseberries on top is however almost certainly native to this country. All that notwithstanding, no cookery book would be complete without this recipe.

3 egg whites
3 tablespoons cold water
1 cup caster sugar
1 teaspoon vinegar
1 teaspoon vanilla essence
3 teaspoons cornflour

Beat the egg whites very stiff, add the cold water and beat again. Keep beating and add the sugar very slowly bit by bit. I am convinced that this is the secret of a successful pavlova. If you just dump the sugar in and then beat it will not rise properly. When the sugar is properly combined add the vinegar, vanilla and cornflour one at a time. Beat these in also.

Bake on a greased tray or in a flan for 45 minutes at 150° C and then leave to cool in the oven. You can buy removable pavlova moulding rings which are useful if your mixture is a bit runny — but it shouldn't be. The pavlova should of course be covered in whipped cream, flavoured with passionfruit or decorated with peach slices or Chinese gooseberries. (I refuse to call them 'kiwifruit', an ugly name if ever I heard one. The French call them *souris végétales*.) I am told by a French friend that she once had a telephone call from her father in Lyon who in some excitement demanded to know what the previous name for this fruit was for a competition he was entering. She knew the New Zealand name but had some difficulty translating it into French. Eventually she decided that *groseilles chinoises* would suffice.

They really are Chinese, of course, from the Yangtse Valley where they are known as yang t'ao. Their introduction to this country is usually attributed to James McGregor who brought them from China and gave the seed to Alexander Allison of Wanganui, who took his first fruit from them in 1910. It was common folklore in our family however that they pre-date that, and my grandmother always used to say that when she was a child, that is about 1880, they grew wild in Central Otago. It was thought that they were brought by Chinese goldminers in the 1860s. A romantic fable I think. They have been grown commercially at Te Puke since 1937 and we were exporting them as early as 1953 in quite large commercial quantities. Jane Grigson in her *Fruit Book* recollects their availability in England before the Second World War. The Chinese never seem to have eaten them much although one of their writers remarks that they were greatly relished by the monkeys in the mountains of Shensi. Perhaps that tells something about ourselves we really don't want to know. Of course a pavlova is not the only thing for which you can use a meringue, as the following two recipes show.

FIRE IN THE SNOW

This dish entranced my youngest son from the moment he saw it illustrated on the cover of *The Penguin Freezer Cookbook* and nothing would do until I had made it for him. When you make it you will see why it is so named.

3 egg whites
180 g caster sugar
1 teaspoon vinegar
600 g raspberries
2 tablespoons brandy
300 ml cream

Beat the egg whites, sugar and vinegar as described for a pavlova until they are *very* stiff. They then need to be formed into a case. This is rather a fiddly process. One of the best ways of doing it is in a baba mould but better still is to use a large icing bag and nozzle. Make first a circular layer on a greased baking tray and then build up the 'walls' in layers. The intention is to have a hollow shape like a basket. This should then be cooked *very* slowly at 100°C for a couple of hours. When it is cooled the case can be used at once or frozen until needed. It needs careful storing in this latter instance because meringue is very brittle.

Put the fruit in a bowl, sprinkle just a little sugar and the brandy over it and leave it to stand for about an hour to absorb this. Pile it in the meringue case and top with the cream, lightly whipped. A perfect summer dessert. But meringue belongs also to the winter.

RHUBARB MERINGUE WITH CUSTARD

Like a number of other fruits, rhubarb has fallen from favour. Perhaps its appearance once too often on institutional menus or its feeding to children as a carminative has contributed to this. For myself I think its decline has been an accompaniment of the decline of the traditional garden. People no longer have the time or the inclination to look after a few raspberry canes, gooseberry and currant bushes, fruit trees and so forth. Luckily a friend of mine recently bought a house which still had the old garden and with it abundant rhubarb.

As a fruit, it has been around a long time. The classical Greeks imported it from China in dried form. It came to them via the River Volga which they called the Rha and this gave it the name which has come down to us, *rha barbaron*. It was used medicinally down the centuries but from about 1800 has been increasingly eaten as a fruit, especially in tarts. This rather different recipe comes from Eliza Acton's *Modern Cookery* of 1845.

450 g rhubarb stems
250 g sugar
4 egg whites
4 tablespoons caster sugar
2 egg yolks
1 egg
450 ml milk
2 tablespoons sugar
60 g butter
vanilla pod

Cut the rhubarb into short lengths, mix with the sugar and stew gently until a pulp results. Rhubarb generates liquid so there is no fear of burning if you stir it well in the first instance. Let cool and turn into an oven-proof serving dish. Make the custard. Split the vanilla pod and put it in a saucepan with the milk. Bring to the boil and set to one side. Remove the pod.

Beat the yolks and the egg with two tablespoons of sugar until they form the ribbon and then stir into the milk with the butter. Heat over a low heat or in a double boiler until the custard thickens and pour over the fruit in the dish. Allow to cool.

Beat the egg whites until they form soft peaks and then gradually beat in the caster sugar. Spread this over the rhubarb and custard and bake in a pre-heated oven at 180° C for forty minutes. 'The crust formed by the white of egg and sugar,' says Ms Acton, 'which is in fact the meringue, should be of a light equal brown, and crisp quite through. If placed in an exceedingly slow oven, the underpart of it will remain half liquid, and give an uninviting appearance to the fruit when it is served.'

Pears can be presented in the same way. Custard is not to everyone's taste even when prepared properly. Ambrose Bierce in his *Devil's Dictionary* defines it as a 'detestable substance produced by a malevolent conspiracy of the hen, the cow and the cook.' Too much rhubarb and custard at boarding school causes the holding of such opinions I dare say.

Rhubarb can be used for all sorts of things. In the Middle East it is often cooked with meat, particularly lamb, in a dish known as a *khoresh*. It can also be served stewed in a form known as a tansy.

RHUBARB TANSY

450 g rhubarb
100 g butter
50 g sugar
2 egg yolks
125 ml cream
2 tablespoons lemon juice
caster sugar

Chop the rhubarb into pieces about an inch long. Simmer it very gently in the butter until it is cooked then off the heat add the beaten egg yolks, the cream lightly whipped and sugar to sweeten to your taste. Return this mixture to the heat and simmer it gently until it is firm. It can be eaten hot or cold. Sprinkle it with the lemon juice just before serving. There are many other interesting things to do with rhubarb. One of the least usual is to make it into icecream.

Icecreams and Sorbets

We have grown used to mass-produced food. It seems to be one of the natural laws of the universe that whoever makes food in commercial quantities destroys its quality. This law is as immutable and as ancient as the pyramids. It is particularly true of icecream. The tragedy is of course that we have been producing it *en masse* for so long that several generations have now passed without many people ever eating the real thing. This is to cheat children of their birthright. When I gave my smallest son real icecream for the first time he ate it in wonderment. He graduated from there to sorbets. Somewhat to my surprise he prefers these latter and best of all café granita. He thinks it is a chocolate ice-block — which it is, I suppose.

Sorbets (from Arabic *shariba*, also the origin of the word sherbet) have been made for centuries. The Romans enjoyed snow mixed with fruit juice. The Chinese of the Late Han discovered refrigeration using blocks of river ice buried in deep cellars. In the eighth century under the emperors of that most civilised of dynasties, the T'ang, the Chinese were making sorbets. By the eleventh century the habit had spread to Japan, as the diary of the court lady Sei Shonagon makes clear.

Sorbets came to England in the time of Charles II. If you go to the great house of Knole at Sevenoaks you will be able to see an ice house as they existed prior to domestic refrigerators. Icecream recipes began appearing in English cookery books about 1715. Hannah Glasse in the 1757 edition of *The Art of Cookery* describes the equipment then used. America had to wait until 1784 when Thomas Jefferson brought a similar machine home from France. These complicated engines involved ice, salt and a variety of stirring paddles and basins with tight lids. The modern method is much simpler and it amazes me that more people do not make ices. Essentially they are a fruit syrup or purée, partially frozen and beaten several times to break up the ice crystals, with the addition of stiffly beaten egg whites (for sorbet) or cream or custard (for icecream) and a repetition of the same process of freezing and beating. They can then be stored almost indefinitely at the bottom of a freezer and whipped out whenever you feel inclined. Sharper flavours make a very refreshing summer entrée course; with those we have already dealt. Those which follow are all dessert recipes.

APRICOT SORBET

Take a large tin of apricots, about 450 g, and purée the fruit and the syrup in a blender adding a little more sugar to taste if you like. Add to this while it is blending a tablespoon of lemon juice and a few drops of almond essence. Almond is very good with apricots; it brings out the flavour. But don't use too much or you will drown the apricot. Set this in a bowl in a freezer and when it is partially frozen it should be beaten until it whitens and increases in volume. Repeat this a couple of times. Beat two egg whites until stiff and fold them into the partially frozen fruit. Repeat the freezing and beating process and then store in a sealed container until you are ready to use it. If you like you can take it out of the freezer a few minutes before serving so that it softens slightly.

CAFÉ GRANITA

This is even simpler. I pour my leftover coffee from the expresso into a storage jar in the freezer. When I have about a litre I dissolve 200 g of caster sugar in it and add a jigger of rum. I then go through the same process of beating and adding the egg whites.

Both of these sorbets can be turned into icecream by substituting lightly beaten cream for the white of egg. The same can be done with almost all fruits and flavours. Adding a little of the appropriate liqueur gives a fillip to it too. The only fruit I have never been able to successfully make into an ice is pineapple which tends to separate out into fibrous particles, although a number of books give recipes. One of the most interesting of these publications is *The Book of Ices* by Agnes Marshall, original edition 1885, and recently republished by the Metropolitan Museum in New York. It contains 117 different recipes for ices, some of them, e.g. cucumber, distinctly odd to modern taste — but no rhubarb. Cooked rhubarb, which I had imagined would do the same as pineapple, in fact doesn't, but makes a delicious icecream in combination with about 300 g of sugar.

NESSELRODE

This is the most splendid of icecreams and will delight your friends at any summer dinner party. There is a long passage in Proust in which Nesselrode pudding figures largely. It is named for a Russian diplomat, friend and contemporary of the French politician Talleyrand, and involves a custard which makes the smoothest of all icecreams. Make your custard from 300 ml of cream, four egg yolks and about 150 g of vanilla sugar. (i.e. caster sugar in which a vanilla pod has been stored). While the custard is still hot, add about 120 g chestnut purée and mix the two thoroughly. When this has cooled stir in about 100 g of mixed raisins, sultanas, and chopped peel together with about 150 ml of sweet sherry or madeira. You can also fold in some whipped cream (say about 250 ml). Custard icecreams should not be beaten but turned in as they freeze, a process which always starts from the outside.

ORANGE AND CARDAMOM

Cardamom is an Indian spice from Mysore and is an ingredient in some curries. It is a seed with a cool flavour something between mint and eucalyptus. Strangely it is also popular in Scandinavian cooking. You may have some trouble obtaining the pods but most health food shops can get them for you. References to cardamom abound in *The Arabian Nights*; in Egypt the ground seeds are used to flavour coffee. It combines particularly well with orange.

1 tin concentrated orange juice (about 200 ml)
3 eggs
175 g caster sugar
4 cardamom pods
300 ml cream
a little salt

240

Beat the eggs with a pinch of salt. Dissolve the sugar in about half a cup of water and boil it hard for a few minutes to make a syrup. Pour this on the eggs and beat again until it thickens. Remove the cardamom seeds from their pods and crush them. Add them and the orange juice to the syrup and beat again. Freeze and beat several times then fold in the lightly whipped cream.

For serving icecreams different flavours and colours can be layered in a mould and turned out just before serving. This looks very dramatic. It must be eaten at once or it will dissolve into a slushy puddle before your very eyes. An advantage of a custard icecream is that it will keep its shape longer if it is moulded. Of course custards are good to eat on their own or just with fruit, the remarks of Ambrose Bierce notwithstanding.

Custards and Pies

The following is one of those remarkable dishes which never cease to astonish me. I have made it again and again and always the effect on guests is the same. It appears to be simply a very bland custard. They take their first mouthful, and then it hits them: they sit stock still while their whole body suffuses with orange.

ELIZABETH RAFFALD'S ORANGE CUSTARD

This recipe shows where we might find the origins of our own national cuisine if we cared to look — in the eighteenth century in rural England. Elizabeth Raffald was one of an unending tribe of energetic eighteenth-century cooks and cookery book writers. According to Jane Grigson in *English Food* she began work at the age of 15 in 1748. By the time of her death eighteen years later she had organised a large cooked-food shop, set up a domestic servants' employment agency, run two important Manchester inns, financed two newspapers, published the first Manchester street directory, coped with a feckless husband and fifteen or so daughters, become housekeeper of a stately home in Cheshire, and best of all published a cookery book, *The Experienced English Housekeeper*. That was in 1769, the same year in which James Cook reached New Zealand for the first time. It is arguable which of those two events of that year added more to the sum of western civilisation but if forced to choose I'd take the cookery book every time. It is from it that this recipe ultimately comes.

zest and juice of an orange
juice of a lemon
tablespoon brandy
125 g caster sugar

6 large egg yolks
600 ml of cream
crystallised orange peel

Blanch the orange peel by simmering it in water for a couple of minutes, otherwise it will be bitter. Drain it and chop it in a blender with the brandy, fruit juice, sugar and yolks. Blend very thoroughly until the zest is entirely indistinguishable. Bring the cream to the boil and add it gradually to the other ingredients. Pour into an oven-proof serving dish. Stand this in a pan of hot water and bake it at 160° C for about half an hour. The result will be a pale, just-set custard. This combination of eggs and cream is irresistible although expensive. The six egg whites can be frozen and used for sorbet or fresh for a pavlova. Sprinkle the custard with the crystallised peel before serving. This custard needs nothing else. It is as quintessentially English as the following dish, also a custard, is quintessentially Greek.

GALATO BOUREKO

They had this on the menu at my favourite Greek restaurant and then one day it wasn't there. I asked the waiter why and he shrugged and said that no one ever ordered it except me so it wasn't worth making it. 'All they ever ask for is baklava.' Silly them.

Filo pastry used to be hard to get, but now most delicatessens have it.

20 sheets of filo
170 g butter
600 ml milk
180 g sugar
3 eggs
60 g semolina
vanilla

Syrup:
300 ml water
180 g sugar
teaspoon lemon juice

Heat the milk to boiling and remove from the heat. Beat the eggs and sugar until the mixture is creamy. Add the vanilla and then beat in the semolina. Return the mixture to the heat in a double boiler and cook it slowly until it thickens; remove it from the heat and keep stirring it until it has cooled somewhat. Spread a buttered baking dish with five sheets of pastry so that they cover the bottom and sides, brushing each sheet with melted butter as you go. Pour in the custard. Cover the custard with the remaining sheets of pastry, one at a time, each one lavishly brushed with melted butter. Sprinkle a little water on the top sheet and bake the pie in an oven at 180°C for about one and three quarter hours. Serve cold.

Filo pastry, if you have not come across it before, is plain, paper thin in sheets and very Greek. Making it is really a job for an expert. I watched one once in the market at Chania, taking a lump of pastry the size of a cricket ball and tossing it from hand to hand, and along his arm, twirling it in the air, until it got flatter and flatter and thinner and thinner. Then he stretched it on a round metal table until it was as thin as tissue paper. A most impressive performance which invariably drew a crowd. If you can't get filo this custard is almost as good cooked on a flaky pastry base. The syrup is made by boiling the three ingredients until they thicken. It can be served hot with the *galato boureko* or poured over it. Syrup seems to be a concomitant of all Greek desserts and is rather sweet for me. Sometimes I dispense with it altogether.

Sweet, filled pies on pastry crusts were once common to all Europe but are found in northern cuisine now mostly in country cooking. It has not always been thus of course. From medieval times to the eighteenth century no feast would have been complete without a pie, although the ingredients seem rather odd to our taste — vegetables (including sweet potatoes), fruit (both dried and fresh) and meat mixed indiscriminately. Gervase Markham speaks of one such which includes artichokes, potatoes, dates, beef, raisins, spices, white wine, rosewater, cinnamon and sugar. It also had an iced top. By the eighteenth century however such promiscuous mixtures were falling out of favour and a meal was more likely to end with a tart of fruit, custard or, interestingly, cheese. A choice prompted by one of those curious quirks of human development in which technology creates unconsidered consequences. The building of the canal system allowed for the easier movement of fruit from south to north and as a result fruit pies became a widespread feature of English metropolitan cuisine. They were often sprinkled with candied roots and peels. We are familiar with some of these candies still, but others are now almost obsolete, such as angelica, or entirely unknown in cooking, such as eringo or bugloss. Root of lettuce was also candied. The following recipe might have originally contained any of these but is now usually made with angelica.

CREAM CHEESE AND HONEY PIE

This requires the simplest of pastries and illustrates the proportions needed for any pastry. They can be expanded indefinitely, and a variation in the proportions of fat to flour or a change in the type of fat determines the type of pastry. Generally speaking, but not invariably, the more fat you put in, the flakier the pastry. Pastry making is very easy and the result much superior to the bought variety, although the latter is convenient if you are in a hurry. Mix 120 g of flour with 60 g of butter and a little water. Knead thoroughly into a well-mixed dough and spread it over the base of a flan. Incidentally, I don't care how much of a whole food fanatic you are you *mustn't* make your pastry from wholemeal flour. It will come out like lead. Possibly the development of flaky pastry had to await the development of a technology able to grind flour to the required degree of fineness.

250 g cream cheese
150 ml cream
2 eggs
4 tablespoons sugar
4 tablespoons honey
cinnamon
chopped angelica

Blend all these ingredients thoroughly and pour the smooth result into the pastry case. Cook in a pre-heated oven at 190°C for about 45 minutes. The top will puff up beautifully. If it seems to be browning too much, gently lay a sheet of foil over the top. This pie can be eaten warm or cold. I prefer the latter with cream. It will deflate as it cools, but that's nothing to worry about.

This is a quintessentially eighteenth-century dish. It was the eighteenth century too which gave rise to the cheesecake as we should know it (and not as we have come to know it recently, from the freezer in the supermarket). John Farley in his *London Art of Cookery* gives eight quite different cheesecake recipes. The following is one of them.

JOHN FARLEY'S CHEESECAKE

pastry as for previous recipe, in proportion
250 g cream cheese
50 ml cream
1 tablespoon rosewater
4 egg yolks
60 g melted butter
100 g crushed almonds
100 g caster sugar
100 g macaroon crumbs
grated nutmeg

Line a flan with the pastry and blend the other ingredients. The eighteenth century was inordinately fond of macaroons and it's certainly true that they impart a delicious taste of coconut to any dish in which they are included. They are a bit hard to find but if you can't then almost any coconut biscuits will do. Pour the mixture into the pastry case and cook at 190° C for about 40 minutes. Eat warm.

The survival of cheesecakes as a specifically American delicacy is probably a result of that peculiar phenomenon, the conservatism of colonial societies, which cling to the habits of the old country long after the old country has given them up. The Ionian Greeks were exactly the same. Just as cheesecake was a phenomenon of the seventeenth and eighteenth centuries, so was the apple pie. America was being colonised about then; the pie travelled to the New World with the colonists and stayed to become a native.

In fact fruit in undried form, and especially apples, was regarded with suspicion until Stuart times. Apples in a raw state were blamed in medieval times for spreading the plague and were shunned for other extraordinary pseudo-medical reasons. In 1569 the sale of soft fruit in the streets of London was actually forbidden by ordinance. If eaten at all, apples were stewed for as long as five hours to get rid of their alleged baneful and poisonous influence. They gradually lost their unenviable reputation and as they became favourites the cooking time was correspondingly reduced. The spices used have remained largely the same, however, from the medieval period to the present day.

APPLE PIE

This recipe comes from New England but might as easily have come from the diary of Jane Austen who wrote therein: 'Good apple pies are a considerable part of our domestic happiness.'

pastry as for Cream Cheese and Honey Pie, *but with slightly more butter*
1 kg apples

1 quince
60 g flour
90 g caster sugar
teaspoon cinnamon
2 cloves
120 ml sour cream

Line a pie dish with the pastry. Peel and core the apples and slice them. Wash the grey down off the quince and also peel, core and grate it. Lay the slices of apple and grated quince intermixed on the pastry base. Mix the other dry ingredients and sprinkle them over the top. Pour over the sour cream and bake at 200°C for about 15 minutes, then reduce the heat to 180°C and bake until the crust is nicely browned. This will take about another twenty minutes or so. Serve hot. In some parts of New England this pie is known as a pandowdy. Adding a quince may seem odd, but once you try it you will never bake an apple pie any other way. Quinces, unfortunately, are not easy to obtain. I have a friend with a tree and beg one from time to time. Our neighbours also had one when I was a child but I was sternly and solemnly warned that the quinces were poisonous. They rotted on the ground.

In classical Greece it was the fruit of love and sacred to Aphrodite. An atavistic memory of that association may explain the aversion of those frowning puritan neighbours. Paris awarded one to Aphrodite in the famous contest which sparked the Trojan war, and they may have been the golden apples of the Hesperides. Quinces probably came to Europe from Persia where they were central to the cult of the goddess. They figure quite prominently on the wall paintings of Pompeii where they are associated with bears for some reason no one can fathom. Quinces were shared by the bride and groom in Roman marriage feasts, a custom which survived in Europe until the Middle Ages. It is described in an anonymous manuscript as 'coming to marriages wherein as our ancestors did fondly and with a kind of doating, maintaine many rites and ceremonies, as the eating of a Quince Peare to be a preparative of sweete and delightful dayes between the married persons.' It is not to be confused with the japonica or false quince, the fruit of which is entirely uneatable, being both bitter and as hard as iron.

PUMPKIN PIE

Another survival from New England — this vegetable was thought to be a native of that area. Contrary to popular belief, however, it was known in Europe long before Columbus nor does its name derive from Amerindian *pompion* (entirely apocryphal) but from French *potiron*, and ultimately from *pepon*, Greek for melon. I prefer the alternative French word *citrouille* which expresses the colour much better.

Whenever I travel up the Horowhenua coast from Wellington it is always the pumpkins which attract me most at the roadside stalls near Otaki and Levin. Most people, I regret to say, have been put off pumpkin by eating it under compulsion as children as a disgusting soggy mess. They can be weaned back onto it via this pie recipe which was given to me by my neighbour Susan Robertson. Pumpkin can also be made into a very tasty mousse.

pastry as for Cream Cheese and Honey Pie
800 g pumpkin, peeled and chopped
2 eggs
½ teaspoon cinnamon, ginger, nutmeg
100 g caster sugar

tablespoon golden syrup
100 ml cream
100 ml milk

Line a pie dish with the pastry. Cook the pumpkin until soft and then blend with the other ingredients to a smooth cream. Pour into the pie case and bake in a pre-heated oven at 200° C for fifteen minutes then reduce to 180° C for a further thirty minutes. By that time the filling will be firm and the top will have slightly caramelised. Serve hot or cold with cream. It is understandable that this has become a Thanksgiving dish in New England. The first summer in the pilgrim settlement, 1621, the crops were very poor and if the settlers hadn't been able to call upon local Indian produce, the folk at Plimouth Plantation would have starved. Among this provender was pumpkin, although they did not cook it as a sweet pie but with vinegar and a little beer as a tart 'spoon meat'. If you should happen to be on Cape Cod at the appropriate time in October each year you can call at the recreated settlement and observe this dish being made as it would have been for the first Thanksgiving. The subsequent transmogrification of it into pumpkin pie establishes a link with the earlier European tradition of sweet pies using vegetable as a base, probably quite important in an agricultural subsistence economy in which preserving food for winter use was difficult.

SPINACH TART

The diarist John Evelyn in his *Acetaria* includes a singular recipe for a sweet tart based on vegetable greens — 'chervil, spinach, beet or whatever herbs you please'. In Provence on Christmas Eve there is traditionally a meal eaten before going to midnight mass and equally traditionally this still includes as a centrepiece this sweet tart. I like to make it each year when the first sweet spinach arrives in the shops.

250 g spinach
250 g cream
60 g caster sugar
a few drops vanilla essence
2 egg yolks
30 g flour
candied peel
pastry

Cook, drain and finely chop the spinach. Make a custard by bringing the cream, sugar and vanilla to a simmer. Remove from the heat. Whisk the flour and egg yolks until they are smooth and then whisk into the hot cream mixture and return to the heat, stirring until it thickens. Cool and mix with the spinach, stirring in the peel. Line a flan with the pastry and pour in the mixture. You can make a pastry lattice over the top if you like. Pre-heat your oven to 190°C and bake the tart for about 30 minutes. Your friends will be very surprised by this dish which I make for vegetarians when they come to dine. The practice of using vegetable bases to dishes to give bulk still survives too in for example carrot cake or potato bread. Rather more conventional in the pie department is the cherry tart which follows.

CHERRY TART

In medieval symbolism the cherry denotes transitoriness, as does the blossom of the same tree in Japan. This should not surprise us. The short-lived cherry blossom is an obvious reminder of the mortality of all things, even the most beautiful. It is preferable to wait for fresh sharp-flavoured cherries for this dish rather than to use the tinned variety which are invariably drowned in a sweet syrup and lose their flavour during the tinning process. Cherries were first cultivated by the Babylonians. Traditionally they were introduced to Europe by the gourmet Lucullus, a general who came across them in Pontus, where he spent a decade from 74 BC fighting Mithridates. In England in the seventeenth century, Robert Herrick wrote poems about them.

150 g flour
100 g butter
2 tablespoons caster sugar
egg yolk
tablespoon lemon juice
700 g stoned cherries
150 ml cream
2 eggs
90 g caster sugar

Make a short pastry by combining the first five ingredients into a soft mixture and line a flan with it.

Stoning the cherries is a fiddly job but not so difficult if you have an olive pitter. Pack the fruit in the pastry case. Beat the eggs, cream and sugar together and pour them over the fruit. This should just fill the case. Bake for 20 minutes at 200°C. The tart will puff up as it cooks but shrink again as it cools. I like to serve it cold in summer, warm in winter.

This mixture of fruit-in-a-custard open tart we tend to think of as being particularly French but the truth is that the French have retained a culinary custom we have lost. In the eighteenth century the same combination was used in raised fruit pies and known as a 'caudle' in England.

RASPBERRY CAUDLE

The nice thing about early January each year is the ready availability of fresh and relatively cheap raspberries, ever my favourite soft fruit. Then I don't feel so guilty about using them so extravagantly in a pie. The lard pastry is the same essentially as that used for raised game pies.

500 g plain flour
125 g butter
125 g lard
5 tablespoons hot water
700 g raspberries
125 g sugar
250 ml cream
2 egg yolks

In a bowl make a well in the flour and put the butter and lard in it chopped. Pour the hot water in and combine into a soft dough. Put aside a third of this for the lid and line a buttered pie mould with the remainder. Fill this case with the raspberries and sprinkle in the sugar. Fit the lid and make a hole in the top. Use one of the egg whites and a little sugar to glaze it. Put in the fridge for about an hour to 'set' before baking. Bake at 215°C for about 15 minutes and reduce to 190°C for about 30 minutes more. Just before that time is up bring the cream to boiling and beat the yolks vigorously into it off the heat. Pour this through a funnel into the hole in the top of the pie onto the fruit. Let it cool slightly and then remove the mould — carefully — and serve.

The same thing can be done very successfully with gooseberries or with something new and interesting on the local market, blueberries. These latter are of course well-known in Europe and America. In Ireland they are traditionally gathered at Lammas. They combine very well with mint.

Another pastry which goes very well with some fruits is suet, although this surprises those who think of it in terms only of steak and kidney.

SUSSEX POND PUDDING

This is a traditional pudding which should never have gone out of favour. It is in many cookery books but I do not ever remember having it as a child, nor do any of my acquaintance.

250 g flour
125 g suet
milk
200 g butter
200 g raw sugar
2 limes

Limes are sometimes hard to get; a large lemon will do or a couple of tangerine oranges for that matter. Mix the flour and suet with enough milk to make a soft dough, about 100 ml should be quite sufficient. Line a pudding basin, well greased, with about two-thirds of it. Chop up the butter and put it with sugar inside this, together with the citric fruit, well punctured in several places with a skewer. Take the rest of the dough and roll it out to a lid, pressing it firmly into place to seal in the ingredients. Fit on the lid and steam it at a simmer for about three hours although you can be fairly flexible about that; very convenient for a dinner party. To serve it put a deep bowl over it and turn it out after loosening it all round with a knife. The butter and sugar will have melted into a rich sauce and the sharp flavour of citrus will have impregnated the whole dish. The fruit itself cannot be eaten and should be discarded.

I really don't know why we don't eat more limes in this country. They grow very successfully here and their flavour is much finer than lemon, although rather stronger.

Suet can also go in a dish itself of course, as well as in the pastry.

FIGGY PUDDING

As they say in the traditional carol: 'Now bring us some figgy pudding.' For many years I sang that and had no idea what it was until I found this recipe. No need to confine it to Christmas of course although it's more suitable for winter than summer and most *unsuitable* for anyone on a diet.

75 g each of figs, seedless raisins and dates, chopped
2 tablespoons chopped mixed peel
100 g flour
1 teaspoon baking powder
pinch of salt
100 g breadcrumbs
100 g suet
50 g brown sugar
1 beaten egg
150 ml milk

Mix all the ingredients together thoroughly. Grease a pudding basin and fill with the mixture. Cover and steam for four hours. Leave it to cool a little and then turn it out. My grandmother always served a pudding of this sort with custard, but I prefer cream.

Some people of course cannot even tolerate the thought of a steamed pudding. My friend Bill Thomas, who went to a boarding school, turns pale at the very thought. Perpetrators of institutional cooking have a lot to answer for on the great day of judgement. Properly made, steamed puddings are delicious, especially the next one which is, ironically, institutional of its invention.

DEACON PORTER'S HAT

I had always been intrigued by the name of this traditional New England dish but couldn't find its derivation anywhere. Eventually I asked a friend in Massachusetts and she explained as follows. The Deacon in question was Andrew Porter, a founder and trustee of that venerable institution Mount Holyoke Female Seminary. Always in public he wore a very tall straw hat, as was the fashion in his day. Traditionally this pudding is steamed in a long cylindrical mould and when it was first served one noonday dinner in 1837 a student involuntarily cried: 'See, the Deacon's hat.' And so it has been called ever since.

300 g flour
teaspoon baking soda
teaspoon each of cinnamon, nutmeg, ginger and ground cloves
100 g suet
100 g molasses (or treacle)
100 ml milk
50 g raisins
50 g chopped nuts

Combine all the ingredients thoroughly in the order given and steam in a greased covered bowl for at least three hours. Traditionally it is served hot with a chilled Hard Sauce. That is to say a creamed mixture of butter, sugar, cream and rum or brandy. I don't know what the Deacon would have thought of it, but it's altogether too rich and sweet for me. The most superior dessert pastry of all is in my view *choux* and so I have left the best until last.

PROFITEROLES

When I lived in Britain I travelled a great deal and was constrained therefore to eat many restaurant meals. In a strange town or city this is something of a problem; one doesn't know which are good and which are bad, although I quickly learned to consult that excellent publication *The Good Food Guide*. That then created another order of problem. Which of the good restaurants to go to? My solution was unorthodox but simple. I telephoned them and asked if they had profiteroles. If they did I went. The devil would get me cheap. I would sell my soul for a profiterole. The quantity given here is said to be sufficient for six persons but if it is then they don't like profiteroles as I do.

Choux Pastry:
  25 g butter
  6 tablespoons plain flour
  2 eggs
  pinch of salt
  150 ml water

Put the water, butter and salt in a saucepan and bring them to the boil. Add the flour and cook for a few minutes until the mixture leaves the sides of the pan. Don't let it burn. Let it cool a little and then beat in the eggs one at a time. The secret of choux pastry is in beating it until the batter is smooth, shiny and extremely stiff. To get to that it must be beaten for at least ten minutes. Unless you have the wrists of a weightlifter you should use an electric dough hook for this.

Put the mixture on a greased tray in spoonfuls or by using a forcing tube. Keep them well separated because they will swell up as they cook. This amount makes about eighteen in all. Bake them in a hot oven at 230°C for ten minutes then reduce to 190°C for half an hour. Don't open the oven door while they are cooking. Let them cool in the turned-off oven with the door slightly ajar. When they are completely cooled you should split them and fill the centres, which will be hollow, with whipped cream. They can then be put back together and stacked in a serving dish in the refrigerator until you are ready to pour on the sauce.

Chocolate Sauce:
  1 tablespoon cornflour
  pinch of salt
  2 tablespoons cocoa
  3 tablespoons sugar
  600 ml milk
  few drops vanilla essence

Mix the dry constituents and then add a little of the milk to make a smooth paste. Bring the rest of the milk to the boil. Take off the heat and mix in the other ingredients. Return to the heat and cook gently until it thickens. When it has cooled pour it over the profiteroles and refrigerate until ready to serve. And invite me to dinner.

Wine & Cheese: Cakes & Ale

If all be true that I do think
There are five reasons we should drink;
Good wine — a friend — or being dry —
Or lest we should be by and by —
Or any other reason why.
— Henry Aldrich (1648 — 1710)

'WINE CHEERS THE sad, revives the old, inspires the young, makes weariness forget his toil, and fear her danger, opens a new world when this, the present, palls.' That's what Lord Byron says anyway, and who am I to disagree with him?

During the meal most of those present will be drinking wine and afterwards you will be drinking coffee. Sometimes, for whatever reason, you will want to end your meal with cheese (with or without fruit, with or without dessert) and on special occasions you will want to eat special foods such as cake. During the celebration of the beheading of Marie Antoinette, for instance, is the most suitable of all dates to celebrate with the eating of cake. . . . This last chapter is devoted to some notes and a few recipes to help you in choosing your wines and ending your meal.

Wine and Cheese

I belong to a curious hybrid generation when it comes to wine. When I was a child the drinking of wine was the furtive and eccentric pastime of a strange cult. Consequently I didn't actually drink it until I was an adult, unless you count a curious substance known as 'sherry' which we drank in tiny quantities at Christmas out of peanut butter tumblers, thinking we were the very devil. Sometimes women in particular diluted it with lemonade and drank the resulting concoction with every evidence of enjoyment. This is still how my mother celebrates Christmas and her birthday. It is a matter of some wonder to me that she does not fall down dead on the spot as a result. This substance called sherry bore little resemblance to the fortified wine of that name that I now buy from my shipper. And my father would have laughed aloud at anyone who drank real wine at all, let alone those who admitted discussing the merits of particular varieties.

Curiously enough, the first such wine I ever drank was Italian Chianti. I think this was because I had somehow developed the idea that the taste of wine had something to do with the bottle being surrounded by straw and then used to put a candle in afterwards. Anyway I liked it and I have been drinking it ever since.

Why the habit of drinking wine has generally caught on is something of a curiosity. In Australia it is easy to understand, since a very high proportion of southern European immigrants have arrived there in the last forty years; we were foolish enough not to have this influx. My friend Jim Henderson puts it down to a generation of ex-servicemen who developed a taste for wine in Italy during the Second World War, who worked on the population like leaven in dough. He may be right. In any event we are now a nation of wine bibbers. By 1978 we were drinking 10.84 litres a head each year and it has gone up steadily since to 14.5 litres by 1981 and about 16 litres at the time of writing this. Our wine industry is now big business.

Unfortunately the growth in wine drinking has been accompanied by an aggressive marketing campaign in which bulk consumption has outstripped quality. Too much of the wine drunk in this country is of that variety disparagingly and correctly described as 'chateau cardboard'. In some countries that which is so packaged would not be permitted by law to be described as wine at all. Doubtless we will grow out of it as we grew out of the 'sherry' of my childhood. Good wine drinking habits however are inhibited by two further considerations. One of these is the curiosity of our tax laws. The tax on wine increases with quality. The result is that the levy on a bottle of good wine is almost twice that on a carton of low quality 'wine'. This keeps the price of the bulk marketed commodity down. If you recollect that only 12% of the price you pay for wine is for the substance you drink and that 40% is for something called 'distributive margins' you will undoubtedly be able to draw your own conclusions as to why this lacuna continues.

In the second place, as with so much else in this country, the drinking of wine is not so much a source of pleasure as of competition. People seek to impress one another by seeing who can serve the most expensive wines. I'm not too concerned about them of course as long as they confine their silly activities to foreign wines; most of them are quite unaware that the

European wines for which they pay the earth are actually very *vin ordinaire* in their own countries and that the French in particular retain for export some wines they laugh about as *bon-bon anglais*. Very sensibly they keep the best for themselves.

One should as far as possible drink the *vin du pays* and that applies to this country too. The difficulty is that most reds require at least two or three years to mature before they are worth drinking. Because more and more people are buying good local reds for cellaring (which is expensive) it is becoming correspondingly more difficult to buy a decent bottle when you want it as most of us are constrained to do. The only answer is to find a good supplier and to offer up each day a little prayer to Saint Crapulous (the patron saint of hangovers) that the trendy wine bores will not find it. I have one who is perfectly satisfactory and I'm not telling a soul where he is, particularly as he is extremely knowledgeable on wines and gives me excellent advice. That's particularly important because whatever we may pretend most of us don't actually know as much as we should about our own wines.

Aside from relying on your supplier there are two other things to do. Keep an eye on the newspaper reports, and find out which wines have won the medals at the two annual competitions. Buy up a few bottles of the reds in particular as quickly as you can before the price goes sky-high and/or they vanish from the shelves. Then make a little resolution not to drink them until they are ready. And the second thing is to lay hands on a crib. There are several of these, published more or less annually, listing the available wines and giving a brief assessment of each. If you take one with you whenever you buy wine you won't go far wrong and you will be very quickly able to annotate it with your likes and dislikes. Beyond that you are as much in the dark as I am. Consequently I have asked my friend Fiona McAlpine who has lived for some years in France and who is much more knowledgeable than I to contribute the next few pages, not only on wine but on cheese, a subject concerning which there is even more lamentable ignorance.

This of course is inexcusable because we have been making cheese for a very long time. When I was a child there were apparently only two cheeses available. These were 'mild' and 'tasty'. I recollect very well that when blue vein cheese was first marketed my father solemnly warned me not to eat it because the blue effect was achieved 'by threading copper wires through it'. He truly believed this. In the intervening thirty years we have turned out some good local cheeses but now, alas, we are the victims of our own invincible ignorance. The cheese industry is consolidating. Driving down the west coast of the North Island these last few years I have been depressed by the numbers of derelict small dairy factories. The emphasis is on consolidation and standardisation in large production units for the sake of export and, in the words of the song 'we won't know what we've lost till it's gone'. Smaller producers are finding it harder and harder to survive.

I should also like to add a note on beer. Some few dishes profit from being eaten with beer, particularly in summer or if they are of very strong flavour, such as an English curry. It is a pity therefore that beer is virtually unprocurable in this country. You have probably just re-read that statement in some surprise. But if you have lived in Britain and are familiar with the Campaign For Real Ale, you will know what I mean. Good beer is ruined by two things: filtration and pasteurisation, which removes or kills all the natural yeasts and solids which make beer beer, and pressurisation, which then artificially restores the 'fizz'. In Britain about a third of the pubs, twenty thousand of them, still offer beer which does not suffer these disabilities. Some several hundred independent breweries turn out excellent and clearly distinguishable beers.

Alas, we do not enjoy that advantage. We have two major beer producers who control all but an infinitesimal part of the business. I would be ashamed to offer their product to any of my English friends. It is as if we made wine by collecting the entire grape harvest, putting it in one enormous vat, throwing in sugar, and marketed the result. For want of anything better some people would drink it but we wouldn't call it wine. If you must drink beer the best thing to do is to brew your own. It's simple enough and not only is it much cheaper when you have got the brew right, but it is much better on the palate.

But that said, back to wine and cheese. I cannot agree with everything that Fiona McAlpine says. I do not accept for instance that there are *no* good New Zealand sauternes — there are a few. I sometimes drink fortified wines, particularly in winter when the main course has been game. Malt whisky is the nectar of the gods (although blended is not). But one of the great pleasures of wine and of food is that it is one of the few human activities in which prejudice and even downright bigotry are to be actively encouraged. At least, it is better that that should be so than that people should be tepid in their opinions on wine and food. That said, let me leave you in Fiona's capable hands in the meantime.

****

I cannot imagine eating dinner without drinking wine. From a banquet five course meal for friends served with the best silver, crystal and linen and its sequence of cherished vintages to the freeze-dried stew eaten in a tent by the light of a bicycle lamp, accompanied by whatever widely-sold dry red we are able to find; from the epicurean delight of smoked fish eaten in the last rays of the early summer sun high above the Kaipara harbour with a fresh clean white wine from Waimauku to the warm comfort of fish and chips cut by the faithful cask of white burgundy in the fridge; from the simple meal for two, when we might bring out a bottle of Cabernet to see how it's getting along to the even simpler meal for two after dashing from work to see a film or to go to a concert and getting home at ten-thirty or eleven; taking the cheeseboard to bed with the house claret, than which no more sensuous delight can be indulged in. The only place (apart from prison) where one cannot drink wine with one's dinner is in a youth hostel, which is probably why I am a law-abiding citizen and do not belong to the Youth Hostels Association.

Many drinks are no doubt 'better for you' than wine: milk, if you happen to be one of those imperfectly weaned adults whose stomachs can actually stand it; fruit juice — until you've read the latest scare about fruit juice, which is that the acid eats away at the enamel of our teeth, and that we should really be eating proper fruit to get the fibre; water, which alone of the common cold drinks goes with food — except for cheese. It is sad but true for fitness freaks — those latter-day puritans among us — that no drink actually goes with food, complements its flavours, complements what it does to the body, except for wine. Fruit juice is too sickly, and so detracts from the flavour of food. All those things we were told about sweets spoiling our appetite for dinner apply to fruit juice. As for milk: if you want to put a restaurant full of French diners off their food, walk in and order oysters with hot chocolate and watch the restaurant empty like the dining room of the Cook Strait ferry as it rounds Baring Head.

What about water? Yes, up to a point, but when it comes to cheese I can do no better than to quote Pierre Androuet, who runs Paris' cheese restaurant. When asked whether one could drink water with cheese, he replied simply 'never'. They don't mix well in the stomach. Androuet's only counsel is to eat cheese and drink nothing: 'it can be done' but, he concluded, 'humans have not yet found anything better than wine to accompany cheese.'

The delight of food is truly complemented by the delight of wine, whether one is on one's own or with family and friends. The complex flavours of wine, which is a natural product fermented, are matched by the complex flavours of good food, in which natural products are cooked, rotted or both. Different flavours are married, and the simple natural product becomes a product of human complexity. And, as with everything human, one never knows quite how a wine will turn out, just as the interaction of the people around the table is a never wholly predictable and never wholly repeatable complex of flavours and savours. If only we had as much control over our vintage conversations as over our vintage wines!

Our relationship to wines is like our relationship to those to whom we serve them, particular and local. Ultimately we all have our favourite wines just as we have our favourite people. Neither might be those who 'deserve' our preference. Those who try to organise our preferences by the criterion of greatness will tell us that there are four and only four great wine-producing areas in the world, and that two and a half of them are in France: Bordeaux, Burgundy and half of the Rhine. When, after seven years there, I left France for New Zealand in 1979 I brought with me a number of cherished bottles, largely of the red wines of Bordeaux, the remnants of my cellar and companions to wines I had known and loved, or I would not have troubled to bring them. Some came by sea, some were tucked into my suitcase and came by air. I was astonished to discover that these wines no longer tasted the same as their twins in France. They hadn't gone off, they weren't bad, they just tasted different. From this I concluded that wine does not cross the equator successfully and turned my attention to local wines. After all, I scorned buying the pasteurised, plastic-wrapped supermarket-orientated French versions of processed cheese that local delicatessens touted as French cheese. Not only was most of it not what any French person over the age of six would regard as real cheese, that is cheese that could grace a cheeseboard, but that which *was* real cheese was often unrecognisable, like those pathetic wedges of Brie in their clingwrap, their natural development arrested, hard and dead in the middle, ammoniacal and oozing at the edges. To be a real cheese snob, one has to buy only the best and freshest, preferably local produce from a *fromager* who ages cheese in his cellars as carefully as a London wine merchant ages wine, and sells it at the exact moment it is ready for eating.

When I was travelling through France, no less important than the cathedrals, churches, museums and châteaux was the visit to the local market, if I was lucky enough to strike market day, and to the best local cheese shop otherwise. My rule of thumb was that if I had never heard of a particular cheese I would buy it — especially if it was labelled 'fermier', the most local of local produce, hand-made on the very farm and most certainly from unpasteurised milk. The memory of that astonishing fortress, the cathedral of St Cecilia at Albi, is inextricably linked to two unrepeatable taste sensations: a *Pyrénées fermier*, quite unlike the Pyrénées cheese obtainable in Paris, and a *Salers fermier*, a cheese which I had never seen in Paris. These are both uncooked pressed cheeses, as is our familiar cheddar. There the resemblance ends. Both the Albigensian cheeses had a subtle and delicate tang, an earthy freshness of hill country pastures that our cheddars don't even aim for. I returned to Paris and consulted Androuet's dictionary of cheeses where in bold type were the words 'let the word Salers be engraved on your memory'. He needn't have worried, it already was.

The question of cheese when it comes to wine is a crucial one, because the crescendo of wines throughout a meal depends very much on whether we are going to reproduce France's great tradition, with at the very least soup or hors d'oeuvre, a main course served not with a plate of vegetables but accompanied with the one garnish that will set it off, a salad to cleanse the palate, the cheeseboard then fruit or dessert. In this case the cheese is chosen in such a way that there is not a sudden drop of register in the flavours, and in the succession of wines, so that a main course of poultry or fish is followed by mild cheeses and light wines, a main course of a highly flavoured casserole is followed by strong cheese and heavier wines. In almost all cases, except for some local variants caused by the preference for drinking local wines, the wine drunk with cheese is red. The cheese neutralises the acid from the vinaigrette which dressed the salad, and so prepares the stomach for the dessert. The English habit, if cheese is served at all, is to have it at the end of the meal, when the red wine has been finished with the main course (one hopes! One does see in restaurants here the unedifying spectacle of people saving some wine to go with their pudding. It doesn't.). It is impossible to cap the sweetness of dessert with the tannin and acidity of a good red wine.

The English have traditionally drunk port with their cheese — at least for fifty per cent of the diners. But even the best port, the port from Douro in Portugal, is sweet, since its fermentation of the wine is stopped by the addition of brandy before all the natural sugar in the wine has been used up, and vintage port thus contains from 6 to 8% sugar. It is not surprising that the French classify port as a 'vin doux', literally a sweet wine, and regard it as an apéritif like vermouth or Dubonnet. It hardly does anything for a cheese worthy of the name.

New Zealanders eating, understandably, in the English tradition, tend to stick to three courses and omit the males-only course entirely. Sometimes one will be offered cheese at the end of a meal, without wine, and with salty crackers that manage to mask the flavour of the cheese altogether. One wonders why. Adherence to the great tradition of French cuisine is something that serious cooks already practice at the level of individual dishes; it would seem logical to complete the process with the careful orchestration of a French menu.

There would be two gains by this. The first is that this is a dairying country and one that should be diversifying into an interesting range of gourmet cheeses. From the farm goudas and edams of Whangarei, passing through the various goat cheeses of the Auckland area to Evansdale of Dunedin, this is beginning to happen. And the nicest thing about the Evansdale cheese is that it isn't called by a foreign name. It is content just to be itself, the cheese that the type of cows and the type of grass and the soil and climate of Dunedin make it.

A cheese course would incidentally encourage the production of more red wines here. The second gain lies in drawing out the meal. The common table links, unites, while the move for coffee to separate chairs, perhaps even a separate room, inevitably disrupts. The dinner is over, soon it will be time to go, the coffee is a peroration, a departure signal, a stirrup cup. The extra course prolongs the ambience, sustains the conversation. It is not a course which needs to be eaten quickly. Cheese can be eaten in small fragments from the mildest to the strongest, wine can be sipped. It is a worthier drink to spend time over than liqueurs.

So let us adapt the grand tradition of France to our excellent meats, fresh vegetables and fruits and burgeoning cheeses, and let us match them with

our flourishing wines. The grand tradition but particular savours, particular variants that one will only taste here.

There are two kinds of New Zealand wine — those that are called after a certain vinifera grape or grapes, such as Cabernet Sauvignon, and those that are not, such as dry red. If the wine is named in English it will not be named after a grape, for the simple reason that England cannot be considered a wine-producing country. If the wine is named in what appears to be French however that is no guarantee that it is named after a grape. A French name such as 'chasseur' (which means hunter) gives a certain cachet to a wine which would be more accurately known as 'medium white'. For gourmet occasions the wines which are made from named grapes, the classical wine-producing grapes of Europe, will be preferred. I shall consider first of all the reds.

Easily first in the league here is Cabernet Sauvignon, the great claret grape of Bordeaux. In France it is usually blended with other grapes, notably Merlot and Malbec, and so we find here blends such as Cabernet Malbec or Cabernet Merlot. It makes a full-bodied but dry wine, and generally the oak casks in which Cabernets are matured leave a slightly woody taste. Cabernet is the red to drink with red meats — beef, mutton, venison — and with cheese. The only way really to enjoy a New Zealand Cabernet is to have a cellar, as it is simply not possible to buy Cabernets more than two or three years old and claims are made that the best will last from fifteen to twenty years, although since good Cabernet has been being made in New Zealand only since 1965 this may be more in the nature of a pious hope.

A Cabernet may follow any wine but it is difficult to see what wine would follow a Cabernet, as New Zealand does not yet produce a true dessert wine like Sauternes of which we may be proud.

Australian Cabernets will be so labelled but the different soil and climate produce a totally different kind of wine. New Zealand wines labelled 'claret' particularly if they come from the boutique wineries, may well contain a proportion of Cabernet and be solid everyday reds but beware of cask wines labelled 'claret'; they might be anything, a throwback to the days when New Zealand wines, in order to be marketed, had to pretend to be equivalent to European wines.

Australian wines labelled 'claret' may contain Cabernet but are more likely to contain a high proportion of Australia's workhorse grape, Shiraz (from the Rhône valley, also known as Hermitage). Shiraz also forms the basis of many Australian burgundies. The corresponding French wine is of course Bordeaux, but the better ones — if you can get them — will not say Bordeaux on the bottle but the name of the village or château from which they come. The trick is to look for the Bordeaux bottle in which most of our Cabernets are also bottled. It has distinct shoulders and a straight neck. Something simply labelled 'Bordeaux' is a very ordinary wine. If you're going to drink French wine do it well and go for the château-bottled or do a step down to the area (Médoc; St Emilion). Open the bottle for a French claret some two to three hours before drinking (I like two and three quarter hours for a Médoc) but for a New Zealand Cabernet I have found one and a half hours to two is sufficient. And yes, 'room temperature' may seem absurd in Auckland in the summer but there is surely somewhere cool you can keep your open bottles of wine without resorting to the refrigerator.

The dispute between the great wines of Bordeaux and the great wines of Burgundy is legendary but can hardly be transplanted to New Zealand wines for the simple reason that the big Burgundy grape, Pinot Noir, does not do so well here and does not produce wines of comparable quality. A Pinot Noir will be a softer wine than a Cabernet but the best of them will have a complex flavour and although there is common agreement that New Zealand Pinot Noirs have yet to find their form, I have kept Pinot Noirs for three or four years and been astonished at the rich flavour they have developed. A good wine for a main course of red meat, also for the cheese, although a cheeseboard of stronger flavoured cheeses could well graduate from New Zealand Pinot Noir to New Zealand Cabernet. Recognise a Burgundy bottle by its lack of distinct shoulders; the body of the bottle slopes into a neck, like a double bass as opposed to a cello.

Pinotage is a lighter, softer red again. Perhaps its function is to be offered to people who haven't yet realised that real wine is red wine. The grape comes from South Africa and is a Pinot Noir cross.

A small amount of Gamay de Beaujolais is also made here. This is a light red. I think of it as a summer lunch wine.

New Zealand is a country where the somewhat cool climate favours the production of white wines and the route most New Zealanders take into the enjoyment of wines begins with our predominant sweetish whites. In white wine countries like Germany whites are drunk with main courses although it is interesting to observe that Germans eat a lot of pork which is a light meat which can be matched by a white. I have heard German doctors maintain that red wine causes headaches and that the tannin irritates the throat, whereas French doctors will maintain that white wine has a bad effect on the nervous system and that drinking too much white will make one neurotic. In other words the feelings we have about what wine of various colours will do to us depends a lot on our cultural conditioning, on the colour of wine that is most frequently drunk locally, usually because that is what is grown locally. This is one reason for considering drinking whites with a main course, though the gorges of millions of French people might rise. The best way to deal with those entrenched in their refusal to drink red wines is to serve poultry, fish or even pork as a main course. Failing this, whites with the greatest stamina for a main course are Chardonnay, Sémillon and Gewürztraminer — with caution.

Chardonnay is curiously enough the white wine grape of Burgundy. Unlike its red counterpart the grape has flourished in New Zealand and may yet produce world-class whites. It is a hard, dry flinty style and unlike most whites it benefits from aging in wood and another two years in the bottle before it is drunk. If your Chardonnay reminds you of mothballs it is probably too young. Serve lightly chilled so that it tastes cool rather than cold, a suggestion of the cellar rather than of the refrigerator. A Chardonnay will go very well with a first course such as seafood.

Sémillon and Sauvignon Blanc are the white wine grapes of Bordeaux and both show here a much softer quality than Chardonnay. Sémillon here makes a more neutral white than Sauvignon Blanc (also known as Fumé Blanc, not to be confused with Chenin Blanc which can nevertheless show something of the same herbal flavour). For this reason Sémillon is a favourite of mine for serving with hors d'oeuvre whereas I would rather keep the more pungent taste of Sauvignon Blanc for taking on its own as a pre-dinner drink, especially in the summer and especially if the pre-dinner drink is taken to the garden. I have similar feelings about Gewürztraminer, although its spicy character might be carefully matched with a spicy stew. I'm afraid that I find Müller Thurgau, Riesling and Riesling Sylvaner uninteresting, comparatively flavourless and bland or, worse, thin and acidic in taste.

There are however now in the medal-winning category some excellent non-sweet and non-acidic Rieslings, full, rich and still. Australian whites do not benefit from the hotter climate and I see no reason for buying them. German whites could be a temptation; these are after all the light whites our Victorian ancestors drank in England, the parents of our Müller Thurgaus and Rieslings. Perhaps there is some buried ancestral prejudice that has made us as a nation take to these wines so. Knowing one's way around German wines is even more complicated than knowing one's way around French wines; as a rough rule go for a wine that has 'Qualitätswein', or better still, 'Qualitätswein mit Prädikat' at the bottom of the label. Anything less is

'Tafelwein', tablewine, and hardly worth buying when there are so many good local whites.

White wines move down the scale with English names like white burgundy or hock, misused French names which are not grape names, like Chablis, or meaningless 'French' names like Sovelle.

White wine is for me very much a summer drink. Not only with black olives before dinner but also throughout the meal. Before the meal is I think the best place for champagne. They say champagne goes with anything. So does a white cardy. There may be a place for sparkling wines that are not méthode champenoise, but they are too sweet for my table. In summer I like a cold hors d'oeuvre, perhaps a mixture of raw vegetables, what the French call 'crudités', which go well with a Sémillon, Sauvignon Blanc or Chenin Blanc.

The main course too should be light, and this is the time for fish or poultry with a Chardonnay, perhaps a Gewürztraminer, or a good Riesling. Spring and summer are not the best time for cheeses and you may have to be content with such large-production cheeses as camembert or gruyere, served with a Cabernet (for by now the sun will have set and it will be cooler), or perhaps a lighter red such as a Gamay de Beaujolais. Borrow from the nouvelle cuisine the idea of fresh fruit such as grapes and apples with the cheeseboard. Alcohol is probably nicer in rather than with desserts; the best use for liqueurs is in icecream or consider a marinated fresh fruit salad. Kirsch is not the only alcohol for fruit salads; try marinating strawberries in Sémillon.

I myself don't particularly like drinking white wines in winter, any more than I find myself thinking of cold hors d'oeuvre or icecream. On the other hand, lovers of oysters must face the fact that these are a winter delicacy and that their subtle flavour will be simply swallowed up if they are eaten with red wine. A winter dinner begins best with a dry sherry, a palomino or flor fino. The brandy with which the sherry is fortified warms the guest, like an open fire; the dryness does not detract from the food which is to follow. Best of all to nibble on with sherry are nuts; let salty crisps be relegated to student parties. Bristol cream is delicious but I would rather keep it for occasions like my grandmother's bridge parties at the end of which sherry and fruit cake would be served. This is an excellent combination. The French might serve port or vermouth as an apéritif. Sherry is hard to buy in France since it owes its very existence to the Anglo-Spanish trade. There is not much about English food that one misses living in France but one can feel a distinct nostalgia for sherry (as one can for toast and marmalade if one is living in a garret with a gas burner. By the time I had graduated to owning a split-level oven with a grill I had forgotten what the sensation of hot toast was like. Indeed, I had forgotten what breakfast was like). Spirits I look upon as fierce liquor for melancholy men of the north, distilled out of goodness-knows-what by those people so unlucky as not to inhabit a grape-growing area. Despite my name and my heritage I cannot bring myself to like whisky, which is only porridge fermented and distilled.

There is nothing like soup for a winter starter and our ancestors drank sherry with their soup. If I were serving fish and poultry and therefore a white wine with the main course, I would serve a white wine with the soup, which would therefore be a light vegetable soup such as carrot soup. Serving a white wine with the first course is a good strategy in any case, since it allows die-hard white drinkers (who probably do not drink very much anyway) to retain a glass of white wine to drink with later courses. If I were serving red meat or spicy cheese-based vegetarian food for a main course, I might prefer a strongly flavoured soup such as sorrel in which case I could begin with a red wine straight away. I would do this in preference to drinking a white wine in winter.

New Zealand guests have a delightful habit of coming to dinner with bottles of wine: what, I wonder, is the origin of this habit? No sense in taking flowers to someone you know has a garden, but of whose cellar you are unsure. This may mean a variety of reds on the table and often an opportunity for comparative tasting that can be one of the pleasures of the occasion. It may be less correct but it is certainly more friendly to drink the wine which is brought then and there. After all it may be a wine your guests have brought to you because they are curious to try it themselves, picking up something unknown in a wine shop on the way (I do this, particularly when I am on holiday and on the lookout for wines I do not readily find in Auckland). It may be a wine they are anxious to share with you because it is one they are fond of and if you put it away for later you will never remember to tell them what you did think of it. Obviously this requires some juggling with the probabilities at that point before your guests arrive when you are opening the red wines. If you open a red wine as soon as your guests arrive it should be ready to drink by the time you have reached the cheese; this is of course if you see dinner partes as occasions for conversation as much as for food. You can always help the breathing process along by decanting the wine.

If I was brought a white wine in winter I would set it on the table at the beginning of the meal for those who might want it. S/he who brought it might have been trying to protect himself/herself against my red wine habit. Cabernet with the main course and the cheese. Dessert is possibly the one course that ought to be left alone, although one could try an Auslese with a fruit tart or risk a vintage port with plum pudding.

The very finest ending to a dinner in winter is to sit in front of the fire drinking cognac and smoking a cigar. Port too is a good into-the-night drink. One can't drink cognac quickly, so if one tries to alternate brandy with coffee the coffee gets cold. Coffee is a quick goodbye drink, a sober-you-up-for-the-drive-home drink. I'm not convinced that it goes with anything but itself.

THE CHEESEBOARD

The first thing one needs is not a cheeseboard but a *maître fromager*, a cheesemonger to use an old English word. As this is not a category which exists in New Zealand one needs the next best thing, which is a good delicatessen. Look for one where cheese is not sold as an adjunct to pâté, sausage and foreign things in tins, but one where a wide selection of cheeses will be cut off the block for you and wrapped in waxed paper. Waxed paper is the best sign that they take their cheese seriously — plastic film makes cheese sweat, as one discovers when one unwraps bubble-packed feta or gruyère and finds that it is wet. All right for picnics. Alas even quite good delicatessens wrap remnants in clingwrap and balance them unappetisingly on top of a new block. Of course the new block is likely to come wrapped in plastic, if it is a block of cheddar or even of more exotic New Zealand cheese, because it is only a block from a whole cheese. At least the cheese has probably matured more than a 250g plastic-packed segment. A good delicatessen should have whole New Zealand cheeses in their own skins —the farm-style Northland gouda and edam (the Taranaki and Tararua sorts come in coloured plastic imitation skins), blue vein and, if you are lucky enough to live in Dunedin, Evansdale.

The second best sign of a serious interest in cheese is imported whole cheeses: Jarlsberg from Norway, Emmental from Tasmania, Stilton from England, Roquefort from France. These shouldn't be confused with the immense variety of flavoured cheese now being imported whole — cheese with French names and often 'made in Germany' or 'made in Denmark' in the small print. These cheeses are basically soft cheese like cream cheese with layers of walnuts, of salami, or mushrooms, or chives, or anything in the middle, like the jam in the middle of a sponge cake. The fact that they are whole has nothing to do with their maturation processes; it is a marketable size for the international frozen-food market. A range of these is the sign of a delicatessen without the courage of its convictions. If a cheese is a good cheese surely what it should taste of is itself not nuts, nor pepper, nor chives, nor garlic, nor bacon, nor curry, nor yet dried fruit. There is nothing that can replace the true fresh tangy taste of plain cheese.

The cheese to buy is real natural cheese cut to your requirements from a complete cheese which has matured for the appropriate length of time. As this can vary from two weeks to three years or more it is the kind of judgement best left to the cheesemonger. Of course, with imported cheese s/he often doesn't have the room to manoeuvre in exercising this judgement. The cheesemonger should sell the cheese only when it is ready to be eaten and one should buy only a few days' supply at a time.

There are some cheeses which legitimately come in small packets: these are cheeses whose maturation processes involve their being made in small sizes, therefore they can be sold with their rinds intact. The most well-known of these is camembert.

Cheese is made from the curdled milk of cows — or any other animal that's going — sheep (roquefort), goats (feta) or even buffaloes (mozzarella — at least in Italy) — speeded up by the addition of rennet which is essentially a coagulating enzyme from the stomachs of calves. The differences in flavour of cheeses come not only from the sort of cow, the sort of grass she eats, the sort of soil it grows in and the sort of winter feed she gets but also from the sort of human treatment they receive. During the period of the cheese's maturing it is acted upon by micro-organisms and one of the things these micro-organisms do is cause the cheese to form a rind which protects the middle of the cheese. Camembert belongs to the flowery-rind family of cheese, as does brie. This somewhat unfortunate literal translation of the French 'croûte fleurie' decribes the downy cotton-wool outside which results from deliberate treatment with *Penicillium candidum*. French camembert comes wrapped in waxed paper in plywood boxes: the wax-coated foil and cardboard boxes in which East Tamaki markets its camembert are a reasonable equivalent. There is no essential difference between a brie and a camembert except that they are made in different places (traditionally Normandy, and Brie which is northeast of Paris), and therefore taste slightly different. They also happen to be different in shape. A brie is much wider and thinner. That the same company should market not only a 'camembert' but also a triangle it calls 'brie' is therefore something of a joke.

A flowery-rind cheese must be eaten within days of its coming to perfect ripeness. Sometimes a cheesemonger will obtain a brie that has been flown in from France. It will be around 30 cm in diameter but 3 cm or less thick giving the impression of a cartwheel. He should cut a first wedge from it to enable buyers to inspect the product. Buy it when it is soft and golden all through. If it is trying to drool over the edges like a Salvador Dali watch don't buy it. The cheese will be over-fermented and taste of ammonia. And if those drooling edges are only held in by clingwrap and the whole cheese has been sliced up first as if this were a supermarket, refuse to buy it on principle. The 'goat camembert' is, as far as I know, a style of appellation unique to New Zealand. I look forward to the time when it might appropriate to itself the name 'Torbay' after the place where it is made rather than calling itself after a French village.

A second way of causing cheese to have a rind is to wash or brush the cheese with anything from brine to brandy; Danish havarti and French port-salut are two mild, creamy cheeses made this way. It is also a way of making a whole small-sized cheese of which some of the most famous examples must be the world's smelly cheeses like Belgium's Limburger.

A third way is to press the cheese into a cloth and this is what leaves the characteristic woven pattern on the edge of a cheddar or gruyère which is what we are usually thinking about when we refer to 'rind' in English, probably because this is the way all the well-known cheeses of England were made. The pressed cheeses have a harder texture because the pressing squeezes out excess whey. Their rind is natural in that it forms without human additions whether bacteria or baths. The rind ensures an even maturing by regulating the moisture content within the cheese.

A final kind of maturing goes not from the outside in but from inside out and this is where the cheese is innoculated with *Penicillium glauci* or *Penicillium roquefort* to produce the internal moulds of blue vein cheese. Most blue cheeses are nevertheless still pressed like stilton, to create a rind. You may be lucky enough to acquire a whole stilton. It can be done, and stilton travels well to New Zealand, as most of the pressed cheeses will since they require longer maturing. A stilton is matured for six months. Do not however think that the way to eat it is to slosh port into it and eat it with a teaspoon. The Stilton Manufacturers Association says that a good stilton does not need port and a bad stilton will not be disguised by any amount of it.

Pierre Androuet, whom I have already quoted as France's best-known cheese expert, recommends serving at least two cheeses more than the number of guests. There is obviously a point at which this becomes absurd, even impossible, especially given the small range of New Zealand cheeses, which we would naturally prefer to put on our cheeseboards. Yet, of the fabled 325 varieties of French cheese, many are basically similar in type but are made in different localities. I find between three and five is a good number. They should be served on a good-sized board (most cheeseboards sold here are too small), because boards provide a good surface for cutting on and knives don't squeal on them as they do on ceramics. I wash my cheeseboard like any other dish and occasionally oil it with baby oil (not linseed, which is poisonous) to stop it from drying out. I take my cheese out of the fridge when I am in the kitchen attending to the first or second course, unwrap it and let it air at room temperature. This is especially important if any cheese has been wrapped in plastic — even a purist like me finds it hard to avoid these completely! I generally rewrap such cheese in waxed paper when I get them home from the shop. We prefer plain bread with cheese; if crackers are served they shouldn't be salty.

The range of cheese served should extend from mild to strong and the ideal way to eat the cheese is to start with the mildest one and end with the strongest one. Your selection will depend on your guests' tastes, on what is in season and obtainable in your area, and also on what you have had for a main course. A mild fish or poultry main course with white wine might mean that the cheese course could be served with a Gamay de Beaujolais or even a Pinotage and begin with a mild cheese like havarti. This is for friends who have to be led gently into the red wine and real cheese state. They are likely to admire on your board a boursin or its Australian equivalent with the obligatory French name. Over to you if you want to humour them. On the other hand *boeuf à la gardiane* and vintage Cabernet Sauvignon must be followed by a cheese worthy of the wine and with a little more bite, and here you might begin with a well-ripened camembert.

A camembert is always popular even on the neophyte's cheeseboard and has the advantage of being available in supermarkets. I find I have to buy them at least a week early and age them myself outside the refrigerator. Cut the first wedge yourself so that the neophyte will know how to cut it and not cut off a portion which is mostly rind. It is not considered well-brought-up to eat the rind. Never ever buy those foreign 'camemberts' or 'bries' in tins. Not only is the milk pasteurised (increasingly hard to avoid these days anyway) but the cheese has been pasteurised after that so the cheese is doubly denatured. They taste to me of milk powder.

After camembert a mild uncooked pressed cheese is nice — Northland gouda or edam (the widely-marketed Taranaki ones I find too bland), or a fresh mild goat cheese like the one from Miranda Valley. Cheshire fits, although if you buy English Cheshire it has sometimes become quite sharp on the way over. A wedge of Evansdale, to my mind the finest New Zealand cheese, might be all right. Like many cheeses this one varies with age and I have found some sharper than others, although it is an essentially mild cheese. Then a slightly stronger cheese in a different style. If you haven't served one perhaps a goat cheese, a gruyère (I allow myself to buy foreign gruyère-emmental-comte family cheeses: I have to admit that the New Zealand one hasn't got their flavour) or one of our widely available Italian-style cheeses like canestrato which has a nice farmyard taste, although I find that our Italian-style cheeses, like the Evansdale, vary quite widely and their strength is often difficult to predict.

A very tasty cheddar, a feta or a blue cheese is good to finish with, or that southern hemisphere curiosity — esrom. Esrom is of its nature a mild washed-rind Danish cheese but by the time it has reached New Zealand it is very strong indeed. I permit myself to buy it because it is, in this sense, unique to Australasia. Epicure and Bonz are two widely available matured cheddars. The plastic packet in which Bonz is marketed goes against all my principles but if they do not package it in hygienic hermetically-sealed units how will they be able to export? Let alone penetrate the New Zealand supermarket. The quality of the cheeses we import as well as those we must export suffers from the requirements of stringent hygiene and competitive international commerce. The plastic-packeted feta is not surprisingly made from cow's milk but there are at least two goat fetas available and I have very occasionally met a ewe's milk feta which is the original style. Of the blue cheeses our blue vein is one of the sharpest and I must admit a sneaking preference for roquefort or stilton which are among the great cheeses of the world. A whole roquefort bought for home consumption has in my experience lasted for weeks. Should it grow mould, so much the better! Thick and even marbling from the inside to the outside is the mark of a good blue cheese. Whatever actual cheeses you serve the important thing is that they should be fresh, natural and distinctive. Your own tastebuds must be your final arbiter: no one else can actually eat the cheeses for you. Experiment as widely as you can; on holiday hunt out the dairy co-operatives in the country and the delicatessens in the city. All dedicated cheese-lovers should put a tour of the markets of France, especially from the Massif Central to the Pyrénées, on their life's agenda.

****

Festival Food

Fiona McAlpine's idea of cheese being served simply with bread and wine is a most attractive one. But sometimes a little more is called for and on those occasions there should be some special dish. Some of these in fact go very well with cheese.

Actually it's one of the least becoming aspects of twentieth-century life that we are losing the ability to mark the passage of time by ritual. Those rituals which do survive, such as Christmas, tend to do so only on sufferance because they suit the needs of the commercial community. But commercial considerations and the values which grow from these, being the universal solvents of all values, are corrosive of the true ritual meanings of things. One of the best ways of reintroducing these meanings into our lives is through food and this section is devoted to those sweet foods which might achieve that end. Of course one of the interesting aspects of ceremonial food is its intense conservatism. Those things associated with ritual usually survive in a form typical of an earlier age when the rest of the world has long moved on. Almost all of the foods we associate with Christmas, for example, are very medieval in the spices they use and in their combinations of dried fruits and meat in the one dish. They are also, for the same reason, very distinct from the food we eat every day or even at dinner parties, and survive all the more for it in individual collections of recipes. Everyone, I have found, has their own recipe for Christmas cake passed down from generations of yore. But Christmas is not the only festival which can be ritually marked with food. There are Easter and All Saints and a host of others. Finishing a meal on the appropriate date with one of these special foods not only marks the event but itself creates an occasion for a dinner. First comes Easter.

HOT CROSS BUNS

Easter, hard after the abstinence of Lent, has ever been a time for feasting. When I was a child my grandmother made spiced buns but when she grew old and stopped doing it, like everyone else, we bought them ready-made. Now hardly anyone makes them any more. It is time the habit was revived. Actually the association of these particular buns with Easter is relatively recent. Until the Reformation, *all* buns were marked with a cross to ward off evil spirits which might stop them rising. This eventually was thought to be a bit popish and the cross was retained for Easter only. Of course the festival goes back long before Christianity and in the northern hemisphere marks the coming of spring. The early church simply co-opted it. To me it always signifies that summer has finally gone. What better way to mark that than with these buns on Good (i.e. God's) Friday.

500 g plain strong flour
30 g yeast
125 g currants
300 ml milk
teaspoon salt
60 g raw sugar
60 g butter
2 eggs
2 teaspoons mixed spice

Warm the milk and mix a little of it with the yeast. Set it aside to work. Mix the flour, salt, sugar and spices and then in a well mix in the milk, yeast, butter and eggs. Add the currants, ensuring they are well distributed. Cover this dough and let it rise for two hours. Break it down and knead it thoroughly. Divide it into about twenty rounded shapes on a baking tray.

271

Leave to rise again until the dough has doubled its volume. Make the crosses on the top with a sharp knife. Bake in a pre-heated oven at 200° C for about twenty minutes. You can make a glaze of milk and sugar and brush this on five minutes before the end if you like.

The buns must be eaten piping hot from the oven, preferably for breakfast with coffee. Of course they can be made at any time of the year. For Easter Sunday on the other hand you should make a simnel cake (and you will find yourself enjoying it for some weeks afterwards).

SIMNEL CAKE

This was not originally for Easter either but for Mothering Sunday, that is the middle Sunday in Lent. In nineteenth-century tradition servant girls made this cake for their mothers. Very likely it is the last remnant of a women's fertility festival which predates Christianity. It has now been more or less co-opted by Easter. You can of course buy the marzipan but it is much nicer to make your own.

Marzipan:
  225 g ground almonds
  225 g icing sugar
  1 tablespoon lemon juice
  2 egg yolks

Mix these ingredients thoroughly to a stiff paste and divide into two.

Cake:
  175 g butter
  175 g raw sugar
  3 eggs
  225 g self-raising flour
  teaspoon each of nutmeg, cinnamon and mixed spice
  salt
  300 g currants
  150 g sultanas
  100 g figs, chopped
  100 g mixed peel
  a little milk

Cream the butter and sugar then beat in the eggs. Sieve in the dry ingredients and mix thoroughly with the fruit. If it is too stiff, moisten with a little milk. Put half the mixture in a greased cake tin, roll out one of the pieces of marzipan and spread it over, then cover with the remaining cake mixture. Bake at 150° C for 3½ hours. When it is cool, roll out the remaining marzipan and spread it over the top. This can then just be popped under the grill to glaze it lightly. Some recipes also call for the cake to be surrounded by twelve small balls of marzipan, said to symbolise the Apostles. Like most such cakes this can be made in advance and kept in an airtight tin. It improves with keeping.

PARKIN

This is something to eat on All Souls (Hallowe'en) or on that curious festival which has come to replace it — Guy Fawkes. Like Easter, Hallowe'en, that is to say the evening of hallows, the souls of the dead, 31 October, is of pre-Christian provenance. The spirits of the dead walk and are traditionally kept at bay by the lighting of bonfires and the ringing of church bells. Masses were chanted all night for the souls of the dead. Curiously this custom has largely vanished in Europe but remains in residual form in the United States. Parkin, which is a sticky ginger cake, should be made at least a month in advance. The longer it is kept the stickier it gets.

450 g fine oatmeal
225 g plain flour
100 g brown sugar
2 teaspoons ground ginger
1 teaspoon baking powder
225 g treacle
75 g melted butter or lard

Mix all the dry ingredients and then beat in the treacle and butter. This may seem a lot of treacle but it is the key to a successful parkin. You will end up with a sticky stiff mixture. Bake it for 1½ hours at 160°C. Keep an eye on it to see it doesn't burn. It goes superbly with a piece of strong cheese, stilton or a local equivalent.

Of all the festivals however always for Europeans the most important have been those associated with Christmas; in that part of the world it is in the heart of winter. My first experience of a European mid winter was salutary. Nothing was green in nature at all and it was so cold I nearly froze. No wonder people shut themselves in, lit a roaring fire and passed the time in feasting and enjoyment: it's the only thing to do in such a circumstance. Actually Christmas as we now celebrate it was invented by Charles Dickens and Prince Albert. In medieval times all that stuff about trees was quite unknown in England. And of course it started on 24 December and lasted until 6 January, i.e. Twelfth Night. Some of these dates are still celebrated, particularly by the French, with special foods. There is the spinach tart earlier described for Christmas Eve, and a cake with a silver coin or charm for Twelfth Night. Less known is this traditional English dish for 24 December.

CREED WHEAT FRUMENTY

A frumenty or firminty is a survival of a medieval pottage. That is to say a sort of porridge to which other ingredients are added, usually dried fruit but sometimes meat (or both). That is what the Authorised Version means when it refers to 'a mess of pottage'.

225 g cracked wheat
1 litre of water
salt
300 ml of cream
300 ml milk
100 g raisins
100 g currants
50 g sugar
nutmeg
300 ml cream
brandy or rum

Health food shops should have the cracked wheat. Put it in a large casserole with the water and a little salt at 100°C and leave it to simmer overnight. The wheat will absorb all the water and turn slightly jellyish. This is creed wheat. It keeps well in the refrigerator for a few days. When you are ready, add the other ingredients, except for the second cream and the spirits. Cook it gently for a couple of hours. Eat it hot or cold with the cream and spirits, whipped stiffly, and serve with a fruit salad. In Lincolnshire this dish is served to children at the completion of sheep shearing.

CHRISTMAS CAKE

As I have already remarked, there are as many recipes for this as there are households. I have several, which I alternate. This one was given to me after I had enjoyed the end result and said so enthusiastically. Also it is not *quite* as rich as some others.

200 g raisins
200 g currants
100 g sultanas
100 g mixed peel
zest of an orange and a lemon
60 ml each orange and lemon juice
60 ml sherry
60 ml rum
2 tablespoons marmalade
300 g butter
225 g brown sugar
5 eggs
300 g flour
salt
teaspoon cinnamon
teaspoon baking powder
100 g glacé cherries
100 g walnuts

Mix the fruit, zest, juice, jam and sherry and heat together in a covered casserole. When they are nicely warmed let them sit for at least 24 hours. Cream the sugar and butter and then add the dry ingredients. Mix well and then add all the other items including the prepared fruit mixture. Combine thoroughly and cook in a greased tin for about 3½ hours at 150°-180°C. Cover with foil if necessary to prevent burning. This cake so often elicited favourable comment, by the way, that the person who gave it to me keeps copies of the recipe to give away.

RICHARD BOSTON'S CHRISTMAS PUDDING

On Christmas Day itself, of course, if you can stand it the final touch is the pudding. This recipe is a famous one which was first published in *The Guardian* by Richard Boston in a column he used to write. Boston of course was the founder of the Campaign for Real Ale. It has become a national institution in England.

300 g breadcrumbs
250 g brown sugar

250 g each currants, raisins, sultanas
60 g chopped mixed peel
30 g suet
teaspoon salt
teaspoon mixed spice
zest of a lemon
tablespoon lemon juice
2 large eggs
150 ml milk
300 ml stout

Mix all these ingredients thoroughly. Put the mixture into a large, well-greased pudding basin and steam for seven hours. This will serve a lot of people and you can halve the quantities if you like. Many people keep an old silver threepenny piece and this is pushed into the mix. Whoever gets it has luck for the rest of the year. Don't use a coin later than about 1936, however. They made them of silver alloy up until then but have since changed to various forms of cupro-nickel. This will not only taint the pudding, it is probably poisonous as well. When I lived in England I belonged to the National Trust and every year their Christmas catalogue contained a pudding made to an early Victorian recipe. It was delicious and must be very similar to the recipe to be found in Sara Paston-William's *Christmas and Festive Day Recipes* which she prepared for the National Trust. Traditionally these puddings are eaten with a hard sauce. This is too rich for me but I give a recipe for it for those hardy souls who can abuse their interiors with impunity.

CUMBERLAND RUM BUTTER
This should be made in advance and kept in the refrigerator.

225 g unsalted butter
350 g brown sugar
175 ml rum
pinch each nutmeg and cinnamon

Melt the butter very gently, stir in the sugar and let it dissolve. Pour in the rum, add the spices, beat it well and set it in small covered pots. This is also traditionally served on sweet biscuits at christening parties. The theory is: butter for a good life; sugar for a sweet life; rum for a spirited life; and the rest for the spice of life. A pleasant thought. There should also be a recipe for mince pies but the plain fact is that I've never made them. I am always overwhelmed with food when I get to that point at Christmas (and besides I always forget to put down the mince a year in advance). So you will have to find your own way with those. Instead I make a Scots variation on the same theme which is not for Christmas but for New Year.

HOGMANAY BLACK BUN

One Christmas I happened to be in Edinburgh and was surprised to find that the Scots don't make much of it. But a week later I discovered that this was not a function of their much vaunted (and entirely spurious) reputation for meanness. They were simply saving themselves for Hogmanay. I also discovered the disadvantage of being a dark man; I went first footing and was given the traditional dram for bringing good luck. Of course I was merely taking the advice of Robert Burns who remarks somewhere that 'freedom and whisky gang tegither' although I suffered for it the next day. This is probably because I had *not* followed the advice of Isaiah: 'Woe unto them that rise up early in the morning, that they may follow strong drink.' Anyway, all of that aside on New Year's Eve the Scots eat this last survival of the great medieval gilded feast day pies.

Pastry Case:
   450 g plain flour
   salt
   ½ teaspoon baking powder
   200 g butter
   water
   beaten egg for glaze

Sift the dry ingredients together and rub in the butter thoroughly. Add just enough cold water to make a stiff paste. Knead it lightly and leave it in the refrigerator for a couple of hours. In the meantime make the filling.

Filling:
   200 g plain flour
   1 teaspoon each cinnamon, allspice, black pepper, mixed spice
   ½ teaspoon each baking powder and cream of tartar
   salt
   75 g brown sugar
   350 g each raisins and currants
   50 g each candied peel and almonds
   1 egg
   2 tablespoons malt whisky
   3 tablespoons milk

Sift the dry ingredients, then add the sugar, fruit, nuts and peel. Mix thoroughly with the egg, whisky and milk. Roll out two-thirds of the pastry and line a raised pie case. Fill with the mixture and roll out, fit and glaze the lid. Prick with a fork and bake at 180°C for two hours. This is to be eaten cold. Like parkin it is very good with cheese. It is even better however with a dram.

For myself I think spreading the festival over twelve days is much better than cramming it all into one. At the very least one avoids indigestion. And if you want to end it literally with a bang you can wassail your fruit trees. I leave you to find out for yourself what that entails and merely remark that your neighbours will think you are barmy for giving toast soaked in booze to a tree and the police will arrest you for discharging a firearm in a populated area. That doesn't stop them down in Somerset.

Coffee

'Coffee,' said Brillat-Savarin, 'I can no more describe than the perfume of yesterday's violets.' His thoughts are echoed by Talleyrand whose politics one might deplore but whose taste one is obliged to admire: coffee, he said, 'detracts nothing from your intellect; on the contrary, your stomach is freed by it and no longer distresses your brain; it will not hamper your mind with troubles but give freedom to its working . . . molecules of Mocha stir up your blood . . . and you will sit down without distress to your principal repast which will restore your body and afford you a calm delicious night.' I cannot now conceive of finishing a meal other than with coffee. Some speak of a preference for tea and infuse all sorts of herbs, but tea in the evening on a formal occasion is a poor thing, whatever may be its restorative properties in the afternoon, and I say nothing more of it here.

Drinking coffee is not however something we have long done as a nation. I recollect very well my first introduction to that which passed for coffee. Far to the back of the kitchen cupboard I found one day a tall flat-sided bottle with a blue label depicting a military sahib being served by an Indian. 'That's your father's,' said my mother and shuddered. It was a substance which had the consistency and sweetness of treacle, but was bitter, and when mixed with hot water made a drink most foul: essence of coffee and chicory. For many years after my first experiment I declined coffee, thinking that to be it.

But I grew up in the age of the coffee bar and I was constrained by the harsh fashion of youth to try coffee again. It bore no resemblance to that which I had once tried and I began to like it. I also had the good fortune to live in a town with a whole shop specialising in coffee — a most unusual circumstance in the fifties. And so I was able to buy the beans of my choice from among a range of flavours and to grind them for myself. I am now well on my way I am sure to my millionth cup, and could not begin the day without it.

In Arab countries the coffee bean has been available for at least a thousand years; in Ethiopia it has grown wild since time immemorial. It was used initially, it is said, by the sufi dervishes, to keep them awake during long and strenuous religious ceremonies. But it has also been drunk in that part of the world and throughout the eastern Mediterranean as a pleasure for centuries. One of my fondest memories of the Greek islands is of the many idle hours I spent sitting in tavernas alternately sipping ouzo and coffee brewed in the Middle Eastern manner and served invariably with a glass of water and a small bowl of nuts or olives. It's preferable to working, any day of the week.

The introduction of coffee to Europe is a more recent phenomenon. John Evelyn records his surprise when a fellow student at Oxford, a Cretan, brewed coffee in the 1630s. The first English coffee house was opened in the same town in 1650 and by the end of the century London was full of these institutions which became mercantile centres and which led, among other curiosities, to a *Women's Petition Against Coffee* of 1674 which complained that the men were never at home and that their excessive habituation of the coffee houses rendered husbands impotent. I confess that I have never experienced that effect.

In a few years coffee had spread to the rest of Europe, although in the teeth of strong opposition. In France this came understandably from the wine merchants. In Italy rather more eccentrically it came from priests who petitioned Clement VIII to ban it on the grounds that it was the drink of infidels and thus a tool of the devil. His Holiness replied with the Italian equivalent of 'Why should the devil have the best tunes?' and declined their request. In other countries however a less civilised approach was adopted. Frederick the Great of Prussia decreed in 1781 that only royalty and the nobility were to be allowed to drink coffee, presumably on the basis that such pleasures were too good for the masses. He actually employed spies to roam the streets sniffing for the smell of coffee roasting illegally, and heavily fined the offenders.

It was probably in their desperate search for substitutes that German coffee addicts discovered chicory. And of course it is one of the curiosities of humankind that a food developed as a substitute becomes a food in its own right. In France some still drink their coffee flavoured with chicory, to the disgust of many purists, including Otto von Bismarck. A story is told that during the German advance into France in 1870 he was with the army and stopped at an inn for refreshment. 'Bring me all the chicory you have,' he demanded sternly of the terrified innkeeper and when the man did so, trembling with many assurances that this was all he had, Bismarck smiled and said: 'Good. Now leave that here and go and make me a cup of coffee.' There are few things upon which I might agree with Bismarck, but I am with him in this. I confess however to a liking for the addition of a little vanilla pod or cinnamon stick to my coffee.

It is important that you should find a coffee which suits you. Most beans in this country are over-roasted. These are distinguishable by being dark and shiny and make a coffee which is too bitter for my taste. Lighter, duller beans may look less attractive but make a sweeter brew and you will therefore be less inclined to put milk or sugar in it to take away the bitterness (although who can be averse to a little cream?).

There are many coffees, usually to be distinguished not only by the extent of their roasting but by their countries of origin. Originally the names such as Kenya or Mocha or Java or Kona denoted these, but they have now become debased into trade names only and are not a good guide. If you have local shippers who are specialists then it is well worth getting to know them. If you can get some Bourbon Santos from Brazil then you are in luck. Otherwise Medillins from Columbia. But you will be unlikely I think to come across such fine varieties. It is a curiosity of those who would not think twice about rejecting a bad wine that they will pour a bad coffee down their throat without demur. But at least the good wines are available as an alternative. A shipper will direct you to the best which can be got. Otherwise I commend to your attention a little book simply entitled *Coffee* by Claudia Roden wherein you will find a good deal of useful information on what to buy and even how to roast your own if you have a mind to do so, although I have never done so myself. There are one or two rules to remember. You should *never* buy your coffee ready-ground. You should grind it yourself just before you make it. There is a very good and crucial reason for this.

The flavour of coffee is a subtle combination of oils and aromatics. The former are bitter and the latter sweet. Roasting concentrates them and grinding releases them, but the aromatics dissipate within an hour of grinding. Thus if you pre-grind your coffee, all you will get will be the residual bitterness of the oils. If you have ever sat on the bus beside someone with coffee they have just bought freshly ground you will know what I mean. The smell is a delight, and you get the enjoyment, but they get the bitter remains. For the same reason coffee should never be reheated, because all of the sweet aromatics will be driven out in the process. This is why instant coffee is never very good to drink; people who have been brought up on this form of ersatz are often astonished the first time they drink freshly ground coffee.

Instant coffee has had another most unfortunate effect. As it has grown in importance as part of the mass marketing of commodities it has driven off the market the variety of available beans. Most coffee is now grown for this purpose of powdering and thus there is a premium on coarse-flavoured and high-yield varieties. The only good thing about this is that the coffee which grows in Nicaragua is particularly suitable for this purpose. Drinking instant coffee thus may become a political act; it will never I hope become a culinary one.

All of that said, how you brew your coffee is over to you. It should of course be fairly finely ground but to infuse it you have a range of methods available. I use an expresso but that is only a preference of my own and boiling water poured onto grounds or filtered is just as good. Some expresso machines look as if they have been invented by Heath Robinson and will also heat milk for you. Of these I am afraid. The Italians, a civilised people who have the most famous and elegant coffee house in the world (Florians), make some very good and simple machines for coffee. Once you have the substance made, what you put in it is your affair. Richard Burton the orientalist describes in *Love, War and Fancy* the addition of ambergris but that seems to me a most perverse act. Carème, however, always used ambergris. Where he got it is hard to say; not the sort of thing you find on special at the supermarket. Apart from milk or cream and sugar there is also the addition of spirits. At this I draw the line with one exception, *viz.* rum. In my view coffee and rum were made for one another and black coffee with a jigger of rum is one of the benefits of civilisation. However, that mixture is best as a morning drink for winter — it can give you a nasty jolt at the end of a dinner party if you are not used to it. Better perhaps that you should offer your guests a cigar, uncut for preference.

Bring your coffee to the table in a thermos jug and serve it in small cups. That way it becomes the extended social event which it ought to be. It will not get cold and if you make a large jug you will not have to be getting up to make a further pot.

Always bear in mind the words of Eliza Acton: 'There is no beverage which is held in more universal esteem than good coffee, and none in this country at least which is obtained with greater difficulty. We hear constant and well-founded complaints from foreigners and English people of the wretched compounds so commonly served up here under its name.' As true now, I am sorry to say, as when these words were penned by her in 1845.

Envoi

We come now as at the end of every meal to the farewell. The coffee is drunk or grows cold. The conversation dies into the silence of content. We might emulate the Russians who, when embarking on a journey, sit in silence for a moment with those who will remain behind. It is the time to contemplate meals past. These, for me, have included some curiosities. I recollect very well a farewell dinner in Moscow, a small but illustrious gathering which included among others a member of the Politburo who had *survived* under Stalin and, as I later discovered, an officer of the KGB. It was not as terrifying as it sounds; on the contrary it was most cordial. And I have survived the experience. But such meals belong to the main course and its conversation. At the end of the meal one contemplates the best of all meals — that eaten domestically with friends. Truly, since time immemorial, an innocent delight.

FINIS.

Index

beef
in bombard of veal 148-50
with Cabernet wines 261
in cockie-leekie 165-6
in leg of lamb à la royale 136-8
moulded tongue 113-14
in pigeon pie 179-80
potted tongue 117
steak and kidney pie 146-8
stews 150-2
see also steak
beer
in cassoulet of duck 175-6
English 257
in farsed stuffed chicken 165
New Zealand 257
Russian 53
Beeton, Mrs 131, 146
beetroot
bortsch 52-3
Harvard beets 202
medieval salads 223
swekolnik soup 52
Bercy, steak 144-5
beurre montpellier 124
Bierce, Ambrose 238
blachan 33
blackcurrant flummery 230-1
blackberries on trifle 232-3
blini 106-7
blueberry
caudle 250
flummery 230-1
boar in sweet and sour sauce 192-3
bombard of veal 148-50
boning
eel 101
fish 71-2
lamb 132
poultry and feathered game 163-4
borage in salads 222
bortsch 52-3
Boston, Richard, his Christmas
pudding 275-6
botargo 105, 106
bouillabaisse 82-3
Boulestin, Marcel 158
boumiano 210
bourride 83-5
Braine, Ray 183
brawn *see* pig's head cheese
bread
barley 33-4

Brillat-Savarin, Jean Anthelme 25-6,
117, 144, 177, 180, 278
brine 156
broccoli
in barley soup 32-3
with chilli and capsicum 198-9
patina of 35
brussel sprouts 198
with pheasant 181
with venison 189
de Brynne, Alice 162, 179, 226
Bulgarian cuisine
lentil, bean and pepper stew
210-11
burghul 75
butter 116
Cumberland rum butter 276-7
see also ghee

cabbage 196-7
coleslaw 224
and fruit soup 58
medieval salads 223
and paprika 196-7
sauerkraut 197
stuffed cabbage leaves 197-8
café granita 239
cake
Christmas 275
Greek 35
Roman 34
simnel 272-3
calf's head, in mock turtle soup 44-5
callaloo 61
canard en croûte 113
caponata 210
capsicum 196
brocccoli with chilli and 198-9
cardamom 240
with coffee 240
orange and 240-1
Carème, Antonin 13, 17, 281
carenum 34
Caribbean cuisine
callaloo 61
fish stews 78-90
mussels in coconut milk 90
peanut soup 55
carob powder, in salads 223
carrots
in ghivechi 211-12
peas and baby 206